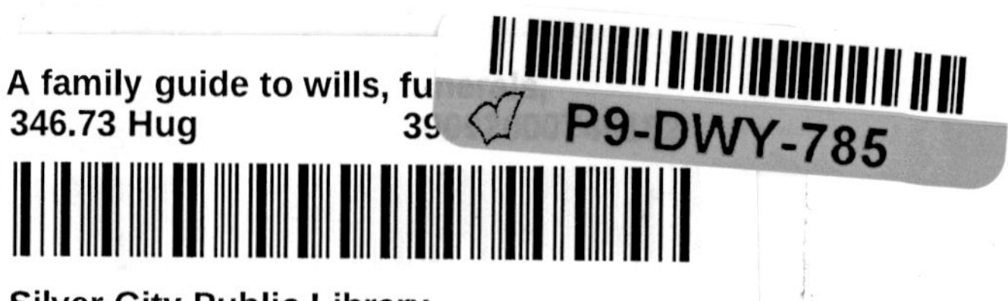

A Family Guide to Wills, Funerals, and Probate

Second Edition

How to Protect Yourself and Your Survivors

THEODORE E. HUGHES
AND DAVID KLEIN

Checkmark Books®
An imprint of Facts On File, Inc.

A Family Guide to Wills, Funerals, and Probate, Second Edition

For information contact:

Checkmark Books
An imprint of Facts On File, Inc.
11 Penn Plaza
New York, NY 10001

Library of Congress Cataloging-in-Publication Data

Hughes, Theodore E.
A family guide to wills, funerals, and probate: how to protect yourself and your survivors / Theodore E. Hughes and David Klein.—2nd ed.
p.cm.
Includes bibliographical references and index.
ISBN 0-8160-4550-X (hbk. : alk. paper)—ISBN 0-8160-4551-8 (pbk. : alk. paper)
1. Wills—United States—Popular works. 2. Probate law and practice—United States—Popular works. 3. Undertakers and underaking—United States.
I. Klein, David, 1919– II. Title.
KF755.Z9 H84 2001
346.7305'2—dc21 00-052813

Checkmark Books are available at special discounts when purchased in bulk quantities for businesses, associations, institutions or sales promotions. Please call our Special Sales Department in New York at (212) 967-8800 or (800) 322-8755.

You can find Facts On File on the World Wide Web at http://www.factsonfile.com

Text design and layout by Erika K. Arroyo
Cover design by Cathy Rincon

Printed in the United States of America

MP FOF 10 9 8 7 6 5 4 3 2 1
(pbk) 10 9 8 7 6 5 4 3 2 1

This book is printed on acid-free paper.

CONTENTS

DOCUMENTS

TABLES

Part I

MAKING LIFE EASIER FOR YOUR SURVIVORS

INTRODUCTION

. . . in this world nothing is certain but death and taxes.
—Benjamin Franklin, 1789

Few of us want to think about death, even fewer feel comfortable talking about it, and fewer still are willing to plan for it. In fact, in an age when life has generally become easier and "sensitive" topics are discussed more openly, death has become increasingly difficult to face, and it has outstripped sex as *the* taboo topic of our times.

This is not to say that people of any period faced death with equanimity. But there are several reasons why the prospect of death is more frightening to us than it was to our parents and grandparents.

To begin with, death is far less familiar today. In our parents' day, almost everyone over the age of thirty had experienced the death of a parent, a sibling, or a close friend. Thus, death was an expected part of daily life, and people learned to accept and cope with it. But in our times the dramatic increase in life expectancy has made our encounters with death far less frequent, and when they occur, we have little experience to help us deal with them.

Our unfamiliarity with death is increased by the fact that most people today die not in their own beds, surrounded by their families, but in hospitals, attended by impersonal professionals during the last hours of their lives and the first hours of their deaths. These strangers often make "professional" decisions that may serve their own interests or reflect their own values rather than those of the dying person or the survivors.

The decrease in family size and the weakening of family bonds have created further problems. No longer can we expect our survivors to find emotional comfort and economic shelter among members of a large, extended family on the family farm or in the family business. Instead, we must make formal, often complex, and legalistic arrangements to ensure that our assets will be safely transferred to our survivors, that our minor children will be taken care of, and that whatever business was interrupted by our death will be brought to an orderly close.

Lastly, in the case of almost every death, the normal process of our survivors' grief and bereavement is interrupted by their need to deal with a number of bureaucracies—banks and brokers, probate courts, federal and state tax authorities, and other government agencies—many of which did not exist or played no part in deaths that occurred a few decades ago.

Perhaps all this explains why many people acknowledge that their deepest anxieties about death center not on their own fate but on what will happen—emotionally, socially, and financially—to those they leave behind. And psychologists who have studied bereavement conclude that the survivors, no matter how intense their love for the deceased, may actually be grieving more acutely about their own plight—emotional, social, and financial.

Our purpose in this book, then, is to relieve to some extent your anxieties about your survivors and to ease their distress about their own situation, at least in its material aspects. To the extent that we succeed, your concern with your death can focus on your emotional relationships with your survivors, and their grief for you will center on the loss of your companionship and not on "the mess we've been left in."

Planning for your own disability and death involves three areas that are only slightly related to each other: (1) making end-of-life health care decisions, (2) managing the transfer of your assets to your survivors as efficiently as possible, and (3) dealing with your bodily remains in a way that you and your survivors feel is appropriate.

The problem of health-care decisions can be substantially alleviated by the preparation of a medical power of attorney—a document that we deal with at length in chapter 3.

The "assets" problem we can deal with objectively and precisely. Assuming that you prefer to leave as much as possible of your estate to your survivors and as little as possible to tax collectors, courts, and lawyers, we can show you the right and wrong ways to achieve this end.

Disposing of your remains and preserving your memory are such personal matters that obviously there can be no right or wrong procedure. Whether you prefer an elaborate funeral service and an impressive mausoleum or a minimal-cost "direct disposal" with a simple memorial service, we have no wish to influence your choice. Yet, whatever your preference, we will note more efficient and less efficient ways of having it carried out.

The easiest way to deal with an unpleasant prospect is by procrastination. And this is probably why most Americans die without a will and without any plans for the disposition of their bodies or their property. Given a life expectancy of some seventy years, most young adults apparently believe that making a will, planning their estate, and doing anything else that forces them to recognize their own mortality can safely be put off until their late sixties.

But those who take comfort from mortality tables overlook a fact that appears daily on the obituary pages: people die at all ages. The most common cause of death before the age of forty is accidents. And because accidents often kill husband and wife simultaneously, designating a guardian for minor children and planning for the management of their inheritance are absolutely essential, even for parents who have not reached the midpoint of their statistical life expectancies.

Planning for your survivors should begin as soon as you have acquired assets that give you even a modest net worth or as soon as you become legally responsible for minor children, through birth or through adoption. Moreover, it should proceed continuously as your net worth and your kinship network change—as you accumulate wealth, as you gain or lose relatives and friends by birth, marriage, divorce, estrangement, or death, and whenever you change your state of residence. This does not mean that you need to devote an inordinate amount of time to planning your estate or contemplating your death or that you ought to revise your will every time you get into an argument at a family reunion. It does mean that you ought to devote perhaps half a day each year to calculating your net worth and reviewing your will, your estate plan, your financial and medical powers of attorney, and your funeral arrangements in the light of any recent changes.

A Family Guide is intended to make all this easier for you by suggesting a systematic course of action. Chapters 1–5 deal with matters that you can and should attend to immediately, no matter what your age. The more effectively you deal with them, the less you will have to do when age or illness makes disability or death seem imminent. What to do when death seems close at hand is dealt with in chapter 6. Again, the more effectively you cope with last-minute problems, the less difficult will be the problems faced by your survivors—problems dealt with in chapters 7 through 10.

If at this point you have not set this book aside, you obviously are willing to face the possibility of your disability or the inevitability of your own death. If you can share its contents with your family and perhaps a close friend and use it to formulate plans that are both satisfying and practicable, what is inevitable will be less painful for all of you.

1

YOUR WILL AND ITS FUNCTIONS

For most people, preparing a will is their first confrontation with their own mortality. This is probably why they tend to procrastinate—and why three out of every four Americans die without one. Yet a will, thoughtfully prepared, can do much to alleviate your fears about death because it enables you to provide for the welfare of your survivors after you are gone and because it assures you that whatever estate you leave behind will be distributed as you would like it to be.

Basically a will has three functions: to designate a guardian for your minor children in the event that you and your spouse die simultaneously, to specify precisely who is to inherit how much of your estate and with what strings attached, and to name a personal representative (formerly called an executor) who will see to it that your estate is distributed according to the terms of your will. These functions will all be carried out whether you leave a will or not, but if you die intestate—that is, without a will—the decisions will be made by the local probate court in compliance with state law—and with consequences that you would probably find quite unacceptable.

If, for example, you and your spouse die simultaneously, the probate court will appoint a guardian for your minor children. But in such circumstances the court is likely to appoint a relative—perhaps a sister whose values and life-style are very different from yours—whereas you might prefer a close friend as the person most likely to rear the children according to your own values.

This loss of control applies also to whatever assets you leave. If you die without a will (dying "intestate"), these assets will be distributed to your creditors and your "heirs at law" by the probate court. Although the intestacy laws vary slightly from one state to another, their common underlying premise is that "blood is thicker than water"—that kinship is the fundamental principle governing the distribution of your estate. Thus, if you die without leaving a will, some state laws specify that up to three-fourths of your estate must go to your spouse, the balance to be equally divided among your children or grandchildren. If you leave a spouse but no children, half may go to your parents. If both your spouse and your parents are dead and you leave no children or grandchildren, everything will go to your brothers and sisters or nieces and nephews. And if you leave neither spouse nor kin, your entire estate goes to the state. If you leave no will, then friends, lifetime partners, stepchildren, or charities get nothing.

It's conceivable that this state-specified plan coincides exactly with your own preferences—in which case you may have no need for a will. But it's more likely that one or more of its provisions will be totally unacceptable. For example, do you want your children to get half your estate (which you could have willed to your spouse)—especially if they are minors, self-sufficient, or alienated from you. If you do want your children to inherit, do you want them to share equally if one of them is a minor or is disabled, retarded, or indigent and the others are adults, healthy, or well off? And, lastly, do you have some nonkin—friends, stepchildren, a lifetime partner, employees, your alma mater, or some charitable institution—to whom you'd like to leave a special gift or a sum of money?

A personal representative appointed by the court in the absence of a will is entitled to a fee and must pay an annual bonding premium, both of which will be charged against your estate. Would you prefer to make your own choice in a way that can keep the fee in the family and save the cost of a bond premium?

Since any of these questions may lead you to make a will, why is it that most Americans die without one? As we have noted, the real reason may be that making a will requires one to acknowledge the prospect of one's own death, but since admitting to a fear of death makes most people uncomfortable, other excuses are commonly offered. Here are some of them, along with counterarguments:

"Why think about it now? There's plenty of time."

Usually presented by young and middle-aged people, this argument overlooks two points. First, death, especially by accident, can come at any time. Perhaps more important, it is people in the younger age groups who are most likely to leave minor or dependent children, and since many accidents kill husband and wife simultaneously, only a will can ensure that the person they choose will be appointed as guardian of the children.

"My net worth isn't high enough to justify the trouble and expense."

Actually, the lower your net worth, the more important it is that you have a will—to ensure that the probate court does not automatically deprive your spouse of half your estate or reduce your estate by the fees of a court-appointed personal representative. And, of course, the question of the guardianship of your minor children becomes more important if the value of your estate is small.

In fact, however, most people underestimate their net worth, not realizing what inflation has done to the value of their real estate, their automobiles, their investments, their stamp collections, and other possessions that have accumulated over a lifetime. Moreover, there is no way for you to estimate accurately what your net worth will be at the time of your death—or even afterward. You may die holding a winning lottery ticket for a million-dollar prize. Or you may die in an accident that results in a successful $500,000 lawsuit for damages arising from your death through another's negligence. Or one of your stocks, whose value has been negligible for years, may suddenly "take off."

"All my property is held jointly with my spouse; thus it will pass automatically to her [him] when I die."

Joint ownership, as we shall see, makes good sense in many marital situations, but despite your intentions, it almost never covers all your possessions and assets. Are your cars owned jointly? What about your collection of guns or clocks? Does the bill of sale for that antique Chippendale table list both of you as owners? Are there some securities that you or your broker neglected to register in joint ownership? Even the most carefully planned estate is likely to include some property that is yours and yours alone. Unless such property is willed to a specific beneficiary, it will be distributed by the probate court in accordance with state intestacy laws.

Perhaps more important, even if absolutely everything is owned jointly, you need to be concerned with what happens to your property if you and your spouse or other joint owner are killed simultaneously or if one of you survives but dies sometime later without having made a will.

WHAT A WILL CAN DO

It would seem, then, that every adult who owns anything of worth or who has a spouse, children, or friends should make a will to ensure that his or her estate will be disposed of according to personal preferences rather than state law. Here, in summary, are some of the issues that a will can settle:

It can name a guardian and an alternate guardian for your minor children and a conservator (also sometimes called a guardian) to manage their inherited assets until they reach the age of majority. Some states, however, permit a guardian to be nominated by a writing separate from a will.

It can designate your primary and contingent beneficiaries: "I give $5,000 to A if he survives my death; otherwise to B."

It can specify charitable gifts—to churches, educational institutions, and philanthropic organizations, for example.

It can make conditional gifts: "I give $1,000 to my nephew Steven Cort if he has earned his undergraduate degree by the time of my death."

It can forgive a debt. If, for example, A owes you $5,000, your will can specify that your estate forgive the balance outstanding at the time of your death.

It can establish a trust and name a trustee for minor children or aged or disabled persons so that they get the benefit of part of your estate but do not have the responsibility for managing it. Such a "testamentary" (will-created) trust can be used to postpone ultimate distribution of an inheritance to children beyond the age of majority, say, to age twenty-five, when they are more mature and less likely to be parted from their money. Without a trust, a child will have complete access to his total inheritance upon reaching the age of majority, which is eighteen in most states. Similarly, a will can transfer some or all of your estate to a living trust that you may have established during your lifetime (see p. 38).

It can name a personal representative (sometimes called an executor) who will be required by law to manage your estate until it is finally distributed. Although a personal representative appointed by the probate court must be bonded (with the bonding premium chargeable against your estate) and is limited in his authority, your will can specify that the bond requirement is to be waived and that his or her authority be far broader than what state law permits.

It can establish the order of survivorship in cases where spouses die simultaneously in an accident, by stating:

> In the event that my wife (husband) and I die simultaneously or under circumstances where it cannot be determined who died first, then it shall be presumed that my wife (husband) survived me, and all provisions of my will shall be construed based on such presumption.

This distinction can be important because in some states, if the two deaths are simultaneous, all jointly owned assets are divided in half, each half requiring separate probate administration. If, on the other hand, one joint owner is regarded as having died later than the other, he or she is deemed to have acquired the entire joint estate and is thus able to pass it on intact to his or her survivors without double probate.

It can disinherit survivors other than a spouse, who normally has a right to override a will that disinherits him or her.

It can revoke all previous wills.

WHAT A WILL CAN'T— OR SHOULDN'T—DO

Because most people have learned what they know about wills from news stories, movies, novels, or television shows, it's not surprising that they have picked up a good deal of misinformation. There are some provisions that should not be included in a will, either because they are clearly illegal and will not be sustained by the courts or because they are simply inadvisable. Here are some examples:

A will may not place a condition on a gift if the condition is generally seen as contrary to sound public policy. Thus, if you leave $5,000 to one of your daughters "provided she divorce the man to whom she is married," the court would hold that the disruption of marriage is against public policy and thus the condition would be unenforceable. Similarly, will provisions that bequeath gifts to illegal organizations, such as terrorist groups, may be successfully contested.

Although it can limit a spouse's share of the estate to the minimum specified by law, a will may not disinherit a spouse entirely. If your surviving spouse is dissatisfied with the provisions in your will, a request to the court will almost certainly result in the spouse's receiving part of your estate. A will may disinherit a child, but the child should be named specifically. Otherwise the child may successfully claim that he or she was omitted unintentionally and is hence entitled to an amount equal to what he would have inherited had the parent died without leaving a will.

A will may not force a gift on an indifferent or unwilling recipient. A beneficiary is under no obligation to accept anything left to him by the will.

A will may not impose penalties on anyone who chooses to contest its provisions. A condition such as "I give my son Jonathan $5,000, but if he contests my will, I direct that he shall receive nothing" will not be upheld if the court feels that the son's lawsuit contesting the will has some merit. Similarly, a will cannot successfully require that anyone contesting the will must pay all litigation costs, including those incurred by the estate.

It is both unnecessary and unwise to disinherit anyone by bequeathing to him or her the sum of one dollar. All beneficiaries must sign receipts for their inheritances before the estate can be closed, and if the beneficiary thus insulted refuses to cooperate, a problem may be created for the personal representative.

There is no restriction against specifying funeral or burial arrangements or anatomical gifts in a will, but both may become irrelevant if the will is not located and read immediately upon your death. (Chapter 4 suggests a more reliable technique for making such wishes known.)

Although a will may specify that some of your possessions are to be given to designated beneficiaries, it should not contain a complete inventory of your assets, since any change in these would necessitate a revision of your will. Assets should be inventoried not in your will but in a letter of instruction (see chapter 4).

You may, if you wish, include in your will whatever statement of your philosophy or "message to the world" you choose, but it is unwise to use your will as a vehicle for venting your displeasure with or animosity against any named individuals. Once the will is probated, it becomes a public document, and any scurrilous attacks it contains will, at best, embarrass your survivors and, at worst, involve your estate in the expensive defense of a libel suit brought by the defamed party.

In disposing of your property, a will must express clear, unambiguous instructions, not mere wishes or hopes. Thus, "I wish my friend John to receive my clock" is an unclear and possibly unenforceable version of "I give John Howard my Chauncey Jerome banjo clock."

WHO SHOULD PREPARE THE WILL?

The foregoing list of dos and don'ts is not intended to encourage you to embark on a do-it-yourself will. On the contrary, it illustrates that a very large number of details, many of them seemingly petty, can render invalid in whole or in part a will prepared without competent professional advice.

Once again, thanks to the mass media, a good deal of misinformation abounds. Is it possible, for example, to make a will simply by writing out your instructions in longhand and then adding your signature? Aside from the technical errors it may contain, such a will—known as a holographic (in your handwriting) will—has no legal standing whatever in about half the states, but in some circumstances it is better than no will at all (see table 1). Oral wills, such as deathbed statements, are even less widely accepted.

Must you, then, pay for the professional services of a lawyer, or can you make your own will by following the instructions or using the forms provided in a number of "how to make a will" books and computer software programs? Unfortunately, there is no unequivocal answer to this question. Many practicing lawyers would caution you against the do-it-yourself alternative—just as most of them are unenthusiastic about the simplified do-it-yourself divorce procedure—but one can hardly assume that their advice is entirely disinterested. The make-your-own-will books and computer software programs are, after all, written by lawyers at least as competent as the general practitioner who has not specialized in estate planning.

On the other hand, many lawyers point out that problems arise not because the do-it-yourself will kits are defective but because readers are careless in following the instructions or unable to apply the general instructions to some exceptional situations. As of this writing, four states (California, Maine, Michigan, and Wisconsin) have adopted "statutory will" forms that comply with the state laws governing wills. Free copies are available from members of the state legislature.

TABLE 1
State Requirements Governing Wills

	Minimum Age to Make a Will	*Number of Required Witnesses*	*Recognizes Holographic Wills*	*Recognizes Oral Wills*	*Conditions Imposed on Oral Wills**
Alabama	18	2	No	No	
Alaska	18	2	Yes	Yes	6, 8, 17, 19
Arizona	18	2	Yes	No	
Arkansas	18	2	Yes	No	
California	18	2	Yes	No	
Colorado	18	2	Yes	No	
Connecticut	18	2	No	No	
Delaware	18	2	No	No	
District of Columbia	18	2	No	Yes	6, 7, 8, 12, 16
Florida	18	2	No	No	
Georgia	14	2	No	Yes	7, 12, 17
Hawaii	18	2	Yes	No	
Idaho	18	2	Yes	No	
Illinois	18	2	No	No	
Indiana	18	2	No	Yes	3, 4, 6, 9, 11, 12, 17, 19, 21
Iowa	18	2	No	No	
Kansas	18	2	No	Yes	6, 7, 12, 17, 21
Kentucky	18	2	Yes	No	
Louisiana	16	2	Yes	No	
Maine	18	2	Yes	No	
Maryland	18	2	No	No	
Massachusetts	18	2	No	Yes	6, 8
Michigan	18	2	Yes	No	
Minnesota	18	2	No	No	
Mississippi	18	2	Yes	Yes	7, 10, 12, 19

TABLE 1
State Requirements Governing Wills *(continued)*

	Minimum Age to Make a Will	*Number of Required Witnesses*	*Recognizes Holographic Wills*	*Recognizes Oral Wills*	*Conditions Imposed on Oral Wills**
Missouri	18	2	No	Yes	2, 6, 11, 12, 17, 19, 21
Montana	18	2	Yes	No	
Nebraska	18	2	Yes	No	
Nevada	18	2	Yes	Yes	3, 7, 12
New Hampshire	18	2	No	Yes	7, 10, 13, 15, 19
New Jersey	18	2	Yes	No	
New Mexico	18	2	No	No	
New York	18	2	Yes	Yes	9
North Carolina	18	2	Yes	Yes	7, 12
North Dakota	18	2	Yes	No	
Ohio	18	2	No	Yes	7, 12, 14, 16, 19
Oklahoma	18	2	Yes	Yes	3, 8, 11, 12
Oregon	18	2	No	No	
Pennsylvania	18	2	No	No	
Rhode Island	18	2	No	No	
South Carolina	18	2	No	No	
South Dakota	18	2	Yes	No	
Tennessee	18	2	Yes	Yes	3, 6, 11, 12, 17, 19, 21
Texas	18	2	Yes	Yes	7, 10, 13
Utah	18	2	Yes	No	
Vermont	18	3	No	Yes	1, 6, 15, 19
Virginia	18	2	Yes	Yes	6, 8
Washington	18	2	No	Yes	3, 5, 6, 7, 12, 17, 19
West Virginia	18	2	Yes	Yes	6, 8
Wisconsin	18	2	No	No	
Wyoming	18	2	Yes	No	

* Key to Conditions Imposed on Oral Wills

1. Limited to $200.
2. Limited to $500.
3. Limited to $1,000.
4. Limited to $10,000.
5. Unlimited if testator is in military service.
6. Limited to only personal property.
7. Available only during last illness.

8. Testator must be in military service.
9. Testator must be in military service during wartime.
10. Testator must be at home or other place of death.
11. Testator must be in contemplation or fear of death.
12. Requires two witnesses.
13. Requires three witnesses.
14. Witnesses must not be beneficiaries of will.
15. Must be reduced to writing within 6 days.
16. Must be reduced to writing within 10 days.
17. Must be reduced to writing within 30 days.
18. Must be reduced to writing within 60 days.
19. Must be probated within 6 months following death.
20. Expires 1 year after testator's discharge from service.
21. Cannot be used to revoke a written will.

Our advice is that *if* your assets are not large and varied, *if* the provisions you intend in your will are fairly conventional, and *if* you have the time and patience to read and follow sometimes complicated instructions, you may safely write your own will, using a book or software on the subject or perhaps following the form shown in figure 1, below. But these are rather significant *ifs*, and you may decide that the relatively modest cost of professional preparation is a bargain in terms of the sense of security it can provide.

Figure 1

WILL

LAST WILL AND TESTAMENT OF JOHN J. JONES

I, JOHN J. JONES domiciled in Lansing, Michigan, declare this to be my last will, hereby revoking all previous wills and codicils.

FIRST

1.1 *Payments of Debts and Taxes*: I direct my Personal Representative to pay all of my legally enforceable debts, expenses of last illness, funeral and burial expenses, and expenses of administering my estate. I direct my Personal Representative to pay all taxes imposed by reason of my death upon any transfer of property includable in my estate, as an expense of administration, unless voluntarily paid by some party.

SECOND

2.1 *Specific Bequest*: I give and bequeath my stamp collection to my son, WILLIAM B. JONES, if he survives me; otherwise this gift shall lapse.

2.2 *Disposition of Residue*: I give, devise, and bequeath all of the rest, residue, and remainder of my estate, real, personal or mixed, wherever situate and whether acquired before or after the execution of this will, to MARY K. JONES (hereafter "my wife"), if she survives me.

2.3 *Alternative disposition—Residue*: If my wife does not survive me, then I give, devise, and bequeath all of the said remainder of my estate to my chil-

Figure 1

WILL *(continued)*

dren surviving me, in equal shares, provided, however, the issue of a deceased child surviving me shall take and share equally the share that their parent would have taken had he or she survived me. If my issue do not agree to this division among them, the decision of my Personal Representative shall be in all respects binding upon my issue.

THIRD

3.1 *Survivorship Defined*: In the event that my wife and I die under circumstances where it cannot be established who died first, then it shall be presumed that my wife survived me and this will and the dispositions hereunder shall be construed on that presumption. No person other than my wife shall be deemed to have survived me or to be living at my death if he or she shall die within ninety (90) days after my death.

FOURTH

4.1 *Personal Representative*: I nominate my wife as my Personal Representative, to serve without bond. If my wife predeceases me, declines to act, or having qualified, resigns, dies, or is removed, I nominate Capitol Bank and Trust Company, Lansing, Michigan, as my Personal Representative.
4.2 *Powers*: I give my Personal Representative all powers of administration granted to independent personal representatives as set forth in the Michigan Revised Probate Code at the time of execution of this will, including the power to sell any real or personal property, and for that purpose I hereby incorporate those powers by reference.
4.3 *Guardian and Conservator*: In the event that my wife fails to survive me, I nominate and appoint my brother and his wife, Richard A. Jones and Elizabeth Jones, Cleveland, Ohio, as Guardians of the person and Capitol Bank and Trust Company, Lansing, Michigan, as Conservator of the estate, of any of my children who is a minor at the time of my death.

____
John. J. Jones

On March 1, 2—, the above testator signed the foregoing instrument (typewritten on two [2] sheets of paper, upon the bottom of each of which he/she also signed) and declared that he/she signed it freely and voluntarily as his/her Last Will; we witnessed the signing in the presence of said testator, and we now, on the same day, sign as witnesses in the presence of said testator and of each other; to the best of our knowledge, said testator is now 18 or more years of age, of sound mind, and under no constraint or undue influence.

Witnesses:	Addresses:
Roberta Roe	Lansing, Michigan
Belinda Blue	Lansing, Michigan

WHAT YOUR LAWYER NEEDS TO KNOW

Although fees for the preparation of simple wills don't vary widely from one lawyer to another, all lawyers earn a living by selling their time. Your bill may be smaller, therefore, if you come prepared with all the information your lawyer is likely to need. A complete listing of your assets, for example, will not only shortcut a long question-and-answer session but will avoid omissions and oversights that require subsequent visits, correspondence, or telephone calls. You may, when you enter the lawyer's office, have only a vague idea of what a "contingent beneficiary" is, but you ought to have clearly in mind all the individuals to whom you intend to leave something. Here is some of the information that your lawyer is likely to need for preparation of even the simplest will. A listing of the personal and property information needed by your lawyer is set forth in figure 2.

YOUR PERSONAL REPRESENTATIVE (EXECUTOR)

Be prepared to name a person (or a bank) who will, on your death, see to it that your assets are collected and inventoried, your legitimate debts paid, your assets distributed according to your wishes, and your estate closed. If your estate is large and complex, you may prefer a personal representative with considerable experience in estate management—a bank, a trust company, or a lawyer. But bear in mind that the personal representative is entitled to a fee ranging from 1 to 5 percent of the value of the estate, that any individual personal representative must be bonded (to protect your estate from his possible fraud, embezzlement, or negligence), and that both the fee and the bonding premium are paid with funds from your estate.

If your estate is relatively simple, you may prefer to choose a trusted friend or a member of the family—even one of your beneficiaries if you foresee no conflict of interest with the other beneficiaries. Such a person should be younger—or at least no older—than you and possess good judgment and reasonable competence in ordinary business transactions. Some states require that the personal representative be an adult resident of your state.

Friends or relatives may choose to waive the fee, and your will can stipulate that they need not be bonded—unless you feel that bonding will protect your estate against their possible negligence.

In addition, if you choose a trusted and competent person, you can give that person, through your will, considerably more authority to settle your affairs than is granted to the personal representative by the laws of most states. Obviously, you should get the person's consent before naming him or her in your will. And if you choose an individual rather than a bank, be prepared to name an alternate, since the first-named personal representative may not outlive you or may for other reasons be unable or unwilling to assume the responsibility. Banks, on the other hand, are "immortal" and hence dependable, but neither banks nor lawyers may be the best possible personal representatives for small or simple estates; because their fees are often based on the size of the estate, they may not be motivated to work as quickly or efficiently as they would for a large one.

Guardian and Conservator for Minor Children

If you have minor children, your will should name a guardian for them—someone who will take over your role as parent until each child reaches the age of eighteen. Some states permit parents to name a guardian in a writing separate from a will. You may have read novels or seen movies in which the twelve-year-old daughter heroically undertakes the rearing of her younger siblings, but the fact is that your minor children cannot legally be enrolled in school or consent to medical treatment, among other things, except through an adult guardian authorized by the court to act in their behalf. This is why the probate court will select a guardian if your will fails to nominate one.

Here your choice is entirely unlimited, and the guardian, unlike the personal representative, need not be a resident of your state. You may choose a relative or perhaps a close friend. Parents of teenage children sometimes list three or four persons as acceptable guardians and permit the children to make the final choice. Some parents choose an adult child as guardian for their minor children, but this can be risky; even if the current sibling relationship is very sound, the sudden increase in authority endowed by the guardianship can threaten it. In all states a child, upon reaching fourteen, has the right to veto the parents' choice of guardian and to nominate a substitute; if the probate judge agrees that the proposed substitution is in the best interests of your child, your original nomination may be overruled.

Figure 2

ESTATE PLANNING QUESTIONNAIRE

CONFIDENTIAL INFORMATION FOR ESTATE PLANNING

Date ____________________

Individual	*Husband*	*Wife*
Name	____________________	____________________
Also known as	____________________	____________________
Social Security no.	____________________	____________________
Birth date	____________________	____________________
U.S. citizen	❑ Y ❑ N	❑ Y ❑ N
Living parents	____________________	____________________
Former spouse	____________________	____________________
Business address	____________________	____________________
Telephone number	____________________	____________________
Fax number	____________________	____________________
E-mail address	____________________	____________________
Home address	____________________	____________________
County of residence	____________________	____________________
Date of marriage	____________________	____________________

Children

Living children (indicate children from a prior marriage and adopted children)

Name	Birth date	Social Security No.	No. of children
____________________	__________	______________	______________
____________________	__________	______________	______________
____________________	__________	______________	______________
____________________	__________	______________	______________
____________________	__________	______________	______________

Deceased children ____

Living children of deceased child ______________________________

Note: If there are no living children or grandchildren, list the brothers and sisters (living and deceased) of the husband and the wife.

Agents and brokers

Safe-deposit box	❑ Y ❑ N	Location ____________________
Accountant	❑ Y ❑ N	Name ____________________
Insurance agent	❑ Y ❑ N	Name ____________________
Stockbroker	❑ Y ❑ N	Name ____________________

Figure 2

ESTATE PLANNING QUESTIONNAIRE *(continued)*

CONFIDENTIAL INFORMATION FOR ESTATE PLANNING

Date ____________________

Real estate (including land contracts)
Description
(include owner: H-husband, W-wife, J-joint) Mortgage balance Market value
______________________________________ $ ______________ $ __________
______________________________________ $ ______________ $ __________
______________________________________ $ ______________ $ __________
______________________________________ $ ______________ $ __________

Cash (checking, savings, CD, money market, credit union) Location of account
(include owner: H, W, J) Amount
____ $ __________
____ $ __________
____ $ __________
____ $ __________

Stocks and bonds (if in a brokerage account, list firm name)
Listed securities (H) ____
Listed securities (W) ____
Listed securities (J) ____
Closely held (family) securities ____

Life insurance (include insured, insurance company, insurance type, owner, and beneficiary) Face amount
____ $ __________
____ $ __________
____ $ __________
____ $ __________

Retirement benefits (list company)
IRA (list location, type (Roth, non-Roth), and amount _____________________
____

Miscellaneous
Household furnishings, autos, collections ______________________________
Money owed by others to you ______________________ $____________
Miscellaneous (trusts, etc.) _______________________ $____________
Expected inheritances ____________________________ $______________
List all gifts made by you over $3,000 in value (date and beneficiary)
____
Any gift tax return filed ❑ Y ❑ N Years filed __________________
List significant debts or obligations other than mortgages listed above
____

Your principal criteria in choosing a guardian are likely to include the prospective guardian's personality, ethical values, and child-rearing style as well as his or her current relationship with your children. But financial stability cannot be entirely disregarded. Guardians are entitled to reimbursement from the child's inheritance for all reasonable costs incurred in maintaining and educating the child and providing medical and other services, but since the cost of rearing a child from infancy through college is currently estimated at about $190,000, anyone undertaking a guardianship takes on a substantial financial burden. This burden should be lightened as much as possible by life insurance and other assets, especially since a guardian is not entitled to compensation. Needless to say, you will want to obtain in advance the consent of anyone you plan to nominate.

If, on the other hand, you are providing very amply for your children, the question arises as to who should control their inheritance—not only to oversee disbursement for current expenses but also to conserve or increase it through effective investment strategy. The person you select to take this responsibility is called a conservator. You may, if you wish, choose the same person to serve both as guardian and conservator (or, for that matter, as personal representative), but since skill in child rearing is not necessarily related to financial acumen, you may prefer to appoint a separate person: perhaps a bank if the inheritance is a large one. The conservator, like the personal representative, is entitled to a fee for managing the child's estate.

The responsibility of the conservator, like that of the guardian, terminates when the child reaches maturity—the age of eighteen in most states. If you have left your children a substantial amount of money and if you think that, at age eighteen, the child is not likely to be mature enough to use it wisely, you can, in your will, set up a trust (see p. 38) for each child, specifying that the child not have access to the trust assets until whatever age you choose. In the interim, the trust's assets will be managed by a trustee of your choice, who thus fulfills the function of a conservator but without the time limits, probate court oversight, and other restrictions imposed on a conservator.

Beneficiaries

Although you undoubtedly know whom you intend to make your *primary* beneficiaries (presumably your spouse and children, perhaps a favorite niece or nephew), it is important to have in mind also several *contingent* beneficiaries—that is, beneficiaries who will be "next in line" should a primary beneficiary die before you do. If you are married or have a lifetime partner, then perhaps the most obvious contingent beneficiaries are your children. Even if they are primary beneficiaries, as well, your will can specify that whatever part of your estate you have willed to your spouse is to go to your children (though not necessarily in equal shares) should your spouse predecease you.

But what if a married daughter—even though she is thirty years younger than you—should predecease you? Do you want her share to go to her surviving spouse or to a trust for your daughter's children, with someone else appointed as trustee? All of these specifics should be clearly spelled out in your will.

Lawyers are not congenital pessimists, but they are trained to identify and plan for contingencies, no matter how improbable. Although it is highly unlikely—short of a catastrophe at a family reunion—that most of your primary beneficiaries will die before you do, you ought to provide your lawyer with a least one level of contingency for each separate gift. For example, "I give $10,000 to A, provided he survives me; otherwise to B."

Given the decreasing size of families, the dispersal of the extended family, and the prevalence of divorce and cohabitation, you may find yourself running out of relatives before you have exhausted all possible contingencies. But bear in mind that if all your reasonable contingencies do become exhausted and if you do not have any surviving relatives who step forward to claim your estate, the residue of your estate is forfeited to the state through what is called escheat procedures. This may not strike you as an unmitigated disaster, but if you prefer to avoid it, you can always add as contingent beneficiaries various friends, charities, or other organizations.

Specifying Money Bequests

Because you may not die for fifty years or more after making your will, you have no way of estimating the ultimate value of your estate. This is of little consequence if you have only two or three primary beneficiaries, because in such circumstances you are likely to specify your bequests in terms of percentages or fractions of the total estate: "75 percent to my wife, Mary, the remaining 25 percent to be divided equally between my son, John, and my daughter, Helen."

If, however, you make a number of small bequests, you need to decide whether to express them in dollars or in percentages. If, for example, you'd like to leave a favorite nephew $1,000, which now represents 1 percent of your current net worth, should you describe the bequest as "$1,000" or as "1 percent of my estate?" If, fifty years from now, $1,000 shrinks to one-fifth of its current value, the gift will be insultingly small; on the other hand, 1 percent of your total estate may at that time represent an amount much larger than you intended. There is no general answer to this dollars-versus-percentage issue, but it needs to be considered for each of your smaller bequests and reconsidered each time you revise your will.

Specific Property Gifts

Aside from gifts of money, real estate, or securities, you may want to give certain of your possessions, large or small, to specific people, whether or not they are beneficiaries of other gifts. Your gun collection, for example, may be given to a fellow member of your gun club; your grandmother's gold brooch may be given to your daughter rather than to your son. If, before you die, any of these things pass from your possession—through loss or theft, for example—you need not revise your will; the gift "fails" and the intended recipient will have no claim against your estate.

List of Assets

Although a complete inventory of your assets has no place in a will (because it is likely to change significantly before you die), it's useful to show one to your lawyer before he draws up your will. (The form shown in figure 2 can be used for this purpose.) To begin with, the inventory will give him a general idea of how complex your will needs to be. Perhaps more important, if your estate is a large one, he may have a number of useful suggestions for avoiding taxes and other problems by reducing the size of your estate—a subject dealt with in chapter 2.

If you feel uncomfortable about disclosing to your lawyer the full extent of your assets because you suspect he will not keep the information confidential, you ought to find yourself another lawyer. Making an estate plan, including a will, is a "moment of truth," and concealing any relevant information can only frustrate your plan and jeopardize the interests of your beneficiaries.

Your lawyer and almost certainly your spouse or partner should be included in your "circle of confidentiality" with respect to your will, but whom else to include is a matter for careful judgment. You may want to elicit specific preferences from your children about some of your possessions, or you may want to discuss with your alma mater the exact terms of a proposed bequest, but generally speaking, a will should be considered a very personal affair. It is not uncommon for elderly persons to use the provisions of their will as threats or rewards in their dealings with their likely beneficiaries, but such behavior benefits nobody.

SIGNING AND PROTECTING THE WILL

Armed with the information described in the preceding pages, you should be able to answer expeditiously whatever questions your lawyer asks. The technical details of compliance with state law can be left to him, and your next step is to read the draft of the will (at home, relaxed, and probably in consultation with your spouse) to make certain that it specifies precisely each of your directions. The signing of the will is best done in the lawyer's office, because he is familiar with the state requirements for signing and witnessing. There is no need for the witnesses to read the will; they are witnessing your signature only, although they must understand that what you are signing is your will.

Some lawyers draft wills naming themselves as the personal representative or as the lawyer who will be employed to probate the will. There is no reason for you to commit your estate to employing a specific lawyer. You may move from the community or change lawyers for other reasons, and a specific commitment would then require revision of the will.

Although you will receive copies of the will, you should sign only the original, to avoid problems of retrieving and destroying several signed copies if you later decide to revise or revoke it. The signed original should be kept where it is (1) safe against fire, theft, or other loss; (2) readily retrievable by you; (3) confidential; (4) likely to be located after your death by your survivors. The storage location that probably best meets these criteria is the will depository maintained by most county probate courts. For a small one-time filing fee, you can file the will until it is probated or revoked. During your lifetime, only you have access to it. On your death, however, copies become available to your survivors for use in the probate process.

Storing a will in a safety deposit box is a common practice, but it has one disadvantage: on hearing of your death, the bank is sometimes required by law to seal the box until a representative of the state treasury can inventory its contents. In such circumstances, your survivors will need to apply for a court order permitting them to retrieve the will.

Storing the will at home, along with other important papers, is a common practice, but a desk drawer or filing cabinet may provide insufficient privacy or protection against fire and theft. And storing it in your lawyer's office, as some lawyers recommend, may place you under an obligation that you may find awkward if you move or establish a relationship with a different lawyer. Moreover, if the lawyer has possession of your will, your survivors may, upon your death, feel some obligation to hire that lawyer when, in fact, they would prefer to use another.

AMENDING OR REVOKING YOUR WILL

As we have noted, it is important to make a will early in life because death can occur at any time. But the statistical probability is that you will live for many years after signing your will and that many of the circumstances on which you based your original will may change. The value and complexity of your assets, for example, may increase. A beneficiary may die; a beneficiary's needs may increase or diminish; your feelings toward a beneficiary may change drastically. You may divorce your current spouse, or separate from your unwed partner, or you may adopt a child, or you may want (or need) to change your will's designations of personal representative, guardian, conservator, or trustee. It is also possible that you will move to another state and that your will may need revision to comply with the new state's laws since not all states recognize the validity of a will you executed when you lived elsewhere. Obviously, then, a will is not something that you can sign and then put away with a sigh of relief. It requires periodic review, and each review may lead to minor changes or major revisions.

Like the original will, changes and revisions should be executed promptly and not be put off on the grounds that you are in good health at the moment. Bear in mind that a will can be executed or amended only when you are mentally competent and that mental incompetence—as a consequence of senility, mental illness, or coma caused by accidental injury, for example—can precede your death by many years. In such a situation, a guardian or a conservator may be appointed to handle your business affairs, but neither representative has the authority to amend or revoke your will.

Codicils

If your will requires only a minor amendment—a change in the amount you've bequeathed to a specific beneficiary, the addition of a gift to a charitable institution, or a change in the designation of the guardian—you can make the change by means of a codicil. A codicil (see figure 3) is simply an amendment to the original will. Like the will, it must comply with state law regarding witnessing and other formalities, and it will be probated together with the will.

Although there is no limit to the number of changes that can be embodied in a codicil or, indeed, to the number of codicils that can be a attached to a will, the presence of a large number of codicils can complicate the probate process. There comes a point at which it is more efficient and no more expensive to amend the entire will—a procedure that is essentially the same at the preparation of the original will.

Revocation

There are several ways in which your current will can be revoked. You can, at any time, simply destroy it (or instruct someone to destroy it in your presence), but this leaves you without a will. Or you can sign a new will that states specifically that it revokes all previous wills. It is also possible that some portions of your will may be automatically revoked by law. If, for example, you have left everything to your spouse and you divorce and die before revising your will, the laws of many states will revoke the gift to your former spouse unless your will specified that your estate is to go to your spouse even after divorce.

Figure 3

CODICIL

FIRST CODICIL TO LAST WILL OF JOHN J. JONES

I, JOHN J. JONES declare this to be the First Codicil to my Last Will dated March 1, 2000.

FIRST

I hereby revoke in their entirety Items 2.1 and 4.3 of my Last Will dated March 1, 2—, and substitute in lieu thereof new Items with the same numbers, which Items shall read as follows:

> 2.1 *Specific Bequest*: I give and bequeath my stamp collection to my daughter, SALLY L. JONES, if she survives me; otherwise this gift shall lapse.
>
> 4.3 *Guardian and Conservator*: In the event that my wife fails to survive me, I nominate and appoint my friend, and his wife, Alfred R. Miller and Susan T. Miller, Detroit, Michigan, as Guardians of the person and Liberty Federal Bank, Lansing, Michigan, as Conservator of the estate of any of my children who is a minor at the time of my death.

SECOND

I republish and reaffirm my said Last Will as herein modified, amended, and supplemented by this First Codicil as if the same were set out here in full and do incorporate the same by this reference thereto.

____

John J. Jones

On February 15, 2000, the above person signed the foregoing instrument (typewritten on one [1] sheet of paper) and declared that he/she signed it freely and voluntarily as the First Codicil to his/her Last Will; we witnessed the signing in the presence of said person, and we now, on the same day, sign as witnesses in the presence of said person and of each other; to the best of our knowledge, said person is now 18 or more years of age, of sound mind, and under no constraint or undue influence.

****WITNESSETH****

Witnesses:	Addresses:
____________________ Robert Roe	Lansing, Michigan 48905
____________________ Belinda Blue	Lansing, Michigan 48905

Obviously, the most efficient and orderly way for you to manage your affairs is to update your will periodically, by signing a codicil or a new will. If you do this conscientiously, your will should accurately reflect your most recently expressed wishes.

LOOKING AHEAD TO PROBATE

Although the preparation of your will may strike you as a generally grim process, the review of your assets it requires you to make may lighten your spirits considerably. Many people who are forced into this inventory of their accumulated possessions experience pleasure and pride because their net worth turns out to be more substantial than they had anticipated.

But this justifiable satisfaction should be tempered by one important consideration: the higher the total value of the assets that you intend to bequeath by means of your will, the more complex and expensive will be the process of probate administration after your death. This means that your beneficiaries will have some of their inheritance eroded by administrative, legal, and court costs and that months, or sometimes years, may lapse before they actually have their inheritances in hand.

If the prospect of probate-court expense and delay concerns you, your best strategy is to reexamine the inventory of your assets with a view to transferring them to your beneficiaries *by some means other than your will.* Bear in mind that your will can transfer only those assets that are in your name at the time of death. Thus, if you transfer the bulk of your assets into joint ownership or the trustee of a revocable trust, you retain control of them while you are alive, but they will not be yours to bequeath by will when you die. If you do this effectively, it may be that upon your death you own nothing that is in your name alone—in which case your will, no matter what it specifies, will not require probate. Or you may own so little that the remaining assets are eligible for transfer by an informal "small estate" probate process that is both swifter and cheaper than full probate administration. The next chapter discusses the various ways by which you can reduce the size of your probatable estate.

2

AVOIDING PROBATE ADMINISTRATION AND DEATH TAXES

The probating of your estate is not your responsibility, because it cannot take place before your death. Since it will be taken care of by your survivors, it is explained in detail in chapters 9 through 11. But the way in which you manage your assets and the form in which you own them from now until the time of your death will determine whether or not your estate will require probate administration, and how complex the probate process is likely to be. This is why making a will discharges only one of your responsibilities to your survivors. Another—at least as important—is to arrange your assets in ways that reduce the difficulties your survivors will have to face in order to inherit them.

THE PROBLEMS OF PROBATE

Briefly, probate court administration of your estate is the legal procedure by which the state ensures that after your death your creditors will collect their lawful debts, the state and federal governments will collect the taxes due them, your rightful beneficiaries will be identified, and the balance of your estate will be distributed according to the terms of your will or, if you did not leave a will according to state law. The entire procedure is supervised by a county court, usually called a probate court but in some states referred to as a surrogate, orphans', or chancery court.

Formal probate administration is always time-consuming, usually expensive, and often enormously frustrating. To begin proceedings, the probate judge must appoint a personal representative who will manage, liquidate, and eventually settle your estate. The personal representative will have to be compensated and, unless your will specifies otherwise, bonded, the costs of which, in addition to court costs, will have to be paid by your estate. The personal representative is required to notify your creditors and invite them to submit their claims, and the costs of this notification (by mail and by newspaper advertisement) are also borne by your estate.

If the personal representative needs the help of accountants, lawyers, or realtors in managing and selling your assets, their professional fees will be added to the cost of the probate procedure. And since the entire process will take not less than six months and may continue for several years, there is a possibility that your survivors may have to wait a long time for their inheritance.

In addition to the considerable costs in money and time, probate administration has other disadvantages. For one thing, because the probate process is a matter of public record, anyone can find out what you owned, what your debts were, and who inherited how much of your assets. This information may encourage claims, illegitimate as well as legitimate, against your estate, and it may expose your beneficiaries to annoying solicitation by charities and other "worthy causes" or by schemers of various kinds. Moreover, your personal representative, no matter how conscientious, may not handle your assets wisely without the benefit of your guidance, especially if your estate includes a flourishing business or securities with which he is unfamiliar. All these considerations make the avoidance of probate highly desirable, and the enormous success of Norman Dacey's *How to Avoid Probate* substantiates this.

The requirement that an estate be probated is not directly related to its value. A multimillion-dollar estate may, if it is properly planned, avoid probate, while an estate worth only $5,000 may have to undergo full probate administration. In trying to avoid probate, therefore, you must bear in mind that probate administration involves basically those assets *owned by you at the time of your death*. This means that anything you give away, place in joint ownership, hold in a pay-on-death bank account or transfer-on-death securities account, or transfer to a trust of some sort is not a *probable asset* because it is not in your name at the moment of death. Thus, in order to avoid probate, you should rearrange legal ownership of as much of your assets as possible without at the same time giving up control over them or the income that they may be producing.

It's rarely practical, of course, to rid yourself of all your possessions simply to avoid probate, and this isn't really necessary. Most states provide simple, inexpensive, and quick procedures for the settlement of so-called "small estates" without lengthy probate administration. Thus, you may be able to avoid the difficulties and delays of probate by transferring some of your highly valuable assets but retaining those whose value does not exceed the \$500–\$140,000 limits that various states impose on the use of the "small estate" procedure (see chapter 11 and tables 8 and 9). In this chapter we describe the various transfer options that can be used to avoid probate.

REDUCING YOUR PROBATABLE ASSETS

Depending on your state of residence, your estate may require probate even if the value of your probatable assets is no more than \$500. For this reason, we will here describe the various strategies and devices that can effectively reduce the value of your probatable assets—preferably without depriving you of control or income. The tax implications of each of these will also be discussed.

GIVING IT AWAY

Since your probatable assets consist only of those assets that you own at the time of death, the simplest way to reduce their value is to give some of them away while you are still alive. In a sense, of course, even a trivial gift, such as a \$25 birthday check to a child or grandchild, reduces your probatable assets, but there may be good reasons for making larger gifts. If an adult child of yours is in financial difficulties or has an opportunity to make a business investment, for example, giving the money while you are alive instead of willing it gets it to the recipient in time of need and allows you to experience his or her gratitude and to witness the results of your benevolence. In addition, giving your assets away protects them from claims of your creditors or an estranged spouse or child.

Giving away a major part of your assets, however, is a strategy that few of us can afford until death is imminent. For this reason, we shall deal with it, along with its tax implications, in chapter 6.

Joint Ownership

Probably the most widely used tactic for avoiding probate is to transfer assets into joint ownership, because upon the death of one joint owner the assets pass automatically to the surviving joint owner or owners without probate and regardless of any contrary instructions in the deceased's will. Joint ownership can apply to any type of property—real estate, household contents, bank and money market accounts, securities, motor vehicles, collectibles, etc.—and it may exist between any two or more persons, whether or not they are related. Joint ownership is, moreover, simple and inexpensive to establish. For a bank account, it requires only the signing of a new signature card; for real estate, simply the preparation and recording of a new deed; for securities, a cost-free change in registration of the certificates or the brokerage account.

Because joint ownership is so easy to establish and because it performs many of the functions of a will but avoids probate, it has been called "the poor man's will." But although you may derive considerable advantage from establishing joint ownership of your house and your securities with your spouse, or bank accounts with one or more of your children, you need to be aware that this form of ownership has some inherent and unavoidable limitations and disadvantages as a probate-avoidance technique.

To begin with, joint ownership can jeopardize your control over the assets, because a transfer into joint ownership is irrevocable and cannot be "unwound" without the consent of all joint owners. Thus, if you establish joint ownership of assets with your spouse and you ultimately divorce, complications are almost inevitable. If you place real estate or securities in joint ownership with a minor child, they may not be sellable until the child reaches majority, because a minor is legally incapable of making this kind of transaction. If you place assets in joint ownership with a second spouse, you automatically cut off any children born to you and your first spouse (unless, of course, you survive the second spouse).

Joint ownership, moreover, is inflexible. Once it is established, not only can you not change your mind—as you can with a will—but you may have problems in shifting the assets into more attractive investments, transferring them to a trust, or liquidating them, because such changes may require the consent of all the owners.

Perhaps more important, complications may arise from the fact that the sequence of deaths of the joint owners is unpredictable. For example, you may transfer your house into joint ownership among yourself and your two adult daughters, intending that they and their children share the ultimate proceeds equally, after your death, which you assumed would occur before those of your children. If one of the daughters predeceases you, however, ownership passes entirely to the surviving daughter, who is under no legal obligation to share half the proceeds with the children of the daughter who died.

If you and your spouse own assets jointly and die simultaneously, the assets become probatable. On the other hand, if your spouse survives you, but not long enough to have made a will or to make further changes in ownership, the assets will pass, if you are childless, to his or her next of kin and not to yours.

In view of all this, before you establish joint ownership of a substantial part of your assets, you need to assess the soundness of your marriage or your relationships with any other prospective joint owners as well as you need to retain control and flexibility. The best plan may be to transfer some of your assets into joint ownership and retain a comfortable balance that you can convert to joint ownership when death seems more imminent than it does at the moment, meanwhile considering some of the less problematic probate-avoidance alternatives described later in this chapter.

The tax consequences of joint ownership are somewhat complex. In general, establishing joint ownership with someone who did not contribute to the purchase of the asset constitutes a gift of half its value. Hence, if you set up joint ownership of an asset worth more than $10,000 with anyone but your spouse (who benefits from an unlimited gift tax "Marital Deduction"), you may be subject to a gift tax for half the value of the gifted asset. If the gift consists of a bank account, this tax is not due immediately, and you need not file a gift tax return until the joint owner either liquidates the asset or puts it into his or her own name. If the gift involves real estate or securities, however, the gift is effective immediately and any gift tax is payable immediately.

As to the federal estate tax, upon your death the total value of jointly held assets will be regarded as part of your taxable estate except to the extent that the surviving owner contributed to its acquisition. If the surviving joint owner is your spouse, however, only half of the asset's value will be subject to estate tax, regardless of whether the spouse contributed to its acquisition.

Pay-on-Death (P.O.D.) Bank Accounts

One way of achieving the advantages of joint ownership while avoiding its disadvantages is to establish a pay-on-death bank account. This account, available at no cost from banks, savings and loan associations, and credit unions, permits the owner to retain complete control over the account balance (and responsibility for taxes on its earnings). But on the death of the original owner, the account balance automatically passes to the named beneficiary without probate administration. Should the owner need the money in the account or change his mind about the beneficiary, he is free to spend the money or change the beneficiary. To take over the account on the owner's death, the named beneficiary need only visit the financial institution and identify herself.

Choosing Beneficiaries

Residents of community property states who name someone other than their spouse as a P.O.D. beneficiary should inform the spouse. In these states, a spouse who is dissatisfied with her inheritance may be able to claim a specified percentage of the deceased spouse's property. But since most spouses receive more than their entitled share, a court challenge is unlikely. And in some states P.O.D. accounts are not subject to a spouse's claim.

Although there are few restrictions on the choice of beneficiaries, some issues warrant consideration. It is legal, for example, to name a minor as P.O.D. beneficiary, but if the account is worth more than a few thousand dollars, and if the child is still a minor and unmarried at the time of your death, it is wise to arrange for an adult to manage the money. If this is not done, one of two results may occur. (1) If the amount is small—generally a few thousand dollars, depending on state law and bank practice—the bank may turn it over to the child or the child's parents. (2) If the amount is substantial, the parents must go to court to petition for a guardian or conservator to collect and hold the money. (If the parents are dead, a guardian presumably will have been appointed.) The delay and expense of a court proceeding can easily be avoided by naming, as the P.O.D. beneficiary, an adult as custodian for the child under the Uniform Transfers to Minors Act (see p. 45).

More than one P.O.D. beneficiary can be named on an account simply by listing their names on the account but, unless it is otherwise specified, each beneficiary will inherit an equal share of the balance. If state law does not permit differentiating among beneficiaries, the owner can, of course, establish a separate account for each beneficiary.

An alternate beneficiary—that is, someone to inherit the account balance should your first choice not survive you—is not permitted. It is widely believed that if three beneficiaries are named and if Number 1 predeceases the owner, then Number 2 inherits Number 1's share. But in fact Number 1's share will be divided equally among the surviving beneficiaries. If this is not the owner's intent, he should immediately name a new beneficiary to replace the one that predeceased him.

Advantages

Aside from the ease of establishing it, one advantage of the P.O.D. bank account is that F.D.I.C. coverage, which normally protects only the original owner of the account up to $100,000, is automatically extended to protect the beneficiaries if they are a close relative—a spouse, sibling, grandchild, or parent of the deceased. In addition, if the account restricts early withdrawals—a certificate of deposit, for example—the early withdrawal penalty will probably be waived should the owner die before the penalty expires.

Disadvantages

One disadvantage of a P.O.D. account is that it is limited to bank products, which almost invariably offer a lower yield than other investments. Depending on the state of the economy and the stock market, you may prefer to use a transfer-on-death (T.O.D.) securities registration, which is nearly as easy to establish but is used to transfer securities rather than bank products (see p. 38).

Some types of bank accounts cannot be automatically transformed into P.O.D. accounts. If, for example, a joint bank account specifies "right of survivorship," one of the owners may name a P.O.D. beneficiary, but the surviving owner retains the right to change or eliminate the designation. In a community property state, of course, half of the account balance already belongs to the spouse, and a P.O.D. beneficiary can be named for the other half.

Perhaps a more serious shortcoming of a P.O.D. bank account is that the owner may not impose any conditions for the beneficiary to meet before receiving the money, as is possible with a revocable living trust (see below). If this limitation is not important to the owner, the P.O.D. bank account is a far less expensive way to achieve the goal of avoiding probate.

Transfer-on-Death Securities Registration

Transfer-on-death (T.O.D.) securities registration, similar in many respects to the P.O.D. account for bank products, is used for stocks and bonds held in a brokerage account. It is available in all states except Lousiana, New York, North Carolina and Texas, and the District of Columbia. As in the case with the P.O.D. bank account, T.O.D. securities registration is set up by naming a beneficiary or beneficiaries on the brokerage account preceded by the phrase "Transfer on death to . . . "

Like the P.O.D. account, the T.O.D. securities registration may have multiple beneficiaries, but unlike the P.O.D. account, it may name alternative beneficiaries if allowed by the brokerage firm.

It is possible, of course, to keep the securities at home or in a safe deposit box rather than in the broker's street account, but if several securities are involved, registering them with T.O.D. beneficiaries would require dealing with the transfer agents for each security. Keeping the securities in a broker's street account reduces the effort substantially.

In addition to the advantages of the P.O.D. account, T.O.D. securities registration has the additional advantage of prompting the owner to keep his investments in the broker's "street" account rather than in a safe deposit box or a desk drawer. This means that when income tax is due, the broker will provide the owner with a comprehensive Form 1099 to submit with his tax return, sparing him the laborious task of compiling one that includes his every investment. It also means that selling a security does not involve the sometimes frantic task of finding the security certificate and mailing it to the broker within the current three-day limit for settling security transactions.

The Revocable Living Trust

A probate-avoidance device that is far more flexible than joint ownership is the revocable living trust, which is coming into wider use as increasing numbers of people recognize its advantages. A revocable trust is a legal entity ("The Roger J. Smith Trust") to which you can transfer assets in any amount and of any kind: real estate, motor vehicles, bank and brokerage accounts, securities, etc. Because the assets thus transferred are no longer owned by you, they are not subject to probate; instead, upon your death they remain in the name of the trustee or the successor trustee, who must distribute them to the trust's beneficiaries according to the terms of the trust agreement (see figure 4).

During your lifetime, however, you retain full control over the trust assets and their income—you can sell them, remove them from trust ownership, add new assets to the trust, and use any income produced by the trust. In addition, you have the right to change the beneficiaries, the share of trust assets that each is to receive, or the conditions under which they will receive their shares. These changes, made by amending the trust agreement, are at least as easy to make as changes in your will.

A typical trust agreement names one or more trustees and one or more successor trustees who assume responsibility when the original trustees die or become incapacitated. You may, if you wish, designate yourself as the original trustee and the principal beneficiaries of the trust (your spouse and children) as successor trustees. If, however, you have a disabled child or a spouse who is inexperienced in managing assets, you may prefer to designate, either as trustee or successor trustee, a bank, a trust company, or even a close friend.

The trust agreement should also specify the length of the trust's life, the rate of compensation (if any) for the trustees, the range of discretion the trustees are to have over the trust's assets, and the terms of conditions under which the trust's assets are to be distributed to its beneficiaries. You may specify, for example, that some or all of the beneficiaries must attain the age of thirty before receiving their share or that the share of one of them must be used in whole or in part for a specified purpose, such as college tuition or payment toward purchase of a new home.

Assets not currently held in the trust can be "poured over" into the trust on your death. You can, for example, designate the trustee or successor trustee of your trust as the beneficiary of your life insurance policies or IRA, Keogh, SEP, and 401k accounts, in which case the proceeds will be delivered, without probate, to the trustee

Figure 4

REVOCABLE LIVING TRUST

DECLARATION OF TRUST made on the date set forth below by __________________and __________________ hereafter called "Trustees", with reference to the following facts:

(a) __________________ and ____________________ are lifetime partners and hold title to all of their property as joint tenants;

(b __________________ and ____________________ are their only children; each of them has children;

(c) and would like to avoid probate, not only in the event of the death of disability of one of them, but also on the death of the survivor of them, but want assurance that, in the event of the disability of one or both of them, property will be applied toward his, her or their care and, upon the death of the survivor of them, will be distributed to their issue who survive such survivor, per stirpes;

(d) The parties have decided upon holding such property in joint tenancy, with full rights of survivorship, and without any mention of a trust on the record, but with a declaration and acknowledgment that those who succeed, or the one who succeeds, to the title on the death or disability of another or others are, or is, actually holding as trustees, or trustee, for the purposes and on the conditions hereinafter set forth.

THE PARTIES AGREE:

1. ESTABLISHMENT OF TRUST. Any property assigned, heretofore or hereafter, by and/or to the Trustees, as joint tenants or otherwise, shall be deemed trust property and Trustees agree to hold the same in trust for the purposes and on the conditions hereinafter set forth.

2. RESERVATIONS. ______________________ and ______________________ (or the survivor of them) reserve(s) the right to amend or revoke this trust and Trustees agree to reassign or reconvey to them or the survivor of them any property affected by the exercise of such right.

3. TRUSTEE. If one acting as a trustee shall become disabled as defined in the paragraph entitled "DISABILITY" in Article V, he/she shall be deemed to have resigned.

If none of the parties is acting as a trustee, the personal representative of the last to act or, if he has none appointed within thirty (30) days after he ceases to act, ____________________ shall become trustee by filing with a beneficiary hereunder a written acceptance of trust.

Individual trustees shall be reimbursed for their reasonable out-of-pocket expenses, but shall receive no additional compensation for their services. A corporate trustee shall be entitled to reimbursement for expenses and fees in accordance with its published fee schedule in effect at the time the services for which the fee is charged are performed, and if there is no such fee

Figure 4

REVOCABLE LIVING TRUST *(continued)*

schedule then in effect, such fees as, from time to time, are recognized in the area as ordinary and reasonable for the services it performs.

4. DISTRIBUTION.

INCOME: While both ________________ and ________________ are living and not disabled, all of the net income shall be paid to them or at their direction. If both of them become disabled, Trustees shall, in their discretion, apply income for their benefit or accumulate income and thereafter treat it as corpus. After the death of ______________ or ____________

Trustees shall likewise pay or apply net income to or for the benefit of the survivor of them.

CORPUS: Trustees may pay to either ________________ or ________________, from the corpus of the trust from time to time, such further accounts (even to the exhaustion of the trust) as in their discretion they deem necessary or advisable to properly maintain him or her in the style to which he or she is presently accustomed, and shall do so if he or she becomes disabled; such payments may include amounts to or for the benefit of persons dependent upon them for support and premiums on life insurance on either of them or such persons whether or not such policies are payable to this trust.

ON DEATH: Upon the death of ______________ or _____________

Trustees shall pay the expenses of his or her last illness and burial and all debts and taxes and other charges against him or her or arising because of his or her death which shall seem proper; upon the death of the survivor of them, Trustees shall pay such expenses, debts, taxes and charges arising because of the survivor's death and shall pay over all remaining property, both corpus and accumulated income, to the issue of ______________ and ________________, surviving such survivor, per stirpes, their children to be the stock.

Notwithstanding the foregoing, if any distributee has not attained his majority, his share shall be continued in trust, with Trustees accumulating income and distributing to him so much thereof and of corpus from time to time as they deem for his best interests and welfare and upon his reaching his majority, paying over to him property, if any remaining; and, in the event of his death, paying property on hand to his personal representative.

5. MISCELLANEOUS.

SURVIVAL DEFINED. No person shall be considered to have survived another if he or she shall die within thirty (30) days after the death of the other.

DISABILITY. If two medical doctors determine that a beneficiary or a trustee is suffering from physical or mental disability to the extent he or she is incapable to exercising judgment about or attending to financial and property transactions, such determination reduced to writing and delivered to any

Figure 4

REVOCABLE LIVING TRUST *(continued)*

beneficiary or contingent beneficiary under this agreement, or to another trustee, shall be conclusive for the purposes of this agreement.

6. ADMINISTRATIVE POWERS. Trustees shall have the power to retain, sell, invest and reinvest, loan, improve, lease and borrow.

7. ACCOUNTING. So long as ________________ lives and is not disabled, Trustees need keep no accounts because of the control which he or she has retained. However, in the event of the disability or death of Trustees shall keep an account of receipts and disbursements and of property on hand at the end of the accounting period and shall deliver copies to the beneficiaries or if one is a minor, to one with whom he or she makes his home.

8. EXCULPATORY. No purchaser from or other person dealing with Trustees shall be responsible for the application of any purchase money or other thing of value paid or delivered to them, but the receipt of Trustees shall be a full discharge; and no purchaser or other person dealing with Trustees and no issuer, or transfer agent or other agent of any issuer of any securities to which any dealing with Trustees should relate, shall be under any obligation to ascertain or inquire into the power of trustees to purchase, sell, exchange, transfer, mortgage, pledge, lease, distribute or otherwise in any manner dispose of or deal with any security or any other property held by Trustees or comprised in the trust estate.

The certificate of the Trustees that they are acting according to the terms of this instrument shall fully protect all persons dealing with Trustees.

9. CONFLICT OF LAWS. All questions concerning the validity, construction and administration of the trust shall be deterrnined under the laws of the State of Michigan.

IN WITNESS WHEREOF, the parties have executed this instrument.

Date: ____________________

Witness:

______________________________ ______________________________

______________________________ ______________________________

STATE OF MICHIGAN } SS
COUNTY OF ____________

On before me, a Notary Public, in and for said County personally appeared __________________ and __________________ to me known to be the same persons described in and who executed the within instrument, who acknowledged the same to be their free act and deed.

Prepared by: ______________________________

Notary Public

County, Michigan
My Commission Expires:

for distribution to the beneficiaries along with the other trust assets. If, in addition, you designate the trust as your sole beneficiary in your will, the trust will acquire any probatable assets you may own at the time of your death. In such a situation, the trust agreement serves, for all intents and purposes, most of the functions of a will.

Although it is thoroughly effective for avoiding probate-court administration of your estate, the typical revocable living trust offers you no advantages whatever with respect to taxes. Because you have control of the trust's assets and the use of their earnings, you remain liable for all income tax. You do not pay gift tax on assets you transfer to the trust, but all trust assets are included as part of your taxable estate for federal estate-tax purposes. Beneficiaries of a revocable trust normally must pay any applicable state inheritance taxes.

In addition, the revocable living trust offers you no protection against creditors' claims. If, for example, an automobile accident in which you are found negligent results in a judgment against you that exceeds your liability-insurance coverage, assets owned by the trust can be attached to satisfy the excess liability. Although in some states creditors cannot make claims against trust-held assets, in general a trust does not offer you the "limitation of liability" that a corporation provides for its shareholders. As "Roger J. Smith, Trustee of the Roger J. Smith Trust," you remain vulnerable to any claims made against either the trust or yourself as a private person.

As you may have concluded at this point, the revocable living trust offers you the same basic advantage as joint ownership: the avoidance of probate. Why, then, go to the trouble and expense of setting up a trust? The answer is that a trust offers you two advantages not available through joint ownership. First, it enables you to retain full control over your assets, including the right to change beneficiaries at any time. Second, the trust enables you to designate a disinterested trustee to manage your assets in case you become disabled. Moreover, the trust avoids the disadvantages and limitations of joint ownership.

Setting up a trust is not a do-it-yourself project, because a trust agreement should be custom-tailored to your specific needs and assets. The process is, however, relatively simple for a modest estate, and a lawyer should not charge you for more than three to six hours of his time for preparing the documents. As an understanding of the advantages of the revocable living trust has proliferated, so, too, has the number of firms advertising, in print and on the Internet, their services in preparing such trusts. Although some of these firms are undoubtedly reputable, an increasing number have come to the attention of state and federal consumer protection agencies for various negligent or fraudulent actions, among them deceptive fee schedules, failure to transfer assets into trust ownership, using "one size fits all" boilerplate provisions instead of an individually prepared document, and negligence in monitoring changes in trust holdings.

In general it is wiser to use a lawyer experienced in estate planning rather than one of these commercial firms.

Totten (Bank Account) Trusts

If your assets at the moment are not valuable enough to justify the setting up of a revocable living trust, you can sample its benefits in a limited way by establishing a miniature form of revocable trust, known as a bank account, or Totten, trust.

The Totten trust is, however, limited to banks and this means that your assets must take the form of savings accounts, interest-bearing checking accounts, certificates of deposit, or other investment instruments offered by banks. Aside from this limitation, it offers some of the basic advantages of a full-scale revocable trust: during your lifetime, you enjoy full control and use of the assets, but upon your death the full balance of the account passes directly to the beneficiaries without the need for probate.

The tax implications are the same as those for a conventional revocable living trust: you pay any income tax during your lifetime, and on your death the account may be subject to federal estate and state inheritance taxes. And, as in the case with any revocable living trust, the money remains subject to the claims of your creditors.

A Totten trust costs nothing to set up; all you need to do is sign a signature card provided by the bank and designate on it the beneficiary. Although some bank tellers are unfamiliar with it, you are almost certain to find it available at a local bank if you inquire persistently.

The Irrevocable Living Trust

Like the revocable living trust, the irrevocable living trust is an effective means of probate avoidance. In addition, it can reduce both income and death taxes. Its basic (and for most people insuperable) disadvantage, however, is reflected in its name: transfers of your property to it are irrevocable. You can never change your mind or, in fact, exercise any significant control over assets in an irrevocable trust. In a very real sense, you have given them away forever.

Irrevocable trusts have traditionally been used by the rich to reduce their income taxes while still keeping certain assets in the family. When assets are transferred into an irrevocable trust, tax on the income they produce is payable either by the trust itself or by family members in lower tax brackets who derive income from the trust. Transfers of assets worth more than $10,000 / $20,000 annually are taxable as gifts, but if you do not exceed this annual gift-tax exclusion, you can build up the trust assets substantially over a period of years without paying any federal gift tax. Because the trust is irrevocable, its assets are not counted as part of your estate in calculating possible estate taxes. And, here again, the beneficiaries pay no inheritance taxes, as they would had they inherited the same assets through your will.

The reason why people of modest means do not use this type of trust is that in order to enjoy the income-tax relief it affords, they must not use either assets or income from the trust personally or to support anyone (such as a child) whom they are legally required to support, to pay life insurance premiums or any other obligations, or to accumulate income for later use. In short, the tax advantage requires that they part forever with assets that they may need for their own current support and eventual retirement.

If you are considering the establishment of a trust to care for a disabled child or to protect a surviving spouse against financial inexperience, bear in mind that the revocable living trust automatically becomes irrevocable on your death and hence may serve the same purpose without the lifetime disadvantages of irrevocability. The "price" you pay for revocability is essentially a matter of income tax and possible federal estate tax, and the flexibility you get in return for this price may well be worth it.

Custodial Accounts for Minors

Just as the Totten trust serves as a "miniature" revocable living trust for people of moderate means, so, too, there exists a "miniature" irrevocable trust: the custodial account authorized by the Uniform Gifts to Minors Act or the Uniform Transfers to Minors Act, one of which laws has been adopted by every state. This type of account, which is available for bank accounts, securities, and, in some states, all types of real and personal property, permits you to play the role of benevolent parent or grandparent and, at the same time, reduce your income and estate taxes as well as avoid probate.

Under the Uniform Gifts to Minors Act, for example, you can set up an account in a financial institution (or register securities) in the name of an adult who serves as custodian of your gift to the minor. Gifts of less than $10,000 / $20,000 a year per beneficiary are not subject to federal gift tax, and the account is not included in your taxable estate if you do not serve as its custodian.

No matter who makes the gift to your child, income tax on the first $1,400 of the account's earnings is payable by the child—at a rate presumably lower than yours—but the rest is payable at his parents' highest tax rate until the child reaches the age of fourteen. At that time, tax on the entire income from the account is payable at the child's rate. Because $28,000 at 5% will not generate over $1,400 annually, in the custodial account, most parents can realize a tax saving on the account without concern that its yield will add to their own tax burden.

Of course, since such accounts are gifts to the minor, neither you nor any custodian may use either the interest or the principal for your own purposes. The account assets may be used to pay for certain extraordinary expenses of the minor—summer camp fees, music lessons, college tuition—but not for food, clothing, medical expenses, or other items that parents are normally required to provide for minor children.

A custodial account can, of course, be added to at any time. If, for example, you are currently accumulating a nest egg for a child's college education, converting it into a custodial account accomplishes the identical purpose but relieves you of liability for income tax on the earnings. On the other hand, the account's assets become available to the minor child when he or she reaches age 18 (21 in some states), whether you are alive or not, at which time there is no safeguard against irresponsible dissipation of the money, as there can be in a formally established irrevocable trust.

Life Insurance

Although life insurance is usually bought to protect your survivors in the event of your untimely death, it also offers a way to avoid probate, because the proceeds of a life insurance policy pass directly to the beneficiary designated in the policy and are not considered probate assets unless you have designated your own estate or its personal representative as the beneficiary.

Although not considered part of your probate estate, life insurance proceeds *are* considered part of your taxable estate for federal estate-tax purposes. You can avoid this exposure to tax by transferring ownership of the policy while you are still alive to one of your survivors—presumably a beneficiary named in the policy. After the transfer, you may continue to pay the premiums, but the new owner must possess what the IRS terms all "incidents of ownership," which include the right to change beneficiaries and even to cancel the policy. To transfer ownership of a policy, you need only ask your agent or the company for an assignment form, sign it, and return it to the company, keeping a copy for your records.

The gift of a life insurance policy is governed by some limitations. First, like any other gift, it will be subject to federal gift tax if its cash surrender value exceeds the $10,000 / $20,000 annual exclusion. (Term policies, of course, have no cash surrender value at any time.) Premiums that you continue to pay on policies that you have transferred are also considered gifts, but they are not likely to exceed the $10,000 / $20,000 annual exclusion. Moreover, if the policy is transferred within three years of your death, it will be presumed by the Internal Revenue Service to have been made "in contemplation of death," and the full death benefit will be included as part of your taxable estate.

If you do not give away your insurance policies, it is important that you keep the designation of beneficiaries up to date, because if all designated beneficiaries die before you, the insurance proceeds will be paid to your estate and thus become probatable and, where applicable, subject to state inheritance tax. If you have set up a revocable living trust, you might consider naming the trust as sole beneficiary of all your life insurance, so that upon your death the proceeds pass, via the trust, to its beneficiaries, thus avoiding both probate administration and state inheritance taxes, if any. This tactic will not, however, avoid federal estate tax unless the assets pass to your surviving spouse, who has the benefit of the unlimited marital deduction.

If your life insurance proceeds constitute the major part of your assets and if you do not otherwise plan to establish a trust, you might consider establishing a revocable life insurance trust to serve

TABLE 2

Legal Consequences of Various Forms of Ownership

Form of Ownership	*Subject to*		*Control During Your Lifetime*	*Bequeath-able by Will*	*Subject to Creditors' Claims*		*Availability to Beneficiaries*
	Probate	*Federal Estate Tax*			*Before Death*	*After Death*	
Asset solely owned	Yes	All	Full	Yes	Yes	Yes	Delayed
Asset owned jointly with spouse	No (1)	One-half	Divided	No (1)	Yes	No (2)	Immediate (1)
Asset owned jointly with non-spouse	No (1)	All (3)	Divided	No (1)	Yes	No (1)	Immediate (1)
Assets in pay-on-death bank account	No	All	Full	No	Yes	No	Immediate
Assets in custodial account for minors	No	None (4)	None (4)	No	No	No	Immediate
Life insurance owned by insured	No (6)	All	Full	No (6)	No	No (6)	Immediate
Life insurance owned by other than insured	No (6)	None (8)	None	No	No	No (6)	Immediate
Life insurance payable to insured's estate or personal representative	Yes	All	Full	Yes	Yes (7)	Yes	Delayed

Assets in a revocable living trust	No	All	Full	No	Yes	Possibly (9)	Immediate (5)
Assets in an irrevocable living trust	No	None	None	No	No	No	Immediate (5)

1. Provided that you are survived by a joint owner.
2. Unless debt was incurred by both joint owners.
3. Except to the extent your estate can prove that a surviving joint owner contributed to the acquisition or improvement of the asset.
4. Unless you are a custodian as well as a donor.
5. Subject, however, to all of the terms of the trust, which may include a provision postponing distribution of the property.
6. Provided that you are survived by a beneficiary designated in the insurance policy. Otherwise the proceeds become a part of your probatable estate.
7. Limited to the cash surrender value of the policy.
8. Unless you assigned the policy to another within three years of the date of your death.
9. Several states expose the assets in a revocable living trust to creditors' claims.

as the beneficiary of all your policies. Such a trust is useful for the care of a disabled child or the protection of a financially inexperienced spouse. Moreover, because it is revocable, you can terminate or modify it at any time prior to your death.

Family Annuities

If you intend ultimately to leave your estate to your children and if the children are now adults and economically stable, you might consider transferring your estate by means of a family annuity. In principle, the family annuity is similar to annuities offered by insurance companies and other financial institutions: in return for a substantial amount of assets (which may be in the form of real estate, a business, or a securities portfolio), your child guarantees you a monthly income as long as you or your surviving spouse live. This agreed-upon monthly income may be larger or smaller than, or equal to, the current yield of the assets. On the death of the surviving spouse, the payments stop, and the child who was making the payments retains the assets.

Because the family annuity is a contractual arrangement, the assets that you turn over to your child are neither probatable nor subject to federal gift and estate taxes. Perhaps more important, you are relieved of income tax on the transferred assets, and the monthly payments you receive get favorable income-tax treatment as an annuity—most of each payment is regarded as a return of "basis" and is therefore tax-free. For this reason, the family annuity is particularly suited for transferring to an adult child assets that have appreciated substantially while you have owned them: the capital gain will be spread over your remaining lifetime.

On the other hand, the family annuity may have as many disadvantages for your child as it has advantages for you. To begin with, the child will be taxed on the income he receives from the assets, but he can claim no deduction for the payments he makes to you. Moreover, if the current yield on these assets falls below the agreed-upon payments, the child must use his own resources to make up the difference. Lastly, if the child eventually sells the assets, he may be subject to a heavy capital-gains tax, because his cost for them will be only the sum of the monthly payments made to you.

There is a further possible disadvantage to you. For you to qualify for favorable tax treatment, the family annuity must be an unsecured transaction. Although you may trust your child fully, there is always the risk that the child may lose the principal through mismanagement or may die before you do, in which case you will have to make a claim against his estate for the remaining monthly payments.

In general, the family annuity is useful if you are in a much higher tax bracket than your child. If this is not your situation now, you may want to keep it in mind for the future, since it can be set up at any time.

FEDERAL GIFT AND ESTATE TAX

If you give someone money or property during your life, you may be subject to the federal gift tax. The money and property you own when you die (your estate) may be subject to the federal estate tax. The following will give you a general understanding of when these taxes apply and when they do not. It explains how much money or property you can give away during your lifetime or leave to your heirs at your death before any tax will be owed.

Most gifts are not subject to the gift tax and most estates are not subject to the estate tax. For example, there is usually no tax if you make a gift to your spouse or if your estate passes to your spouse at your death. If you make a gift to someone else, the gift tax does not apply to the first $10,000 you give that person each year. Even if tax applies to your gifts or your estate, it may be eliminated by the unified gift and estate tax credit, discussed later.

Generally, you do not need to file a gift tax return unless you give someone, other than your spouse, money or property worth more than $10,000 during a year. An estate tax return generally will not be needed unless your estate is worth more than the applicable exclusion amount for the year of death. (See table 3.)

THE UNIFIED GIFT AND ESTATE TAX CREDIT

A credit is an amount that eliminates or reduces tax. A unified credit applies to both the federal gift tax and the federal estate tax. You may subtract the unified credit from any gift tax that you owe. Any unified credit you use against your gift tax in one year reduces the amount of credit that you can use against your gift tax in later years. The total amount used against your gift tax reduces the credit available to use against your estate tax.

Previously, the unified credit was $192,800, which eliminated taxes on a total of $600,000 of taxable gifts and taxable estate. The Taxpayer Relief Act of 1997 increased these amounts for gifts made and for estates of decedents dying after 1997. Table 3 shows the unified credit and the applicable exclusion amount for the calendar year in which a gift is made or a person dies.

TABLE 3

Unified Gift and Estate Tax Credit

Year	*Unified Credit*	*Applicable Exclusion Amount*
1998	$202,050	$625,000
1999	211,300	650,000
2000 and 2001	220,550	675,000
2002 and 2003	229,800	700,000
2004	287,300	850,000
2005	326,300	950,000
After 2005	345,800	1,000,000

FEDERAL GIFT TAX

The federal gift tax applies to the transfer by gift of any property. You make a gift if you give property (including money) without expecting to receive something of at least equal value in return. If you sell something at less than its full value or if you make an interest-free or reduced interest loan, you may be making a gift.

The general rule is that any gift is a taxable gift. There are, however, many exceptions to this rule. Generally, the following gifts are not taxable gifts:

1. The first $10,000 you give someone during a calendar year (the annual exclusion)
2. Tuition or medical expenses you pay for someone (the educational and medical exclusions)
3. Unlimited gifts to your spouse
4. Unlimited gifts to charities

THE ANNUAL GIFT TAX EXCLUSION

A separate $10,000 annual gift tax exclusion applies to each person to whom you make a gift. Therefore, you can give up to $10,000 each to any number of people each year and none of the gifts will be taxable. If you are married, both you and your spouse can separately give up to $10,000 to the same person each year without making a taxable gift. If one of you gives more than $10,000 to a person during a year, this may result in gift splitting, discussed below.

Example 1. You give your son a cash gift of $9,500. If it is your only gift to him this year, the gift is not a taxable gift because it is under the $10,000 annual exclusion.

Example 2. You pay the $21,000 college tuition of your granddaughter. Because the payment qualifies for the educational exclusion, the gift is not a taxable gift.

Example 3. In 1998, you give $30,000 to your 25-year-old daughter. The first $10,000 of your gift is not subject to the gift tax because of the $10,000 annual exclusion. The remaining $20,000 is a taxable gift. As explained below, however, you may not have to pay the gift tax on the remaining $20,000. You must, however, file a gift tax return.

Gift Splitting

If you or your spouse make a gift to a third party, the gift can be considered as made one-half by you and one-half by your spouse. This is known as gift splitting. Both of you must agree to split the gift. If you do, you each can take the $10,000 annual exclusion for your part of the gift. Gift splitting allows married couples to give up to $20,000 to any person annually without making a taxable gift. If you split a gift you made, you must file a federal gift tax return to show that you and your spouse both agree to use gift splitting. You must file a return even if half of the split gift is less than $10,000.

Applying the Unified Credit to Gift Tax

After you determine which of your gifts is taxable, you then calculate the amount of gift tax on the total taxable gifts and apply your unified credit for the year. For example, in 1998 you give your daughter, Jennifer, $25,000. You also give your son, Alex, $25,000. You must apply the gift tax exemptions and the unified credit as follows:

> The gift tax on $30,000 ($15,000 remaining from your gift to Jennifer plus $15,000 remaining from your gift to Alex) is

$6,000. You subtract the $6,000 from your unified credit of $202,050 for 1998. The amount of unified credit that you can use against the gift tax in a later year (or against the estate tax on your death) is reduced by $6,000. You do not have to pay any gift tax this year. You must, however, file a gift tax return.

FILING A GIFT TAX RETURN

Generally, you must file a gift tax return using Form 709 if:

1. You gave more than $10,000 (annual exclusion) during the calendar year to someone (other than your spouse)
2. You and your spouse are splitting a gift
3. You gave someone (other than you spouse) a gift that he or she cannot actually possess, enjoy, or receive income from until sometime in the future

You do not have to file a gift tax return to report gifts made by paying someone's tuition or medical expenses. You also generally do not have to report deductible gifts made to charities.

FEDERAL ESTATE TAX

The federal estate tax may apply to your taxable estate at your death. Your taxable estate is your gross estate less allowable deductions. Any unified credit not used against your gift tax during your lifetime will be available for use against your estate tax. Your gross estate includes the value of all property in which you had an interest at the time of death. This may include far more property than is included in your "probate" estate. Your gross estate includes:

1. Property owned solely in your name
2. Half of all joint property you owned with a spouse
3. All joint property you owned with a non-spouse, with some exceptions
4. Property in a revocable living trust established by you during your lifetime
5 Assets in a pay-on-death bank account and a transfer-on-death securities account
6 Life insurance proceeds payable to your estate or, if you owned the policy, payable to your heirs.

TAXABLE ESTATE

The allowable deductions available to reduce your taxable estate include:

1. Funeral expenses paid by your estate
2. Debts you owed at the time of death
3. The unlimited marital deduction (generally, the value of the property that passes from your estate to your surviving spouse)

APPLYING THE UNIFIED CREDIT TO ESTATE TAX

As noted above, any portion of the unified credit not used to avoid gift tax can be used to eliminate or reduce estate tax. For example: Tom Roe gave his son, Tim $100,000 in 1998. This was Tom's first taxable gift. He filed a gift tax return. Tom subtracted the $10,000 annual exclusion and computed the gift tax on his taxable gift of $90,000. The gift tax was $21,000. Tom used $21,000 of his unified credit to eliminate the tax on the gift. If Tom made no other taxable gifts and then died in 1999, the available unified credit that can be used against his estate tax is $190,300. This is the unified credit for 1999 ($211,300) less the unified credit used against the gift tax ($21,000).

FILING AN ESTATE TAX RETURN

An estate tax return must be filed if your gross estate is more than the filing requirement for the year of death. Table 4 lists the filing requirement for estates of persons dying after 1997.

TABLE 4

Estate Tax Filing Requirement

Year of Death	*Filing Requirement*
1998	$625,000
1999	650,000
2000 and 2001	675,000
2002 and 2003	700,000
2004	850,000
2005	950,000
After 2005	1,000,000

Example. Mary died in 1998. Her gross estate totalled $1,325,000. She left a total of $625,000 to her children and the balance, $700,000, to her husband, Joe. The amount that passed to her husband qualified for the marital deduction and, therefore, was not included in Mary's taxable estate. Her taxable estate was $625,000. Neither Joe nor Mary had ever made a taxable gift. An estate tax return must be filed because Mary's **gross estate** exceeded $625,000. However, because Mary's **taxable estate** was not more than $625,000, Mary's unified credit eliminated all of the estate tax.

STATE TAXES

Some states impose a tax on gifts (payable by the donor) and on estates (payable from estate assets), or levy a tax on inheritances (payable by the beneficiary). As tables 5 and 6 indicate, however, almost all states provide exemptions for spouses and blood relatives, the size of the exemption depending on the closeness of the relationship to the deceased. In some states, you may be able to spare your beneficiaries the payment of state inheritance taxes by giving them their inheritance before you die rather than by willing it to them, and in all states you can specify in your will that your estate will pay the tax so that the inheritance passes to the beneficiary undiminished.

TABLE 5

State Estate Tax Rates and Exemptions As of December 31, 1997

State	*Rate (On Net Estate After Exemptions) (b)*	*Maximum Rate Applies Above*	*Exemption*
Alabama	Maximum Federal credit (c), (d)	$10,040,000	$60,000 (c)
Alaska	Maximum Federal credit (c), (d)	10,040,000	60,000 (c)
Arizona	Maximum Federal credit (c), (d)	10,040,000	60,000 (c)
Arkansas	Maximum Federal credit (c), (d)	10,040,000	60,000 (c)
California	Maximum Federal credit (c), (d)	10,040,000	60,000 (c)
Colorado	Maximum Federal credit (c), (d)	10,040,000	60,000 (c)
Florida	Maximum Federal credit (c), (d)	10,040,000	60,000 (c)
Georgia	Maximum Federal credit (c), (d)	10,040,000	60,000 (c)
Hawaii	Maximum Federal credit (c), (d)	10,040,000	60,000 (c)
Idaho	Maximum Federal credit (c), (d)	10,040,000	60,000 (c)
Illinois	Maximum Federal credit (c), (d)	10,040,000	60,000 (c)
Maine	Maximum Federal credit (c), (d)	10,040,000	60,000 (c)

TABLE 5 (continued)

State Estate Tax Rates and Exemptions As of December 31, 1997

State	*Rate (On Net Estate After Exemptions) (b)*	*Maximum Rate Applies Above*	*Exemption*
Massachusetts	Maximum Federal credit (c), (d)	10,040,000	60,000 (c)
Michigan	Maximum Federal credit (c), (d)	10,040,000	60,000 (c)
Minnesota	Maximum Federal credit (c), (d)	10,040,000	60,000 (c)
Mississippi	1% on first 60,000 to 16%	10,000,000	600,000
Missouri	Maximum Federal credit (c), (d)	10,040,000	60,000 (c)
Nevada	Maximum Federal credit (c), (d)	10,040,000	60,000 (c)
New Mexico	Maximum Federal credit (c), (d)	10,040,000	60,000 (c)
New York	2% on first 50,000 to 21%	10,100,000	Varies
North Dakota	Maximum Federal credit (c), (d)	10,040,000	60,000 (c)
Ohio	2% on first 40,000 to 7%	500,000	10,000 (e)
Oklahoma	0.5% on first 10,000 to 10% (f)	10,000,000	(g)
Oregon	Maximum Federal credit (c), (d)	10,040,000	60,000 (c)
Rhode Island	2% on first 25,000 to 9%	1,000,000	25,000 (h)
South Carolina	Maximum Federal credit (c), (d)	10,040,000	60,000 (c)
Utah	Maximum Federal credit (c), (d)	10,040,000	60,000 (c)
Vermont	Maximum Federal credit (c), (d)	10,040,000	60,000 (c)
Virginia	Maximum Federal credit (c), (d)	10,040,000	60,000 (c)
Washington	Maximum Federal credit (c), (d)	10,040,000	60,000 (c)
West Virginia	Maximum Federal credit (c), (d)	10,040,000	60,000 (c)
Wisconsin	Maximum Federal credit (c), (d)	10,040,000	60,000 (c)
Wyoming	Maximum Federal credit (c), (d)	10,040,000	60,000 (c)
District of Columbia	Maximum Federal credit (c), (d)	10,040,000	60,000 (c)

(a) Excludes states shown in inheritance tax table (E43) which levy an estate tax in addition to their inheritance taxes to insure full absorption of the Federal credit.

(b) The rates generally are in addition to graduated absolute amounts.

(c) Maximum Federal credit allowed under the 1954 Code for state estate taxes paid is expressed as a percentage of the taxable estate (after $60,000 exemption) in excess of $40,000, plus a graduated absolute amount. The $60,000 exemption is allowed under the State Death Tax Credit.

(d) A tax on nonresident estates is imposed on the proportionate share of the estate which the property located in the state bears to the entire estate wherever situated.

(e) A credit equal to the lesser of $500 or the amount of the estate is allowed. A marital deduction is allowed in an amount equal to the net value of any asset passing from the decedent to the receiving spouse. But only to the extent that the asset is included in the value of the Ohio gross estate. Property passing to surviving spouse is entirely excluded.

(f) Rates apply only to lineal heirs, for collateral heirs the rates vary from 1% on the first $10,000 to 15% on amounts of $1,000,000 or more.

(g) Exemption is a total aggregate of $175,000 for father, mother, child and named relatives. Property passing to surviving spouse is entirely excluded.

(h) Marital deduction is $175,000.

Source: Commerce Clearing House

LOOKING AHEAD

As you consider the various strategies described in this chapter and summarized in table 2, you may decide that some of them are immediately practicable for you, some are worth considering in later years, when the value of your assets is likely to have increased and the needs of your dependents are likely to have changed, and some are simply irrelevant to your financial or family circumstances.

Obviously, those that are immediately suitable and very simple to implement—transferring some assets into joint ownership, for example, or perhaps transfering ownership of one or more of your life insurance policies—should be done immediately because, after all, you may die tomorrow. On the other hand, there is no reason to postpone certain other actions merely because you cannot take full advantage of them now. Most of them are not all-or-nothing arrangements. You can, for example, set up a custodial bank account under the Uniform Gift to Minors Act with an initial deposit of $25 or less and have it available for much larger deposits later on. Similarly, if you set up a revocable living trust now—even if you transfer only a single bank or brokerage account—it will be ready and waiting for the transfer of all your other assets, even if you do this in thirty years, only a few hours before your death.

As we shall see in chapter 6, many of the strategies that are impractical for you today will become highly practical when death is imminent. But the extent to which you can take advantage of them at that time may depend largely on the plans you make today.

TABLE 6

State Inheritance Tax Rates and Exemptions

Selected Categories of Heirs As of December 31, 1997

	Rate			*Exemptions ($Thousands)*			
State	***Spouse, Child or Parent***	***Brother or Sister***	***Other than Relative***	***Child Spouse***	***Brother Parent***	***Other than or Sister***	***Relative***
Connecticut	2–8%	4–10%	8–14%	Al l	$50	$6	$1
Delaware	2–4	5–10	10–16	70	25	5	1
Indiana	1–10	7–15	10–20	All	100	0.5	0.1
Iowa	Exempt	5–10	10–15	All	All	None	None
Kansas	1–5	3–12.5	10–15	All	30	5	None
Kentucky	2–10	2–10	6–16	All	5(a) (b)	1 (a)	0.5
Louisiana (c)	2–3	5–7	5–10	All	25	1	0.5
Maryland	1	10	10	(d)	(d)	0.15	0.15
Montana	2–8	4–16	8–32	All	All/7	1	None
Nebraska	1	6–9	6–18	All	10	2	0.5
New Hampshire	Exempt	18	18	All	All	None	None
New Jersey	Exempt	11–16	15–16	All	All	0 .5	0.5
North Carolina	1–12	4–16	8–17	All	33.15 credit	None	None
Pennsylvania	6	15	15	All	2	None	None

TABLE 6 (continued)

State Inheritance Tax Rates and Exemptions

Selected Categories of Heirs As of December 31, 1997

	Rate			Exemptions ($Thousands)			
State	*Spouse, Child or Parent*	*Brother or Sister*	*Other than Relative*	*Child Spouse*	*Brother Parent*	*Other than or Sister*	*Relative*
South Dakota	Exempt/3.75–7.5/3–15	4–20	6–30	All	30/3	0.5	0.1
Tennessee	5.5–9.5	5.5–9.5	5.5–9.5	600	600	600	600
Texas	(e)	(e)	(e)	(e)	(e)	(e)	(e)

(a) For all other, the exemption is the greater of the statutory amount or (1) one fourth of each beneficiary's interest, if the decedent dies between July 1, 1995 and June 30, 1996; (2) one half of each beneficiary's interest, if the decedent dies between July 1, 1996 and June 30, 1997; (3) three fourths of each beneficiary's interest, if the decedent dies between July 1, 1997 and June 30, 1998; or (4) each beneficiary's total inheritable interest, if the decedent dies after June 30, 1998.

(b) Exemption is $20,000 for infant child or mentally disabled (natural or adopted).

(c) All tax rates will be reduced by 18% for all estates of persons dying after June 30, 1998 through June 30, 2001.

(d) No tax on transfers of real property and first $100,000 of property other than real property.

(e) The amount due is the portion of the federal credit attributable to property in Texas. Only estates that have federal estate tax liabilities are subject to the inheritance tax.

Note: In addition to an inheritance tax, all states listed also levy an estate tax, generally to assure full absorption of the Federal credit.

Source: Commerce Clearing House and respective State Revenue Departments.

3

PREPARING FOR POSSIBLE DISABILITY

Although no one expects to become seriously injured or critically ill, each of us is likely, if we live long enough, to become incapacitated to some extent before dying. Physical incapacity through injury or illness can occur at any time. Mental incapacity generally occurs later in life, although it too can occur at any time. Both possibilities require advance planning, because, once the incapacity has occurred, planning is impossible. In this chapter we discuss the appointment of a surrogate to handle financial and health care decisions if and when you are no longer able to make or communicate such decisions. We also describe alternatives for paying for long-term health care.

MANAGING YOUR FINANCES DURING DISABILITY

If you become incapacitated you will need someone who can act on your behalf in handling your financial affairs—bank deposits and withdrawals, bill paying, check cashing, investment management, the buying and selling of property, and other transactions. The various techniques discussed below allow you to name a person who will take responsibility for your assets should the need arise. It is important to note that preparations must generally be completed before the onset of your incapacity. Most of the procedures discussed, although widely used, have significant limitations. Nevertheless, each offers a degree of comfort and protection.

Guardianships and Conservatorships

When a person is already incapacitated, a guardian can be appointed to manage his or her personal affairs. If the assets are substantial, a conservator can be appointed for purposes of financial management. Such appointments can be made only by petition to a court, usually the probate court. The petitioner—often your spouse, adult child, a close friend—must file a petition with the court for the appointment. In most cases a lawyer must be retained and compensated to see the process through to completion. If the person for whom the guardianship is sought objects to the appointment, he or she may contest it, usually with the assistance of yet another lawyer. The court may also require the testimony of a physician, who must also be compensated, to establish the patient's lack of competence. The process can be expensive and time consuming, and if the allegedly incapacitated person contests the appointment, emotionally devastating for everyone involved.

Once a guardianship or conservatorship has been established, it is subject to continuous supervision by the probate court. Guardians are required to report any major decisions relating to the welfare of the person under their supervision. Conservators must report every transaction carried out on behalf of the person whose assets and affairs they are managing. Although there may be good reason for this supervision by the court, most people find the entire arrangement bothersome and expensive. More importantly, a person under a guardianship or conservatorship automatically surrenders to the guardian or the conservator most of his fundamental rights.

Representative Payeeships

Several states have established a procedure for the management of money known as "representative payeeship," to be used in connection with state and federal benefits programs. The appointed representative can be a spouse or a child of the recipient. The representative payee receives and manages the money on the recipient's behalf, applying it to the cost of support and health care, and investing any balance.

Representative payeeships are attractive because, compared to conservatorships, they are relatively easy to establish. The government agency making the payment determines whether the representative payeeship should be created, avoiding the need to apply to the probate court. On the other hand, the representative payeeship is limited in scope, since it applies to one benefit only. Thus, it is useful when the beneficiary is relying entirely on veterans' benefits or Social Security, for example, but not if the beneficiary has one or more sources of nongovernmental income.

Shared Ownership

Some people concerned with the possibility of future incapacity convert their solely owned property into shared ownership with a family member, or other person. A bank account, a brokerage account, or even a home can be transferred into joint ownership for its management when disability occurs. But creating joint ownership of assets is difficult to unwind and has several limitations, detailed in chapter 2. In general, shared ownership is not a desirable option if its major purpose is merely to have someone act on your behalf in the event of disability.

Revocable Living Trust

The revocable living trust, also described in chapter 2, is especially useful in cases of incapacity because the trustee or successor trustee can immediately manage, invest, and reinvest trust assets without prior court approval or intervention. However, the incapacitated person must have established and funded the trust before the onset of incapacity, particularly in cases of mental incompetence. Finding a suitable trustee may also be a problem, and if the assets are modest, the expense and time involved in establishing and maintaining a trust may not be worthwhile.

Financial Power of Attorney

A more useful and flexible alternative, the financial power of attorney, has none of the limitations of guardianships, conservatorships, representative payeeships, shared ownership, or revocable living trusts. In this context, the word "attorney" is a misnomer, since the empowered person can be any adult—a relative, a close friend, or even a bank—and need not be (and rarely is) an attorney. Hence, in the discussion that follows, we will refer to the "attorney" as the "agent."

Once executed by you—the "principal"—the power of attorney document authorizes your designated agent to take virtually any action with respect to financial and property management on your behalf except the signing and revocation of your will.

Obviously, then, your choice of an agent is critical. The person selected must be trustworthy and have good business sense, and should be available and willing to serve over what may be an extended period of time. The agent, unless it is a bank, serves without compensation. For this reason a family member, a friend, or any potential beneficiary of your estate may be a good choice. You should also designate a successor agent in case your first choice is unavailable or unwilling to serve when the need arises. It is possible to select two persons to act as co-agents, but doing so can lead to problems if the two individuals cannot agree on a particular course of action, unless the document authorizes each agent to act independently.

One advantage of the power of attorney is that, unlike a guardianship or a conservatorship, it does not require court approval or supervision. A power of attorney also offers both the principal and the agent a greater degree of control. The principal can choose his own agent and specify when and in what circumstances the agent can act. He can revoke the power of attorney document at any time. And while the power of attorney is in effect, the principal can handle his financial affairs however he likes for as long as he remains competent.

Unlike joint ownership, the power of attorney retains for the principal exclusive ownership and control of the principal's assets. And, unlike a revocable living trust, there is no need to change title on the assets. Moreover, power of attorney forms are available at most office-supply stores and usually can be prepared without the assistance of a lawyer. A power of attorney document can be signed by any adult who is mentally competent and free of duress or undue influence. It represents a private agreement between the principal and his designated agent and need not be filed with a court or otherwise made public.

Durable Power of Attorney

Until recently a power of attorney was revoked automatically when the principal became incompetent. Today, however, all states recognize what is called a durable power of attorney, which, if it contains appropriate provisions, survives incompetence until the principal revokes it or dies.

Limited Power of Attorney

The limited of power of attorney restricts the agent's authority to a specific activity—the sale of a house, for example, or the management of a checking account. (See figure 4.) Limited powers of attorney are useful even in the absence of incapacity—when, for example, you are out of the country. The limited power of attorney is durable in that it survives incompetence and at the same time temporary since it expires when the specified transactions have been completed.

General Power of Attorney

The general power of attorney gives your agent the right to handle all your financial affairs and is available in two forms, the present power of attorney, and the future power of attorney. The present power of attorney (see figure 6) takes effect as soon as the document is signed. It is useful for anyone who needs immediate management of his or her financial affairs. The future power of attorney, on the other hand, is written so that it goes into effect only after the principal becomes incapacitated. Because the future power of attorney gives the agent no immediate power, the document should specify that the principal's incapacity is to be determined by a specified physician. Once a physician certifies that the principal can no longer manage his financial affairs, the power of attorney then takes effect.

Acceptability of the Power of Attorney

A power of attorney is useless unless the bank, insurance company, brokerage firm, or other third party is willing to accept and act upon it. Acceptance of a present power of attorney is likely to be routine if photocopies of the document are distributed to the parties involved and if the document contains a clause exempting these persons or entities from any liability they might incur by relying on it. It should also contain a statement that photocopies are valid, although some third parties will accept only the original document. In addition, it should be witnessed and, if real estate is involved, notarized and recorded with the register of deeds where the property is located.

Copies of a future power of attorney should not be distributed except to your personal physician who, when the time comes, will sign a statement certifying your incapacity. In all cases, your agent should receive a photocopy and be informed about the location of the original.

Figure 5

LIMITED FINANCIAL POWER OF ATTORNEY

I, ____________________, the principal, of ____________________ make this power of attorney according to sec. 495 of the Revised Probate Code of Michigan. I also revoke any prior power of attorney I may have made dealing with my financial affairs as described below.

1. APPOINTMENT OF AGENT.

I appoint ____________________ of ____________________ as my agent. If that person fails, for any reason, to serve as my agent, I appoint as successor agent ____________________ of ____________________ .

2. DURATION. This power of attorney shall take effect when I sign it. The power of attorney shall not be affected by my disability.

3. POWERS OF AGENT. The agent can do the following thing(s) for me:

____

____

If I have given the agent the power to transfer real property, the property may be described in an attachment to this form, which may be revised from time to time.

5. COMPENSATION OF AGENT. The agent may receive reimbursement for actual and necessary expenses incurred in carrrying out the above powers. Otherwise, the agent shall not receive any compensation.

6. RELIANCE BY THIRD PARTIES. Third parties can rely on this power of attorney or the agent's representations about it. Anyone who does shall not be liable to me for permitting the agent to exercise powers under the power of attorney, unless they have actual knowledge that the power of attorney has terminated.

7. MISCELLANEOUS. This power of attorney shall be governed by Michigan law, although it may be used out of state. Photocopies of this document shall have the same legal authority as the original.

I sign my name to this power of attorney on ________________ ,2______.

____
Principal

Witnesses:

________________________________ ________________________________

STATE OF MICHIGAN
COUNTY OF ________________ } SS

This instrument was acknowledged before me on ________________ , 2 ____ by

____

Figure 5

LIMITED FINANCIAL POWER OF ATTORNEY *(continued)*

____
Notary Public

__________ County, Michigan

My commission expires __________

Prepared by:

____

____

Figure 6

GENERAL FINANCIAL POWER OF ATTORNEY

I, __________, the principal, of __________ make this power of attorney according to sec. 495 of the Revised Probate Code of Michigan. I also revoke any prior power of attorney I may have made dealing with my financial affairs as described below.

1. APPOINTMENT OF AGENT.

I appoint __________ of __________ as my agent.
If that person fails, for any reason, to serve as my agent, I appoint as successor agent __________ of __________ .

2. DURATION. This power of attorney shall take effect when I sign it. The power of attorney shall not be affected by my disability.

3. POWERS OF AGENT. Except as stated in paragraph 4, the agent can do anything with regard to my financial affairs that I could do, including powers to:

(a) Property management. Buy, sell, give (outright or in trust), hold, convey, exchange, lease, partition, improve, mortgage, option, insure, invest or otherwise deal with my real or personal property (my real property may be described in an attachment to this form, which may be revised from time to time). Make deeds, bills of sale, purchase agreements, land contracts, sales contracts, listing agreements, easements, mortgages, leases, options, security agreements or other documents with regard to my real or personal property.

(b) Investment. Invest or reinvest in stocks, bonds, loans, U.S. government obligations (including savings bonds and treasury bills) and other securities; receive dividends or interest from the securities; vote stock in person or by proxy; deal with the securities directly or through a brokerage firm; make any documents with regard to the securities.

Figure 6

GENERAL FINANCIAL POWER OF ATTORNEY *(continued)*

(c) Business manage. Operate, participate in, reorganize, recapitalize, incorporate, sell, consolidate, merge, close, liquidate or dissolve a business that I might be engaged in; employ agents, officers or directors for the business; make contracts with regard to the business, including buy-sell or partnership agreements.

(d) Borrowing. Borrow money, unsecured or secured by my property; make promissory notes, mortgages, security agreements, guaranties or similar documents in connection with any borrowing.

(e) Debts and expenses. Pay bills, loans, notes or other debts owed by me or incurred by the agent on my behalf; pay all expenses for the support and maintenance of me or my dependents; pay all expenses for the management of my property.

(f) Financial institutions. Open or close an account at a bank, savings and loan association, credit union or other financial institution; make deposits or withdrawals from the account, and make drafts, checks, receipts, notes or other instruments for that purpose; lease, discontinue, enter or withdraw contents from a safe deposit box at a financial institution; carry on any other transactions at financial institutions.

(g) Taxes. Pay federal, state or local taxes I owe, or any interest or penalty on them; make and file tax returns, reports, forms, declarations or other documents for these taxes; claim and cash any tax refund; handle any and all federal, state and local tax matters.

(h) Employee benefits. Exercise all rights, options, powers or privileges for any pension, thrift, stock option or ownership, profit-sharing or other employee benefit plan I am eligible for.

(i) Government benefits. Apply for and receive any government benefits, including social security, that I am eligible for; receive and cash or deposit any benefit check or draft.

(j) Legal and administrative proceedings. Begin, continue, defend, appeal, settle or compromise any legal or administrative proceedings involving me or my property

(k) Insurance. Obtain, redeem, borrow against, amend, cancel, convert, pledge, surrender or change any insurance I have; make any documents, forms or affidavits in connection with any insurance.

(1) Motor vehicles. Apply for or transfer the certificates of title to automobiles or other motor vehicles.

(m) Agents and employees. Employ and compensate real estate brokers, stockbrokers, investment advisers, accountants, lawyers, or other agents and employees.

(n) Other powers. I also give the agent powers to:

Figure 6

GENERAL FINANCIAL POWER OF ATTORNEY *(continued)*

4. RESTRICTIONS ON POWERS OF AGENT. The agent shall not have the power to do any of the following things: a) make a will or codicil for me, b) change the beneficiary of any life insurance, c) have any power or incidents of ownership over life insurance I own on the agent's life, d) exercise any powers that would make my property taxable to the agent for income, gift, estate or inheritance tax purposes, e) other:

____

____

5. COMPENSATION OF AGENT. The agent may receive reimbursement for actual and necessary expenses incurred in carrying out the above powers. Otherwise, the agent shall not receive any compensation.

6. RELIANCE BY THIRD PARTIES. Third parties can rely on this power of attorney or the agent's representations about it. Anyone who does shall not be liable to me for permitting the agent to exercise powers under the power of attorney, unless they have actual knowledge that the power of attorney has terminated.

7. MISCELLANEOUS. This power of attorney shall be governed by Michigan law, although it may be used out of state. Photocopies of this document shall have the same legal authority as the original.

I sign my name to this power of attorney on ________________ ,2_____.

____
Principal

Witnesses:

________________________________ ________________________________

STATE OF MICHIGAN }
COUNTY OF ________________ } SS

This instrument was acknowledged before me on ________________ , 2 ____ by

____
Notary Public

____________________ County, Michigan

My commission expires ________________

Prepared by:

____

____

Revoking a Power of Attorney

A power of attorney, because it is a voluntary arrangement, can be revoked by the principal at any time prior to his or her incapacity. Revocation requires nothing more than the signing of a form called "revocation of power of attorney," which need not be witnessed (see figure 7). If the original power of attorney was recorded with the register of deeds, a witnessed and notarized revocation should also be recorded.

Copies of the revocation should be submitted promptly (by certified mail, if necessary) to the agent and to any third parties who honored the original power of attorney. The original document should be retained with your records. If you revoke a power of attorney in order to appoint a new agent, the new power of attorney document should contain a clause reciting that your previous power of attorney has been revoked and that the current version is effective.

Just as it is required to sign a valid power of attorney, mental competence is required to revoke a power of attorney. If the principal becomes incompetent, subsequent revocation requires an interested person to petition the probate court for the appointment of a conservator, who may then, depending on state law, sign a revocation on behalf of the principal.

Terminating a Power of Attorney

Aside from revocation, there are several ways in which a power of attorney can terminate. A power of attorney terminates automatically on the death of the principal, or when the principal's agent and any third parties involved receive news of the principal's death. A future power of attorney that went into effect when the principal became incapacitated terminates automatically if the physician who certified the incapacity certifies that the principal has regained capacity. A power of attorney automatically terminates if the agent resigns or dies and no successor agent was named in the original document. A power of attorney can be terminated by court order if a claim is made and proven—by a beneficiary, for example—that the principal was incompetent or under duress when the power of attorney was signed.

Although a power of attorney generally avoids probate court intervention in order to deal with disability, it cannot prevent disaffected family members from later seeking appointment of a

Figure 7

REVOCATION OF POWER OF ATTORNEY

I, ________________, the principal, of ________________ revoke my power of attorney dated ________ [and recorded on ________, at Liber ________ Page ____, in the office of the Register of Deeds, ________________ County, Michigan], and all the powers given to my agent ________________ in such power of attorney.

________________ ________________

Date Principal

Witnesses:

________________ ________________

STATE OF MICHIGAN } SS
COUNTY OF ________________

This instrument was acknowledged before me on ____________, 2 ___ by

____
Notary Public

________________ County, Michigan

My commission expires ____________

Prepared by:

____

____

guardian or a conservator to manage the principal or his assets. (In selecting a guardian or conservator, the court may, however, give priority to the agent named in the power of attorney.) Despite this limitation, though, a power of attorney, especially the durable power of attorney, is a useful, effective, and inexpensive means of preparing for possible disability.

ISSUES OF LIFE AND DEATH

There are two documents that can express your preferences about medical treatment or its cessation: the living will and the medical power of attorney. The living will explicitly states your preferences about medical treatment should you become unable to express them when suffering from a terminal illness. The medical power of attorney names another person who will have the right to make medical decisions for you if you become incapable of making them yourself. Both of these documents are called advance directives.

Living Will

Most of us hope our death will be swift or painless, but not everyone will be that lucky. Accidents or diseases like cancer, Alzheimer's disease, and AIDS may lead to physical or mental deterioration. Increasingly sophisticated life-support systems intended to maintain a patient's vital processes during major surgery or while diseases run their course can be used to prolong by days, months, or even indefinitely the lives of patients whose condition is obviously hopeless—sometimes extending the agony of the patient, and nearly always resulting in high medical bills. Many individuals, if faced with such a situation, would prefer a quick and relatively painless death.

The Right To Die

The law distinguishes between active and passive euthanasia. Active euthanasia—the deliberate administration of lethal doses of medication or any other intentional act undertaken to end a terminal patient's life—is illegal everywhere. (Oregon law permits physician-assisted suicide in limited circumstances.) Because humanitarian motives are not a defense, imploring a doctor or friend to end your suffering by killing you, constitutes soliciting the commission of an illegal act, though your request will not necessarily go unheeded.

Passive euthanasia involves the refusal of treatment. It is well established that all patients have the right to be fully informed of the risks and outcomes of every medical procedure, and to refuse treatment. This is known as "informed consent." Thus, if a doctor tells you that you have cancer and suggests that radiation or surgery can prolong your life, you may, provided you are mentally competent, decline the suggested treatment. The right of a patient to refuse medical treatment, even when such refusal means certain death, is absolute.

The right to refuse treatment, however, is useless if the patient is comatose or otherwise incompetent. In all states such cases are covered by "right to die" laws, which specify the circumstances under which treatment may be withheld and designate individuals empowered to make the decision to withhold treatment.

Right-to-die laws, though they differ from state to state, are designed to protect both the patient and the doctor. They protect the patient's right to a dignified death by permitting the refusal of further medical treatment—essentially a reiteration of the principle of informed consent. And they protect the doctor who authorizes passive euthanasia from criminal or civil liability that might otherwise result from his decision. All states require consensus by a group of physicians as well as the patient's family before treatment may be withheld.

Regardless of the laws of your state, if you would prefer to have your life terminated by passive euthanasia, the most effective instrument available to you is a living will, a document that expresses your preference clearly and formally. In most states, a properly executed living will is legally binding on your survivors and doctor. Moreover, in these states, the execution of a living will cannot be interpreted as suicide—important because insurance policies often contain a clause rendering the policy void if the insured commits suicide.

In a few states, living wills are not legally binding. Nevertheless, a living will clearly expresses your preferences to your family, your close friends, and your doctor. This can be extremely important because in some cases both the soon-to-be survivors and the doctor would prefer to discontinue life support but feel restrained by their uncertainty as to the preference of the now-incompetent patient.

Drafting a Living Will

Although wording for a living will varies from state to state, the following instructions should produce a legally acceptable document. The wording should generally follow the sample shown in figure 8.

Your living will should be dated, and the signing should be witnessed by two persons who are not your beneficiaries or related to any of your beneficiaries and are not your physician or employees of your physician.

Some states do not regard a living will as legally binding unless executed after the patient has been diagnosed as terminal. Thus, it may be wise to change the date on your living will annually and then initial the change.

Figure 8

LIVING WILL

I, ______________________________, being of sound mind, make this statement as a directive to be followed if I become permanently unable to participate in decisions regarding my medical care. These instructions reflect my firm and settled commitment to decline medical treatment under the circumstances indicated below:

I direct my attending physician to withhold or withdraw treatment that merely prolongs my dying, if I should be in an incurable or irreversible mental or physical condition with no reasonable expectation of recovery, including but not limited to: (a) a terminal condition; (b) a permanently unconscious condition; or (c) a minimally conscious condition in which I am permanently unable to make decisions or express my wishes.

I direct that treatment be limited to measures to keep me comfortable and to relieve pain, including any pain that might occur by withholding or withdrawing treatment.

While I understand that I am not legally required to be specific about future treatments, if I am in the condition(s) described above I feel especially strongly about the following forms of treatment:

I do not want cardiac resuscitation.
I do not want mechanical respiration.
I do not want tube feeding.
I do not want antibiotics.

However, I do want maximum pain relief, even if it may hasten my death.

Other directions (insert personal instructions):

These directions express my legal right to refuse treatment under federal and state law. I intend my instructions to be carried out, unless I have revoked them in a new writing or by clearly indicating that I have changed my mind.

Signed: ______________________________ Date: ____________

Address: ______________________________________

Figure 8

LIVING WILL *(continued)*

I declare that the person who signed this document appeared to execute the living will willingly and free from duress. He or she signed (or asked another to sign for him or her) this document in my presence.

Witness: ______________________________

Address: ______________________________

Witness: ______________________________

Address: ______________________________

Many hospitals urge patients to sign a living will on admission for almost any but the most routine surgical procedures. In any event, copies should be given to your doctor for filing with your medical record, to one or more members of your family, to your spouse or domestic partner, and perhaps to a trusted (and younger) friend. The original document, along with a list of all persons who have received copies, should be kept with your will, your letter of instruction, and other important papers.

MEDICAL POWER OF ATTORNEY

According to the laws of many states, in the absence of a living will, the termination of life support measures requires written consent, which obviously cannot be obtained from a patient who is comatose or otherwise incapable of communicating his wishes. Some states delegate decision-making in such instances to the patient's parents or next of kin-a classification that does not include friends, no matter how close or long-lived the relationship. Therefore, many people choose to execute a medical power of attorney.

A medical power of attorney authorizes a person of your choice to make all medical decisions for you in the event you become incapable of communicating such decisions yourself. The document, which goes into effect as soon as it is signed and witnessed, retains for you the right to make medical decisions as long as you are competent and transfers this right to the person of your choice if and when you become incapacitated. (See figure 9.)

Figure 9

MEDICAL POWER OF ATTORNEY

I, ________________, the patient, of ________________________ make this power of attorney according to secs. 495 and 496 of the Revised Probate Code of Michigan. I also revoke any prior power of attorney I may have made dealing with my health care as described below.

1. DESIGNATION OF PATIENT ADVOCATE.

I, ____________________ designate ________________ of ________________________ as my patient advocate.

If that person fails, for any reason, to serve as my agent, I designate as successor patient advocate ____________ of ________________.

2. DURATION. This power of attorney shall take effect only when I am unable to participate in medical treatment decisions. That determination shall be made, in writing, by my attending physician and another physician or licensed psychologist. This power of attorney shall not be affected by my disability

3. POWERS OF PATIENT ADVOCATE. Except as prohibited by law or as restricted in paragraph 5, the patient advocate shall make all decisions about my care, custody and medical treatment, including powers to:

(a) have access to medical records and information; give medical waivers and authorizations.

(b) authorize admission to or discharge from health care facilities, including hospitals, hospices and nursing homes

(c) employ or discharge medical caregivers, including physicians, nurses and therapists, and pay them reasonable compensation from my funds

(d) consent to or refuse any medical treatment, including diagnostic, surgical and therapeutic procedures

4. FOREGOING LIFE-SUSTAINING TREATMENT (OPTIONAL). By signing below this paragraph, I give the patient advocate the power to decide to withhold or withdraw treatment that would allow me to die. I acknowledge that such a decision could or would allow my death.

____

Patient

5. Exercise of Powers. In exercising the above powers, the patient advocate shall make decisions according to my best interests, or as instructed by me orally or in writing below:

____

____

6. RELIANCE BY THIRD PARTIES. Third parties can rely on this power of attorney, the doctors' statement or the patient advocate's representations about them. Anyone who does shall not be liable to me for permitting the

Figure 9

MEDICAL POWER OF ATTORNEY *(continued)*

patient advocate to exercise powers under the power of attorney, unless they have actual knowledge that the power of attorney has been revoked.

7. MISCELLANEOUS. This power of attorney shall be governed by Michigan law, although it may be used out of state. Photocopies of this document shall have the same legal authority as the original.

I am 18 years of age or older and of sound mind. I am signing this power of attorney voluntarily and without undue influence, duress or fraud.

I sign my name to this power of attorney on _______________, 2_____.

____
Patient

STATEMENT OF WITNESSES

We are eligible to serve as witnesses. We have witnessed the patient's signature, and state that the patient appears to be of sound mind and under no undue influence, duress or fraud.

____
Signature of Witness

____
Name of Witness

____
City *State* *Zip*

____
Signature of Witness

____
Name of Witness

____
City *State* *Zip*

____
Signature of Witness

____
Name of Witness

____
City *State* *Zip*

DOCTORS' STATEMENT

I, ___________________________ of ___________________________
am the patient's attending physician.

Figure 9

MEDICAL POWER OF ATTORNEY *(continued)*

I, ______________________________ of ______________________________am either a physician or a licensed psychologist.

We have examined the patient and it is our opinion that he/she is unable to participate in medical treatment decisions.

______________________ ______________________________
Date *Physician*

______________________ ______________________________
Date *Physician*

ACCEPTANCE OF DESIGNATION

I have been designated as the patient advocate of the patient making this power of attorney. I accept that designation and agree to act as required by law and as stated below:

(a) This designation shall not become effective unless the patient is unable to participate in medical treatment decisions.

(b) A patient advocate shall not exercise powers concerning the patient's care, custody, and medical treatment that the patient, if the patient were able participate in the decision, could not have exercised on his or her own behalf.

(c) This designation cannot be used to make a medical treatment decision to withhold or withdraw treatment from a patient who is pregnant that would result in the pregnant patient's death.

(d) A patient advocate may make a decision to withhold or withdraw treatment which would allow a patient to die only if the patient has expressed in a clear and convincing manner that the patient advocate is authorized to make such a decision, and that the patient acknowledges that such a decision could or would allow the patient's death.

(e) A patient advocate shall not receive compensation for the performance of his or her authority, rights, and responsibilities, but a patient advocate may be reimbursed for actual and necessary expenses incurred in the performance of his or her authority, rights, and responsibilities.

(f) A patient advocate shall act in accordance with the standards of care applicable to fiduciaries when acting for the patient and shall act consistent with the patient's best interests. The known desires of the patient expressed or evidenced while the patient is able to participate in medical treatment decisions are presumed to be in the patient's best interests.

(g) A patient may revoke his or her designation at any time and in any manner sufficient to communicate an intent to revoke.

Figure 9

MEDICAL POWER OF ATTORNEY *(continued)*

(h) A patient advocate may revoke his or her acceptance to the designation at any time and in any manner sufficient to communicate an intent to revoke.
(i) A patient admitted to a health facility or agency has the rights enumerated in section 20201 of the public health code, Act. No. 368 of the Public Acts of 1978, being section 333.20201 of the Michigan Compiled Laws.

______________ ______________________

Date *Patient Advocate*

The living will, although a useful document, deals only with the question of life or death, and not other medical issues. The medical power of attorney, on the other hand, can deal with a wide range of medical issues. Moreover, it puts the decision making in the hands of someone who knows you intimately and is aware of your preferences. Although you should not designate more than one person, it is wise to select an alternate should your original designee be unable or unwilling to serve when the need arises.

The person you designate, sometimes called a patient advocate or surrogate, can be any adult. The person should clearly understand your wishes and be willing to defend them in the face of what may be strong opposition from family or physician. There is no prohibition against designating the same person named in your financial power of attorney. Most states prohibit the appointment of your physician and other health-care providers. Some states extend that prohibition to anyone caring for you in a hospital or to any beneficiary of your will. Thus, although a family member or close friend may be your preferred choice as patient advocate, in some states you are not permitted to make such a designation if he is a beneficiary of your will.

Because the medical power of attorney can be far more detailed than a living will, you should give your agent as clear an understanding as possible regarding what treatments you prefer to accept or reject in specific circumstances. If you have a massive stroke, for example, do you want to reject aggressive treatment (such as mechanical ventilation or tube feeding) immediately? Or would you prefer that your patient advocate allow such treatment initially, to be terminated later if ineffective? Or do you want to receive treatment for as long as possible? Because it allows you to make all sorts of specifications, the medical power of attorney is far more useful than the living will.

If you are away from home, possibly in another state, your medical power of attorney and your living will may or may not be honored, depending on the laws of that state. They are almost never honored by emergency medical technicians, who by law must presume your consent, stabilize you, and get you to a hospital. Once you are there, however, your medical power of attorney can usually be relied on in the event you are unable to make or communicate health care decisions.

Although the legal requirements for a medical power of attorney differ from one state to another, you do not necessarily need the help of a lawyer in signing one. Forms are sometimes available from your hospital, your local bar association, or the state office on aging. Generic forms, which may not conform with your state's laws, should be avoided. Forms that conform with the laws of your state are available for $5.00 from Partnership for Caring Inc., 1035 30th Street, NW, Washington, DC 20007, 1-800-989-9455.

Once you have signed a medical power of attorney, you should make several copies and distribute them to your physician and to anyone else with an interest in your welfare. Store the original in a safe place, making sure that your loved ones know where it is stored.

Unfortunately, there is no ironclad guarantee that either your living will or your medical power of attorney will be honored. In some states, health care providers are entitled to refuse to comply with it on moral or religious grounds. Some states require an objecting physician to remove himself or herself from the case and transfer it to someone willing to honor the documents, but this is not easily done. In some cases, the hospital's ethics committee may resolve the problem; in others, a lawsuit may be necessary. This is why your patient advocate should be someone who does not shrink from conflict.

FUNDING LONG TERM NURSING CARE

The problem of paying for health care in the event of a prolonged illness is one that everyone may face. Because eligibility for Medicaid-funded nursing care is uncertain, and because neither Medicare nor the various Medigap policies cover all costs associated with a prolonged stay in a hospital, nursing home, or hospice, payment from other sources is almost essential.

Medicaid

Medicare and Medigap do not pay for nursing home care beyond 100 days. Medicaid, a federal program administered by the states, is available for the payment of long term care not covered by Medicare or Medigap. But eligibility for Medicaid requires a low net worth; the threshold is set by the state in which you reside. In general, you may own your house (regardless of value), one vehicle (regardless of value), household furnishings and personal goods (regardless of value), a prepaid irrevocable funeral contract, and funeral insurance. Medicaid's low net worth threshold has caused many people to rearrange their financial affairs to qualify. Assets are given away, converted from nonexempt to exempt assets, or transferred to a Medicaid qualifying trust.

A Medicaid qualifying trust transfers control of a person's assets to a trustee, and gives the trustee authority to make support payments on behalf of the person establishing the trust. On the person's death, the assets are distributed to beneficiaries named in the trust. Increasing numbers of upper- and middle-income people have taken advantage of this type of trust, but both Congress and the states have recently taken steps to limit its use. There is a possibility that in the future it may be completely prohibited.

Long-Term Health Care Insurance

When first sold a number of years ago, long-term health care insurance policies were generally unsatisfactory because insurers were uncertain about the extent of their payoffs and their exposure to liability. Recently, as a result of competition and government monitoring, benefits have improved significantly. But there is still no uniform format for these policies. Thus, any long-term health care policy should, before purchase, be closely examined with respect to the following issues.

Benefits "Trigger"

The "trigger" is the event or condition that must occur before the benefits can begin. There are two approaches to triggering: functional and medical. The functional model identifies six activities of daily living and allows benefits to be paid when the insured can no longer perform a specified number—usually three of the six—without assistance. The medical model requires care to be "medically necessary" before benefits become payable.

Levels of Care

Long-term health care insurance policies generally offer three levels of care: custodial assistance; skilled care (daily care by professionals under a physician's supervision); and an intermediate level somewhere in between. Lower levels of care may be provided at the patient's home or in an institutional setting. Higher levels are almost always provided in a nursing home.

Any policy you choose should provide care at all levels, both at home and in a nursing facility. It should not require that you use a lower level of care before becoming eligible for a higher one. A good policy will offer access to any level of care at any time.

Daily Benefit Amount

The premium of a long-term health care insurance policy is based on the daily payment to which the insured is entitled when policy benefits are triggered. Before choosing the benefit amount, you should inquire about the cost of nursing home care and what contribution, if any, can be expected from Medicaid.

Duration of Benefits

Every policy sets a time limit on the payment of benefits, usually one, two, or five years, and sometimes a lifetime. The longer the benefit period, the higher the premium. Before making a choice, assess your personal situation. Bear in mind that the average length of nursing home care is between two and three years, and that only a small percentage of patients remain in nursing home care for more than five years.

OTHER ISSUES

Other conditions of a policy that need careful scrutiny are the waiting period—the length of time before benefits begin—and the existence of a condition prior to the purchase of the policy. A pre-existing condition should not postpone benefits for more than six months. An "excluded impairments" clause, on the other hand, denies benefit payments for any conditions that existed at the time the policy was issued. Unless the policy contains a "waiver of premium" clause, you will have to continue paying the premium after benefits begin.

SUMMING IT UP

If you wish to authorize another person to deal with your possible future disability or incapacity, a financial power of attorney and a medical power of attorney are generally the tools of choice. If your assets are substantial, complex, and likely to need management, the revocable living trust allows for professional management during your life and is an excellent probate-avoidance device at your death. If extended care seems likely, you should consider purchasing long-term health care insurance.

4

YOUR LETTER OF INSTRUCTION

As we have noted in chapter 1, your will, because it is an important legal document, must be prepared carefully in accordance with certain legal formalities. This means that revising it each time the nature or value of your possessions changes is likely to be inconvenient and somewhat expensive. For this reason, your will should dispose of your possessions in rather general terms and should not attempt to enumerate everything you own. Your will may, of course, bequeath certain possessions (a piece of jewelry, for example, or an antique desk) to a specific person, but it should not attempt to specify the disposition of every stock, bond, savings account, recreational vehicle, or other possession, because these change continuously over time.

Yet it is extremely important that you maintain a current record of everything you own so that your survivors will not overlook items of value simply because they don't know of their existence or whereabouts. It is all very well to assume that your spouse or partner is fully aware of your assets and your liabilities—especially if most of your possessions are owned jointly—but if you both die in an accident your survivors will be unlikely to know what you own and what you owe, unless you have provided them with a current inventory. Such an inventory is known formally as a letter of instruction. (See figure 10.)

There are two further purposes that can be served by your letter of instruction. First, it can express your wishes about funeral arrangements and body disposal. Embodying these wishes in a will is not a good idea, because often the will isn't read until after the

Figure 10

LETTER OF INSTRUCTION

This version of a letter of instruction, adapted from a form provided by Citibank, suggests the various items and the level of detail that should be specified, but you should feel free to adapt it to your own situation and the nature of your assets. People who make frequent changes in their securities or their insurance policies may find that a loose-leaf binder or a box of index cards is more convenient and more flexible.

Name ______________________

YOU CAN EXPECT

From my employer: ______________________________________
(Person to contact, dept., phone)

____
(life insurance) *(profit sharing)*

____
(accident insurance) *(pension plan)*

____
(other benefits)

From insurance companies ______________________________
(total amount)

From Social Security ______________________________
(lump sum plus monthly benefits)

From the Veterans Administration ________________________
(you must inform VA)

From other sources: ______________________________________

UPDATED ______________________
(date)

FIRST THINGS TO DO

1. Call ______________________ to help.
(relative or friend)

2. Notify my employer: ___________________________
(phone)

3. Make arrangements with funeral home. See page _________.

4. Request at least 5 copies of the death certificate. (Usually, the funeral director will get them.)

5. Call our lawyer: ______________________________________
(name, phone)

6. Contact local Social Security office.

7. Get and process my insurance policies.

8. Notify bank that holds our home mortgage.

Figure 10

LETTER OF INSTRUCTION *(continued)*

SOCIAL SECURITY

Name ______________________ Soc. Sec. number:____________

Location of card: ______________________

File a claim immediately to avoid possibility of losing any benefit checks.

Call local Social Security office for appointment. They tell you what to bring. ______________________
(phone)

Expect a lump sum of about $ ______ plus continuing benefits for children under 18, or until 22 for full-time students.

A spouse may receive benefits until children reach 18, between ages 50–60 if disabled, or if over 60.

SAFE DEPOSIT BOX*

Bank: ______________________

Address: ______________________

In whose name: ______________________

Location of key: ______________________

List of contents: ______________________

____

Number:______________________

POST OFFICE BOX

Address: ______________________

Owners: ______________________

Number: ______________________

Location of key/combin. ______________________

*In the event of death, the bank may be required by state law to seal the lessee's box as soon as notified, even if jointly leased.

LOCATION OF PERSONAL PAPERS

Last will and testament: ______________________

Birth and baptismal certificates: ______________________

Communion and confirmation certificates: ______________________

School diplomas: ______________________

Marriage certificate: ______________________

Military records: ______________________

Naturalization Papers: ______________________

Other (adoption, etc.) ______________________

Figure 10

LETTER OF INSTRUCTION *(continued)*

CHECKING ACCOUNTS

Bank: ______________________________

Address: ______________________________

Name(s) on account: ______________________________

Account number: ______________________________

Kind of account: ______________________________

Repeat to cover all accounts of husband and wife.

Canceled checks and statements are in: ______________________________
(location)

SAVINGS ACCOUNTS AND CERTIFICATES

Bank: ______________________________

Address: ______________________________

Name(s) on account: ______________________________

Account number: ______________________________

Kind of account: ______________ Type: ______________

Location of passbook (or certificate receipt):

Any special instructions: ______________________________

____

Repeat for each account.

DOCTORS' NAMES/ADDRESSES

Doctor(s): ______________________________
(name, address, phone, whose doctor)

Dentist: ______________________________

Pediatrician: ______________________________

Children's dentist: ______________________________

CREDIT CARDS

All credit cards in my name should be canceled or converted to your name.

Company: ______________________________ Phone: ______________

Adress: ______________________________

Name on card: ______________________________ Number: ______________

Location of card: ______________________________

Repeat for each card.

Figure 10

LETTER OF INSTRUCTION *(continued)*

LOANS OUTSTANDING
(OTHER THAN MORTGAGES)

Bank: ______________________

Address: ______________________

Name on Loan: ______________________

Account number:______________________

Monthly payment: ______________

Location of papers: ______________________
(and payment book, if any)

Collateral, if any: ______________________

Life insurance on loan? ❑ Y ❑ N

Repeat for all loans

DEBTS OWED TO ME

Debtor: ______________________

Description: ______________________

Terms: ______________________

Balance: ______________________

Location of documents: ______________________

CAR

Year, make, and model: ______________________

Identification number: ______________________

Location of papers: ______________________
(title, registration)

Repeat for each car.

INCOME TAX RETURNS

Location of all previous returns-federal, state, local: ______________

____

Our tax preparer: ______________________

____
(name, address, phone)

Check: Are estimated quarterly taxes due?

SPECIAL WISHES

1. ______________________
2. ______________________

Figure 10

LETTER OF INSTRUCTION *(continued)*

PERSONAL EFFECTS

I would like certain people to be given these personal effects:

Person

My white jade pendant ______________________________

My camera ______________________________

My photography books ______________________________

All my other books ______________________________

Other items ____

INVESTMENTS

Stocks ______________________________

Company ______________________________

Name on certificate __________________________

Number of shares ______________________________

Purchase price and date: ______________________________

Location of certificate(s): ______________________________

Repeat for each investment

Bonds/Notes/Bills ______________________________

Issuer: ________________________________

Issued to ______________________________
(owner)

Face amount: ___________ Bond number: _________________

Purchase price and date: _______________________________

Maturity date: _________

Location of certificate(s): ______________________________

Mutual Funds ___________________________________

Company: ___________________________________

Name on account: _________________________________

No. of shares or units: _______

Location of statement(s), certificate(s): _________________________

Other Investments (U.S. savings bonds, etc.) _____________________

For each, list amount invested; to whom issued; issuer; maturity date and other applicable date; location of certificates and other vital papers

CEMETERY AND FUNERAL

Cemetery Plot: ___________________________________

Location: ______________________________________

Figure 10

LETTER OF INSTRUCTION *(continued)*

When purchased: ____________________

Deed number: ____________________

Location of deed: ____

Other information: ____
(perpetual care, etc.)

Facts for Funeral Director (Bring this with you, and bring cemetery deed, if possible)

My Full Name:___________________________________

Residence: __________________________________ Phone: ____________

Marital status: ________Spouse: ______________________________

Date of Birth: __________ Birthplace: ______________________________

Father's name and birthplace: ____________________________________

Mother's maiden name: __________________________________

Length of residence in state: __________ In U.S.: _______________

Military service: ❑ Y ❑ N When: _____________

(Bring veterans' discharge papers if possible.)

Social Security number: __________ Occupation: ____________________

Life insurance (bring policy if proceeds will be used for funeral expenses):

____
(company names and policy numbers)

LIFE INSURANCE

Location of all policies: ____

To collect benefits, a copy of the death certificate must be sent to each company.

Policy: _________________________________
(amount)

Whose life is insured: ____

Insurance company: _________________________________

Company address: ____

Kind of policy:________________________ Policy number: _____________

Beneficiaries: ____

Issue date: _____________ Maturity date: _____________

How paid out: ____

Your other options on payout: _________________________________

other special facts: ____

____

Figure 10

LETTER OF INSTRUCTION *(continued)*

Repeat information above for each policy.

For ____________________ in veterans' insurance call
(amount)

local Veterans Administration office: ____________________
(phone)

OTHER INSURANCE

Accident

Company: ____________________

Address: ____________________

Policy number: ____________________

Beneficiaries: ____________________

Coverage: ____________________

Location of Policy: ____________________

Agent, if any: ____________________

Car, Home and Household

Give information below for each policy.

Coverage: ____________________

Company: ____________________

Address: ____________________

Policy number: ____________________

Location of policy: ____________________

Term (when to renew): ____________________

Agent, if any: ____________________

Medical

Coverage: ____________________

Company: ____________________

Address: ____________________

Policy number: ____________________

Location of policy: ____________________

Through employer or other group: ____________________

Agent, if any: ____________________

Repeat for all medical insurance policies.

Mortgage Insurance: ____________________

HOUSE, CONDO, OR CO-OP

In whose name: ____________________

Address: ____________________

Figure 10

LETTER OF INSTRUCTION *(continued)*

Lot: ______ Block: _______ On map called; ______________________

Other descriptions needed: ______________________________

Our lawyer at closing: ______________________________
(name) (address)

Location of statement of closing, policy of title insurance, deed, land survey, etc.: ______________________________

Mortgage ______________________________

Held by: ______________________________
(bank)

Amount of original mortgage: _______________

Date taken out: __________

Amount owed now: ______________

Method of payment: ______________________________

Location of payment book, if any (or payment statements): __________

____

Life insurance on mortgage: ❑ Y ❑ N

If yes, policy number: ____________

Location of policy: ______________________________

Notify bank of my death; the unpaid amount will be paid automatically by the insurance, and the house is owned free and clear.

Veterans' exemption claim, if any: ______________________________

Location of documentation papers: ______________________________

Annual amount: __________

Contact local tax assessor for documentation needed or more information.

House Taxes

Amount: __________

Location of receipts: ______________________________

Cost of House

Initial buying price: _______________

Purchase closing fee: ______________

Other costs to buy ______________________________
(real estate agent, legal, taxes, etc.):

Improvements as of __________ come to ______________
(date) *(total so far)*

Itemized House Improvements

Improvement: ____________ Cost: ________ Date: ____________

Location of bills:______________________________

Figure 10

LETTER OF INSTRUCTION *(continued)*

If Renting: ❑ Y ❑ N

Lease location: ______________________ Expires: ____________
(date)

HOUSEHOLD CONTENTS

Names of owners: ______________________

Form of ownership: ______________________

Location of documents: ______________________

Location of inventory: ______________________

IMPORTANT WARRANTIES, RECEIPTS

Item: ______________________

____

(warranty location) *(receipt location)*

funeral. The letter of instruction, on the other hand, can be more readily accessible and is more likely to be read immediately after death. Second, the letter of instruction is the appropriate place for the expression of any personal wishes or messages to your survivors. Your will, if it should require probate, will become a public document, accessible to anyone who is curious about its contents, and for this reason it should not contain any information that you'd prefer to keep private.

Unlike your will, your letter of instruction is not a legally enforceable document, and the instructions it contains are not binding on your survivors. (As we shall see, your survivors are not legally bound to carry out your funeral and burial preferences, whether you include them in your will or in your letter of instruction.) Your will is likely to contain such phrases as "I direct that . . .", but your letter of instruction, despite its name, merely *informs* your survivors and cannot legally *command* them to do anything.

Unlike a will, the letter of instruction is not a legally enforceable document. It may take any of a number of forms. It can, for example, consist of an informal letter to survivors, a file of index cards, a looseleaf notebook, or a computer disk, all of which are relatively easy to update. *The Beneficiary Book* (P.O. Box 500028, San Diego, CA 92150, 1-800-222-9125) offers a comprehensive fill-in-the-blanks letter of instruction in looseleaf form. Personal Record (Nolo Press, 950 Parker St., Berkeley, CA 94710, 1-800-992-6656) is a software program compatible with almost any computer.

Whatever the form you choose, the location of your letter of instruction should be known to those who are closest to you—your spouse, your children, perhaps a close friend, or your lawyer. This does not mean that they need have access to it or knowledge of its contents while you are alive; you can, for example, keep it in a locked desk drawer to which only you have the key or in some other location that is private. But it should be easily and readily accessible so that you can keep it up to date regularly—every time you buy or sell a stock or open or close a bank account—and so that it can be found by your survivors within hours of your death.

Because the letter of instruction is a highly personal document, it is impossible to specify what the "ideal" letter should contain. The following listing, therefore, is suggestive rather than prescriptive. You may not need to include every item, but you should review it to make sure that you have not overlooked anything.

Funeral and Burial Preferences

If you already own a cemetery plot, the letter should indicate the plot number, the name and location of the cemetery, and the location of the cemetery deed. Similarly, if you have made advance arrangements with a funeral home, the location of the contract should be specified. Figure 11 illustrates a sample form.

If you have made no advance arrangements, you may want to express a wish to donate one or more organs or your entire body, or a preference as to the type of funeral service, the person you would like to serve as your eulogist, and the method of body disposal. Although these preferences are not binding on your survivors, there is no reason why they should not comply with them if they are reasonable; most survivors are grateful for this information, especially if you have been reluctant to discuss them openly during your lifetime.

Your Assets—Liquid and Otherwise

Liquid Assets

Although your letter need not account for every penny of your net worth, it should list each bank or credit-union account, certificate of deposit, U.S. savings bond, money-market account, and any other

Figure 11

FUNERAL AND BURIAL PREFERENCES

Check the following Yes/No spaces as they pertain to your wishes.

Yes No

____ ____ 1. I direct that my body be used for medical purposes as follows:

____

____

____ ____ 2. I request postmortem examination be made if desirable.

____ ____ 3. I direct cremation of remains.

a. Ashes to remain

b. If (a) is yes, then the disposition of ashes should be as follows: ________________________________

____

____ ____ 4. I request burial in the following manner:

a. Place of burial: __________________________

b. Address: ______________________________

____ ____ 5. I want a memorial service with no casket present.

____ ____ 6. I desire a funeral with remains present.

a. Closed casket.

b. Open casket.

Funeral Home: __________________________

Address: ______________________________

Phone: _______________

____ ____ 7. Service:

a. House of worship: ________________________

b. Clergy: _______________________________

c. Prelude: ______________________________

d. Solo: ________________________________

e. Hymns: ______________________________

f. Special scripture or poems: __________________

____

g. Other instructions: _______________________

____

____

____ ____ 8. I request that memorial gifts be given to the following organizations: ___________________________________

____

____ ____ 9. Other information: _________________________

____

Date __________ Signed ________________________________

instrument that represents cash. Each year millions of dollars in unclaimed bank accounts revert to state treasuries simply because the original owners or, more often, their survivors have lost track of them.

Because the past decade has seen dramatic fluctuations in interest rates, many people have shifted their cash back and forth among savings accounts, money market funds, certificates of deposit, government bonds, mutual funds, brokerage accounts, and other investments, and some people have hedged by keeping part of their assets in several of these. This is why it is extremely important to pass on to your survivors a complete inventory of your current investments, including the schedule of interest payments and the physical location of the passbook, certificate, statement, or other document.

Stocks and Bonds

If your stock and bond transactions have been handled by one brokerage firm and if your securities are registered in the broker's street account name, your letter of instruction should include (or specify the location of) your most recent monthly statement. If, on the other hand, you have been using several brokers and the stock or bond certificates are in your possession, your letter should include a complete inventory and a schedule of dividend due dates, along with an indication of whether the dividend checks are addressed directly to you or are deposited automatically in a bank or money-market account.

Other Assets

Your letter should include a listing of all other moneys due you—from loans you have made, from rents, royalties, promissory notes, land contracts, etc.—and information as to where the contracts, notes, and other documents are located.

Insurance Policies

Each of your current life insurance policies should be inventoried by company, policy number, face value, and beneficiary designation—with a schedule of premium payments and dividend dates. The location of the policies themselves should be specified. Any loans you have taken against their cash value should be noted.

Medical Benefits

If you are covered by some kind of medical plan, your letter should identify the provider or insurer, the coverages, and the location of the policy. This is important to your survivors not only for the collection of possible benefits resulting from your terminal illness but also for the continuation of coverage for themselves.

Death Benefits

In order to collect your death benefits, your survivors will need your Social Security number, possibly your birth and marriage certificates, and evidence of your discharge from military service. Your letter should indicate the location of all these documents. In addition, it should specify any union death benefits or mortgage or credit life insurance that pays your indebtedness on your death.

Tangible Property

Your letter should also list all of your possessions that involve some form of registration, deed, or title: real estate, motor vehicles, boats, snowmobiles, etc. Because your survivors will need the registration document in order to transfer its ownership, the location of each document should be specified. If these items are covered by insurance policies, the letter should identify the insurer, the number, location, and expiration date of each policy, and the schedule of premium payments. This is especially important with respect to automobile and homeowner's insurance because a lapse in premium payments, which can occur all too easily when your survivors are distracted by your death, can leave important assets completely unprotected.

YOUR LIABILITIES

Although a painstaking review of your checkbook can help your survivors identify your recurring financial obligations, you can make their task much easier by listing in your letter all your current financial obligations: mortgage payments, loan payments, charge accounts, installment payments on cars, boats, and major appliances. In addition to listing each of these obligations, your letter should note whether you alone are responsible for the indebtedness or whether someone else (perhaps your spouse) cosigned for the loan. As we shall see in chapter 10, outstanding debts on cosigned agreements remain the responsibility of the cosigner after your death, but debts incurred by you alone will not have to be paid by your survivors if there is insufficient money left in your estate. This listing will, in addition, help your survivors decide which of your obligations should be paid promptly in order to prevent foreclosure, repossession, or the cutting off of essential services—and which can be delayed until final settlement of your estate.

Your letter should also list any payments you have made or documents you have signed for goods to be delivered or services to be performed in the future: airline tickets you have bought in advance, tour reservations, a purchase agreement on a car not yet delivered, taxes paid in advance of the due date in order to gain an income-tax deduction. Many of these items represent cash that can accrue to your survivors if the agreements or reservations can be canceled promptly.

MISCELLANEOUS

No matter what your life-style, you carry around "in your head" many facts that will not be in the heads of your survivors. You should include in your letter, therefore, any information that you cannot assume your survivors know. The following suggestions should lead you to think of other items:

Keys

Nothing is more frustrating to survivors than encountering a locked drawer or cabinet for which they can't identify a key—or a key for which they can't identify the lock. You yourself have no difficulty in identifying your keys by shape or color, but you can't expect your survivors to do the same. Your letter should specify the location of all important keys and combinations (safe-deposit box, desk drawers, file cabinets, office, safes, vehicles), and each of those keys should be somehow identified. All keys for long-discarded suitcases, padlocks, or typewriter cases should be immediately discarded.

Hiding Places

Even people who rent safe-deposit boxes often have secret hiding places at home—to foil burglars or simply to avoid frequent treks to the bank. For example, some people store the sterling tableware in a cranny behind the furnace, or they cache precious jewelry at the back of the third shelf of the linen closet.

If these hiding places are ingenious enough to fool burglars, they are just as likely to be overlooked by your survivors. Your letter, therefore, should specify their location(s). Of course, if a burglar finds your letter, your hiding place is no longer secure, but since burglars rarely spend time reading private documents, you would do well to avoid the far greater risk that your survivors will overlook some of your highly valued possessions.

Inconspicuous Valuables

The value of some antiques and collectibles is apparent at a glance, but this is not true of others, especially those that require a certain amount of expertise. Your survivors, especially if they don't share your enthusiasm or knowledge, may discard as junk or send to the local thrift shop some highly valuable old clocks, china, paintings, first editions, guns, antique woodworking tools, or other items that you have painstakingly and lovingly acquired over many years.

Your letter, therefore, should identify each of these items and indicate their approximate value and the location of any documents (bills of sale, receipts, customs declarations, etc.) that provide evidence of their provenance. This listing, if it is done with care, can serve a second purpose: by omitting certain items, it can prevent your survivors from assuming that the omitted items have high value as antiques and taking them, with high hopes, for appraisal by antique dealers or auctioneers, only to be told that they should be consigned to the local thrift shop.

On the other hand, certain items with no value as antiques may nevertheless have high personal value: a four-generation family bible, for example; a century-old daguerreotype of an ancestor; a set of metal-working tools crafted by a grandfather as part of his blacksmithing apprenticeship; a type cabinet handed down by a great-grandfather who was a printer. Sketching the history of such items in your letter may not only increase their value in the eyes of your survivors but also strengthen their feeling for the family's history.

YOUR "LETTER TO THE WORLD"

Your letter of instruction also gives you an opportunity to communicate to one or more of your survivors some feelings or ideas that, for one reason or another, you are unable to express in a face-to-face situation. You may, for example, want to use your letter to heal a longstanding breach in a relationship or to explain its causes or origins. You may want to express affection or respect that you are reluctant or embarrassed to express while you are alive. You may want to explain or apologize for certain of your own actions that at one time or another created problems or raised questions for your survivors.

Because this is *your* letter, there are no prescriptions or proscriptions as to its contents. One principle, however, might be worth following: in general, it is wise to avoid vindictiveness or to express hopes or expectations that are unlikely to be fulfilled. No purpose is served by a posthumous revelation that you have always resented your brother because your parents sent him, but not you, to college or by a hope that your thirty-five-year-old daughter will abandon her homosexual relationship and find herself a husband. If you would like to be remembered fondly, it is better to err on the side of tolerance and charity.

KEEPING UP TO DATE

Even if your affairs are quite complicated, completing a letter of instruction involves no more than a couple of evenings of concentrated work. This effort will be entirely wasted, however, unless you keep updating the letter at regular intervals: monthly if you shift your investments frequently; not less than twice a year to account for insurance premiums, automobile changes, and other shifts in your assets and liabilities.

Such changes can, of course, be combined with your other household accounting chores, especially if you keep at least part of your letter in the form of a ledger or loose-leaf account book. A good deal of its contents will be useful to you during your lifetime in budgeting and in calculating state and federal income tax, and the more carefully you maintain your letter of instruction the more time you are likely to save on these other chores.

5

FUNERALS — AND SOME ALTERNATIVES

Unless you are on the verge of death, planning for the disposal of your body and for the rituals that will mark your death may strike you as futile if not downright morbid. And, to a large extent, you're right. Although some people plan their funeral service and their burial down to the smallest detail, there are several reasons why this doesn't make much sense.

To begin with, until you are terminally ill, the time, place, and circumstances of your death are uncertain. You may die while traveling, thousands of miles from home; or, years before you die, you may move far away from your preselected grave site; or the eulogist you have chosen may die before you do; or inflation may drive the cost of your plans far beyond the money you have set aside for them; or the membership of your survivor group may change through death or divorce. Moreover, if you die in certain kinds of accidents—fire, drowning, a plane crash—there may be no body for the survivors to dispose of.

There are other uncertainties, as well. Unless you donate your body for medical research or organ transplant (see p. 110), possession of it passes, on your death, to your next of kin, and with possession goes the right to decide about its disposal. Even if they know your preferences and want to comply with them, they may not be able to afford to. But, more important, they are under no legal obligation to comply, even if money is available.

Given these difficulties, it is not really practical for you to make advance arrangements with a funeral home, a cemetery, and perhaps even a monument firm, specifying exactly what you want from each. Because of continuous inflation, no reputable funeral home will write a future contract that specifies a price in current dollars. Even if you prepay a substantial amount for your funeral, your survivors may be faced with additional charges or, alternatively, with accepting a funeral much simpler than you had specified. It is also possible, of course, that by the time you die the funeral home with which you contracted may have gone bankrupt or out of business, in which case your repayment may be lost entirely.

Advance purchase of a cemetery plot or grave site also presents problems. Many people believe that the purchase of a cemetery plot represents a miniature investment in real estate that can yield a profit if it is not ultimately used. But this is not the case. Your ownership of a cemetery plot is not the same as your freehold ownership of your house and grounds. Ownership of a plot gives you the right to be buried there (in a casket or in a crematory urn), but if you move or change your plans, in some states you may not sell it at a profit, and some cemeteries restrict resale rights to themselves.

Monuments may also be purchased in advance, but what value will they have if you move before you die? They are very expensive to ship, and their resale value is low. As for caskets, not only can you buy one in advance, but you can also buy your choice of two models in kit form by mail order (from the St. Francis Burial Society, 1768 Church Street NW, Washington, DC 20036), but even the most avid do-it-yourselfer would probably not want it in the house, even though the supplier points out that it has interim use as a blanket chest, a wine rack, or a coffee table.

Since most people don't enjoy contemplating their deaths in as graphic terms as funeral planning requires, you may feel that the arguments presented above relieve you of any need to think about the subject. But although it is inadvisable to try to formulate specific plans, it is crucially important, for several reasons, that you make some general decisions and share them with those closest to you.

To begin with, if your survivors have no idea as to your preferences, they are likely to put up little resistance to the arguments of a funeral director in favor of the most expensive funeral they can (or think they can) afford. These arguments center on three areas in which your survivors may be vulnerable: (1) social status and conspicuous display: the implication being that an elaborate funeral and expensive casket will impress the departed's friends and neighbors and express the survivors' love and respect; (2) an appeal to grief and guilt: "Your (parent, spouse, child) deserves the very best, doesn't he? And this is the last thing you can do for him"; and (3) a denial of the reality of death: "A very expensive casket will help protect the cremains against decay."

Now, if you yourself want an elaborate and expensive funeral, no harm will have been done by these arguments. But if you would have preferred something much simpler and less expensive but did not communicate your preferences, money that might have gone to the survivors may go instead to the funeral director.

A second reason for making and sharing your plans may be even more important. Your funeral is for the benefit of your survivors. It will be a significant event that at least some of them will remember for the rest of their lives. This is why it is crucial not only that *they* should be aware of *your* preferences but that *you* should be aware of *theirs*—and perhaps modify yours to accommodate theirs if there are differences. Obviously, if you are so concerned about their feelings that you don't express your own preferences candidly and if they, in turn, are inhibited by the same consideration, no communication will take place. But you may be able to achieve at least something more than polite evasiveness if you center your discussion not on specific funeral details but on the following four general questions:

What kind of ritual do I want to mark my death?

Do you want your family and friends to "pay their last respects" by filing past your open casket and joining a cortege to the cemetery? Or do you want a memorial service conducted by a close friend, without your body present? Or would you prefer a convivial party of your closest friends, with music, drinks, and whatever kind of merriment you usually enjoyed with them—the kind of ending described in the old song:

See what the boys in the backroom will have
And tell them that I'll have the same.

How concerned am I about keeping my body intact?

Your answer to this question will influence your decisions about donating your entire body or some of its organs, cremation, and other options described later in this chapter. It may also influence your choice of casket and grave site, if you believe—against all scientific evidence—that the right choices can prevent decay. Lastly, your answer to this question is closely related to a third question:

How do I define immortality?
Although all of us have some concern with how—and how long—our survivors will remember us, our specific views vary widely. Some people, presumably believing that their physical remains are important, choose a memorably elaborate funeral and a conspicuous grave. (In some cultures a photograph of the deceased is embedded in the headstone, and some American funeral directors offer the survivors, at additional cost, a photograph of the deceased laid out in the casket.) Others, believing that their immortality depends on their works and acts, regard their physical remains as totally insignificant and may hasten the return of "ashes to ashes, dust to dust" by cremation. Still others believe that they achieve some degree of immortality by donating their corneas, kidneys, and other parts to prolong or enhance the lives of others.

How much will the disposal of my remains cost my survivors?
Even if, allowing for inflation, you set aside enough money for a traditional funeral, cemetery burial, and perpetual care of the grave, some of this money could, if you made a less expensive choice, pass to your survivors. From this point of view, then, you are not really "paying your own way." At the time of this writing, the average funeral, including cemetery burial, costs approximately $4,000. If this sum represents only a small fraction of your net worth, both you and your survivors may feel that it is well spent. But if, when you reach old age, your income diminishes and the cost of living goes up, your funeral expenses may be crippling to your survivors, and a less costly alternative may be desirable, if not, indeed, essential.

Once you and those close to you have reached some agreement—or at least compromise—on these fundamental questions, you can intelligently begin to examine specific alternatives. As you will have noted, some of your answers to the questions related to actual disposal of the body; others related to social rituals intended to mark your death. Usually, these two functions are independent of each other, but sometimes one places limitations on the other. A church service with the body present, for example, can be followed either by grave burial or by cremation, but usually not by donation of the body for research. Organ donation for transplant purposes can be followed by a viewing of the open casket, but body donation, of course, can be followed only by a memorial service. Since your body must ultimately be disposed of by one of only a few methods, whereas ritual is available in a wide variety of alternatives or can be dispensed with altogether, we shall review the disposal alternatives first and indicate any limitations they place on memorial rituals. Table 7 provides a systematic overview of the alternatives.

DISPOSAL ALTERNATIVES

Grave Burial

Grave burial is so traditional in Western society that many people do not even consider the alternatives, and today more than 90 percent of Americans choose this method of disposal. The arguments in its favor are so widely accepted that they need only the briefest mention. A grave is believed to provide a "permanent" resting place. A family grave plot, or even a pair of adjoining graves, offers eternal "togetherness" for family members or spouses. And a grave, especially if it is situated in serene and attractive surroundings, is an inviting place for memorial visits by survivors.

But none of these arguments is invulnerable. A grave is not, in fact, permanent. Cemeteries can be, and have been, moved or destroyed to make way for such public projects as reservoirs, hydroelectric plants, and even superhighways. Moreover, the togetherness provided by the family plot becomes less achievable in a society in which one out of every five families changes its address every year and in which divorce and other family changes inevitably reduce people's concern for their ancestors. And even if families remain in place and loyal to the memories of their forebears, many grave sites that were initially serene and inviting become unattractive as a consequence of overcrowding, surrounding urbanization, or sheer neglect.

Those who oppose grave burial offer additional arguments. Cemeteries, they point out, use land that might be put to more socially productive purposes. Cemetery plots are expensive, as are headstones. Cemetery burial usually, though not necessarily, is preceded by embalming, the purchase of an expensive casket, and other elaborate and costly services. Many people feel, also, that burial concentrates attention on a person's physical remains rather than on the meaning of his life—and that, with respect to the body, a swift return to its original elements through cremation is preferable to what Robert Frost has called "the slow, smokeless burning of decay."

On the other hand, your own circumstances and feelings may render these counterarguments meaningless. If you have a family plot (or if you think your family is stable enough both structurally and geographically to justify one), grave burial may be a desirable alternative. If you are a veteran, you are entitled to free grave burial in a military cemetery, although it may be located at a considerable distance from your home—quite possibly in another state.

CREMATION

Cremation, although it is chosen by fewer than 10 percent of Americans, is the most widely used method of disposal in a number of other countries—especially those, such as Japan and England, in which population density has made the use of land for cemetery purposes prohibitively expensive.

For some people, the very word "cremation" brings to mind the horrors of the smoking furnaces of the World War II death camps, but the modern crematorium bears no resemblance to this image. Often resembling a conventional funeral home, with rooms available for viewing the body and for conducting funeral or memorial services, the crematorium contains a high-temperature furnace that in a matter of two or three hours reduces the body to approximately eight pounds of ash. Temperatures are so high that there is no smoke, and the ashes produced by the container or casket are completely consumed. The remaining bones are pulverized and combined with the ashes, and the "cremains" are placed in an urn or other container.

The alternatives for actual disposal of the ashes are several. They may, of course, be buried in a conventional grave. Most cemeteries permit the interment of two cremated bodies in a single grave, and they charge less for the opening and closing of the grave than for a casket. Alternatively, the crematory urn may be kept permanently in a niche in a columbarium, usually operated by the crematorium. Some crematoria scatter the ashes in a memorial garden.

In some states commercial operators—who are often the owners of private aircraft or seagoing vessels—are permitted to charge fees for scattering the ashes from the air or on the waters at locations specified in the letter of instruction or by the survivors. Other states—presumably as a result of lobbying by cemetery interests—prohibit the scattering of ashes, but it is difficult to see how this prohibition can be enforced if survivors choose to do it privately and inconspicuously. None of these alternatives need be chosen before or immediately after cremation. Usually the survivors are given the cremains in a canister or urn, and ultimate disposition can occur at any time after that.

Cremation is usually supported by either or both of two arguments—one philosophical, and therefore unresolvable; the other economic, and therefore testable. The philosophical argument is that the process is swift, clean, and final and that survivors are not stressed by thoughts about a body "amoldering in the ground." Obviously, this argument is entirely subjective.

The economic argument, on the other hand, is one whose validity you can check objectively. Cremation, its proponents argue, is far cheaper than grave burial because (1) no embalming is necessary, (2) a simple, inexpensive container may be used instead of a casket, (3) no cemetery plot or monument is needed, and (4) if death occurs at some distance from home, it is far less expensive to ship "cremains," which can travel by parcel post or United Parcel Service, than to ship a body (which must first be embalmed) in a casket by air or rail.

But these economies are not inevitable, since some of them relate to the ritual rather than to the cremation process itself. If, for example, cremation is chosen in conjunction with a traditional funeral service, the full services of a funeral director may be required, and the only economy is the difference between crematorium and cemetery costs—a difference that may turn out to be negligible. On the other hand, grave burial, if you choose a simple graveside service, need not involve the full range of services offered by funeral directors as part of the "standard adult funeral."

To compare the costs of cremation with those of grave burial, you need to compare (1) the cost of cremation itself plus the cost of an urn and perhaps the placement of the urn in a columbarium or a grave against (2) the total cost of the cemetery plot, opening and closing costs, perpetual care or annual maintenance fees, plus the excess cost of a casket over a crematorium container.

If you have philosophical objections to cremation (only the Orthodox Jews have a religious prohibition against it), the economic argument will obviously leave you unmoved. If you have no particular preferences one way or the other, however, you might consider saying just that in your letter of instruction. Giving your survivors this kind of discretion allows them to compare costs at the time of your death—or to take advantage of the substantial economy that cremation offers if you die away from home.

Body Donation

The donation of your body to a hospital or medical school for research or teaching purposes and the donation of certain of your organs for transplantation are often considered as essentially the same process, but they are not. Although both procedures are covered in the Uniform Anatomical Gift Act, a law adopted by all states, they are in some respects mutually exclusive. If you decide to give any of your organs except your corneas for transplant purposes, your body becomes unacceptable for use in research or teaching. On the other hand, if you give your body for research or teaching purposes, your specific organs cannot be used for transplantation. Hence, you need to consider each kind of donation separately.

People who intend to donate their bodies for research or teaching usually have one or both of two motives: to eliminate all funeral costs and to benefit humanity, usually by giving their bodies to a specific institution or for a specific purpose. Actually, neither of these intentions may ultimately be realized.

To begin with, not all bodies are acceptable, and no institution can be compelled to accept an anatomic gift. If your body has been mutilated by accident or surgery or emaciated by disease, it may not be usable for either research or teaching. For this reason alone, it is important that you have an alternative plan for disposal.

Giving your body to a specific institution is also somewhat uncertain. The need for bodies is by no means as great as it used to be, and it is not uniform in all parts of the country. In anatomy courses for medical, nursing, and dentistry students, sophisticated visual aids have reduced the need for bodies. And the cachet of being able to say, "I'm leaving my body to the Yale Medical School," has given high-status institutions more bodies than they need. As a consequence, reciprocity among medical schools has developed, and as a result of this very sensible arrangement, your body may not end up at the institution of your choice or be used for the purposes you'd prefer.

Although some medical schools will pick up your body from the place of death at no cost to your survivors, others require that it be delivered, and none of them will pay transportation costs if you die in a distant place. And although you have the legal right to donate your body, most medical schools will nevertheless require written consent of your next of kin before making arrangements to accept your gift.

Thus, if you want to donate your body, you can indicate this preference in your letter of instruction and, if you wish, on a Uniform Donor Card (see figure 12), but it is still advisable to choose an alternate method of disposal in case your wishes cannot be carried out for one of the reasons indicated above.

Most medical schools require that your body not be embalmed—although some of them will accept a body that has been embalmed according to their instructions. This restriction on embalming usually precludes any kind of service with the body present, and the usual practice is for survivors to hold a memorial service shortly after the death. After the body has served its purposes in research or teaching, it can be returned to the survivors for burial or cremation; but in most cases it is disposed of, usually by cremation, by the institution to which it was donated, and the ashes are returned to the survivors, if they wish.

Organ Donation

The donation of organs for transplant, in contrast to body donation, is not motivated by the desire to eliminate disposal costs, because it is not a method for final disposal and in no way precludes a traditional service, including viewing of the body. And although the need for bodies fluctuates, the need for all transplantable organs always exceeds the supply, prompting one renologist to display a bumper sticker pleading, "Don't bury kidneys; transplant them."

Donating your organs will almost inevitably prolong or improve someone's life. Your corneas, transplanted, will restore the recipient's sight. Each of your kidneys can literally give an otherwise doomed recipient a new lease on life. Your skin can help the recovery of burn victims, and your bones, your pituitary gland, and other parts can also be used in treatment or research. In fact, it is impossible to list organ donations exhaustively because the technology is evolving so rapidly that any list is likely to be incomplete within a year.

Figure 12

UNIFORM DONOR CARD

UNIFORM DONOR CARD

OF ____________________________________

Print or type name of donor

In the hope that I may help others, I hereby make this anatomic gift, if medically acceptable, to take effect upon my death. The words and marks below indicate my desires.

I give: (a) _______ any needed organs or parts

(b) _______ only the following organs or parts

____

Specify the organ(s) or part(s)

for the purposes of transplantation, therapy, medical research or education;

(c) _______ my body, for anatomic study if needed.

Limitations or special wishes, if any: ______________________________

____

Signed by the donor and the following two witnesses in the presence of each other:

______________________________ ______________________

Signature of Donor *Date of Birth of Donor*

____________________ ______________________________

Date Signed *City & State*

____________________ ______________________________

Date Signed *Witness*

This is a legal document under the Uniform Anatomical Gift Act or similar laws.

For further information consult your physician or

National Kidney Foundation Inc.
1 Park Avenue, New York, NY 10016

Although there are always more potential recipients than there are donors, organ transplant is beset by two problems: most organs must be removed very promptly after death, and a recipient who is biologically compatible with the donor must be readied for the transplant very shortly after the death of the donor. Obviously, this biological and chronological "match" isn't always easy to achieve. It depends not only on the circumstances of your death but also on the efficiency of an organ-transplant network in your community. Hospitals that are part of such a network can, when a donor's death is impending, alert a recipient in the community or plan for shipping the donation promptly to where it can be used.

One consideration that deters some people from becoming donors is the fear that their death will be hastened by physicians eager to get their organs for transplantation. This fear is groundless, because the code of ethics established for transplantation prohibits any physician involved in the transplantation from attending the potential donor. On the other hand, some people fear that they will be kept "alive" artificially until a recipient can be located and prepared. Whether you feel that this fear is justified depends on your definition of "death." Most states now accept the concept of "brain death"—a "flat electroencephalograph" taken several times and indicating irreversible inactivity in the brain. After death thus defined, it is possible to maintain circulation and respiration by artificial means, and this is sometimes done to keep organs in satisfactory condition for transplant. The individual thus maintained, however, is not being "kept alive." He is, in fact and in law, dead.

As you can see, just as it is difficult to donate your entire body to a specific institution for a specific use, so, too, it is difficult to donate specific organs. A better plan, if you intend to be a donor, is to execute a Uniform Donor Card, indicating on it whatever options you prefer. Two of the options—body donation and organ donation—are mutually exclusive, but by checking both of them, you allow the ultimate decision to be determined by the circumstances of your death and thus ensure that your gift will be used optimally.

Donor cards are available from the Kidney Foundation and other sources. Some state motor-vehicle administrations offer all licensed drivers a press-on donor label that can be attached to the reverse side of their driver's license—thus ensuring that the intention to donate will be noticed promptly in the event of accident or death away from home. No matter which form of donor card you use, you can always change your mind: simply deface or tear up the card, or peel the label off your driver's license.

RITUAL ALTERNATIVES

TYPE AND LOCATION OF SERVICE

Unlike the alternatives for body disposal, which are clearly limited, the alternatives for rituals marking your death are virtually limitless, and their various features can be combined in a variety of ways. A religious service, for example, can be held in a house of worship, a funeral home, your own home, a crematorium, or at the grave site. It can be held with an open casket, a closed casket, or with no body present. A memorial service, too, can be held anywhere and at any time after the death, since it usually takes place with no body present. As in the case of body disposal, it is difficult to make precise arrangements before death occurs, but you and your next of kin can and should reach some agreement on a number of preferences.

Although the choice between religious and secular services may seem to depend very simply on the nature of your own religious beliefs, problems can arise if funeral arrangements are left in the hands of children who may have a more secular outlook than you do. In such a situation, the lack of open discussion can cause your children—in an attempt to please you or to please themselves—to err in either direction.

CHOICE OF CASKET

Because the cost of the casket is the largest single component in the total funeral costs and because the price of a casket ranges from under two hundred to several thousand dollars, your choice becomes especially important if you are concerned with sparing expenses for your survivors. There are two bases for choice of a casket: social display and the hope of preserving the body against decay.

Social display is so personal a consideration that no "objective" advice is possible—other than the sometimes overlooked fact that simplicity is always in good taste, whereas ostentation rarely is. On the question of whether an expensively durable casket preserves the body, however, the objective answer is clear: it does not. Enough exhumations have been conducted to support the firm conclusion that no casket can prevent decay and that sealed metal caskets, which are sold on the grounds that they postpone decay, often hasten it.

OPEN OR CLOSED CASKET

Viewing of the body, as we have noted, has been the subject of considerable debate. Those who favor it argue that it convinces the survivors of the reality and finality of the death and that many friends as well as relatives want the opportunity of a "last look." Those who oppose it point out that it places undue emphasis on the physical remains and that it indirectly increases funeral costs because it usually requires embalming and cosmetic restoration and may induce the survivors to choose a more elaborate casket.

If you are considering an open casket, bear in mind that at your death emaciation or disfigurement by accident or disease may make you look somewhat less than presentable. Some morticians, working through photographs, create admirable restorations; others produce grotesque and irreparable caricatures.

FLOWERS OR OTHER TRIBUTES

You may also want to discuss with your survivors the question of whether the mourners should send flowers. This, of course, is the traditional way in which mourners can express their sympathy—and flowers can be used to make a minimum-price casket look somewhat less austere. On the other hand, you may feel, as many people do, that flowers are a waste of money and that your obituary notice should include the phrase "No flowers, please"—and possibly the suggestion that mourners might instead make a contribution to your favorite charitable institution or research foundation.

GRAVESIDE AND CREMATORIUM RITUALS

If you have chosen a ritual, religious or secular, to which all your friends and acquaintances are to be invited, you may prefer that the ultimate disposal process be attended by your family only. Thus, after the service in a church or funeral home, only the few people you have chosen will accompany your body to the grave site or watch it moved into the crematorium furnace. The addition of the phrase "Interment private" to the usual obituary notice will make your preference clear.

POSTFUNERAL RITUALS

Although it is not an integral part of the funeral, a post-funeral gathering of mourners, usually with food and drink, has become traditional. Its primary purpose is to provide support to those who are most severely bereaved, but another is to offer an opportunity for relatives and friends who have not met in a long time to come together in a social way. Because there is no prescribed format for these occasions, you may wish to lay out some specifications of your own—for food, drink, music, etc.

SOME MODERN ALTERNATIVES

The various disposal and ritual alternatives described above are chosen so commonly that they are likely to be available in almost every part of the country. Two further alternatives are not yet available everywhere, but both are likely to proliferate because they appeal to an increasing number of people on both philosophical and economic grounds.

DIRECT DISPOSAL

If you are not concerned with how your body is disposed of or with a ritual that involves the presence of the body, you may be interested in the process called *direct disposal.* Under this system, a commercial firm specializing in the process collects your body from the place of death and transports it directly and immediately to a cemetery or a crematorium. Because many of the usual services provided by a funeral director are entirely eliminated (e.g., embalming and cosmetic restoration) or provided at lower cost (e.g., the use of minimal-cost caskets), these firms can provide complete service for about one-fourth the cost of a standard adult funeral. Memorial services or any other rituals remain the responsibility of the survivors.

Not surprisingly, the funeral industry, perceiving the direct-disposal firms as a serious threat to profits, has lobbied strenuously—and to some extent successfully—for legislative restrictions against them. In California, for example, direct-disposal firms are required to employ licensed morticians even though they provide no professional services. Nevertheless, perhaps as a consequence of the growing secularization of the American public, such firms seem likely to proliferate—not merely because of the substantial economy they offer but also because of the philosophy underlying the entire procedure.

Memorial Societies

Far more widely available than the direct-disposal firm is the memorial society, which originated some fifty years ago as a consumer cooperative aimed specifically at reducing the high costs of funerals and providing its members with dignified funerals at minimal cost. Although, like the direct-disposal firms, memorial societies have aroused the hostility of the funeral industry, its opposition has not been effective enough to prevent their spread, and today several hundred such societies exist throughout the United States and Canada.

All memorial societies are devoted to public service and are operated almost entirely by volunteers, but they differ somewhat in the way they function. Some of them have formal contracts with one or more funeral homes that offer special prices—as much as 50 percent below the typical cost of a funeral—in return for the volume of business assured by the society. Others have no formal contract but deal on an informal cooperative basis with one or more commercial funeral homes, continuously monitoring their services and charges. Still others simply provide their members with advice and alternatives when the need arises. A one-time individual or family membership entitles you to the society's services, and since there is reciprocity among societies in various parts of the country, you do not necessarily lose the benefits of membership if you move.

When these societies originated, the membership they attracted tended to be above the average in income, education, and occupational prestige. Because people with these characteristics tend to prefer the simplest possible alternatives for both disposal and ritual, the memorial societies initially stressed a rather austere style at minimal cost. As they attempted to extend their membership beyond this relatively small group, however, they recognized that members of other cultures and other income groups had very different preferences. As a consequence, many memorial societies have broadened the range and style of service they can suggest. But the common denominator remains protection of the member against exploitation and a reasonable assurance of minimal cost for whatever style of disposal the member chooses.

You may be able to find your local memorial society by checking in the yellow pages of the telephone directory under "Memorial Societies," in the white pages under the name of your community (e.g., Rochester Memorial Society), or by consulting a local clergyman. A centralized source of information is the Continental Association of Funeral and Memorial Societies (2001 S Street NW, Washington, DC 20009), which also offers a variety of publications on the subject.

PLANNING TENTATIVELY

In this chapter we have attempted to present not a detailed description of "how to shop for a funeral" but, instead, a broad overview of current practices and alternatives. Our purpose is to help you make very general decisions rather than negotiate for "prearrangements." If you are seriously concerned about the costs of the kind of funeral you prefer, you might consider setting up an investment account or a savings account of some sort specifically earmarked for your funeral expenses. Such an account may, in fact, keep pace with inflation. An insurance policy bought for the same purpose will not keep pace with inflation but may net a "profit" if you die before your premiums equal its face value.

In general, however, the actual negotiations for funeral arrangements are best left to your survivors, and for this reason we deal with them in chapters 7 and 8. The decisions you make on the basis of this chapter should be tentative, because many unforeseeable changes may occur before you die—changes in your place of residence, in your family structure, in the composition of your survivor group, and even in your religious or philosophical beliefs. Nevertheless, because death may occur at any time, making some general decisions after thoughtful discussion with your spouse and children will inevitably, sooner or later, make the planning of your funeral arrangements easier for them and thus relieve them of some of the stress occasioned by your death.

6

WHEN DEATH SEEMS IMMINENT

If you die suddenly—as a result of an accident, a heart attack, or a massive stroke—whatever estate plans you have made or funeral preferences you have expressed earlier will obviously be unchangeable. But the majority of people don't die suddenly or unexpectedly; either they die of "natural causes" at an advanced age—an age at which death within a few years is reasonably predictable—or they die of a terminal illness such as cancer, liver disease, or kidney failure, from which death may be predictable within a matter of weeks or months.

Learning that you have only a few more months of life is, of course, a devastating experience, but psychologists and others who have studied people in such situations report that after a period of severe emotional upset a state of tranquil resignation almost inevitably evolves. Having reached this stage, the dying person often uses his remaining time not only to "put his house in order" with respect to family relationships but also to fine-tune his estate plan and to make last-minute property transfers that will reduce probatable assets and death taxes and minimize red tape for survivors. Often, too, he can relieve his family and friends of some responsibility by making decisions about future medical treatment and by planning his funeral more precisely than was practical when the time of his death was remote and its place uncertain.

If you are stricken with a terminal illness, however, the likelihood that you will be able to take advantage of these last-minute opportunities will depend on your relationship with your doctor and with your family. According to recent studies of death and dying, doctors are notoriously reluctant to tell a patient that death is approaching—in part because they see such a statement as an admission of personal defeat, in part because such predictions occasionally turn out to be wildly inaccurate, and in part because they believe that such a warning will demoralize the patient.

Some doctors inform the family of a patient's imminent death, but families may be just as reticent as doctors if they share the doctor's concern about the patient's morale. And even if both they and the patient know that life is about to end, they may feel that any discussion of medical treatment or funeral details will somehow hasten the patient's death or that any reference to estate planning or property distribution is in poor taste if not downright ghoulish.

This reticence on the part of doctor and family is not easy to overcome. But if you have executed a living will (figure 8) or medical power of attorney (figure 9), convinced your doctor, throughout your relationship, that you want to be told the truth at all times, and generally responded rationally to bad medical news in the past, you have at least some possibility of being forewarned of your death.

Once you know that death is imminent, the advantage you can take from this knowledge is considerable, but your own reactions may create problems. The awareness that you are going to die can turn your thoughts so thoroughly inward that you may have none for the welfare of your survivors. Or you may become too depressed or angry to be able to function rationally. (Some individuals never attain the stage of resignation that psychologists have identified.) But most people do eventually become reconciled, and many of them derive considerable comfort from the opportunity for last-minute decisions that will either benefit their survivors directly or, at the very least, reduce the number or the difficulty of the tasks that will face them immediately after the death.

Not everything that is suggested in the following pages may be appropriate for you or, for that matter, feasible. Setting up a trust or writing a will for the first time, for example, involves at least two sessions with your lawyer, which may have to take place at your bedside. On the other hand, given some degree of cooperation from your family members, your doctor, your lawyer, and perhaps your accountant, you will probably be able to do more than you think you can.

MATTERS OF LIFE AND DEATH

Your Will

If the value or the kind of property you own has changed significantly since you signed your most recent will or if the membership of your survivor group has changed, now is the time to review and update all the bequests you have made in your will. At this time you may want to reconsider the dollars-versus-percent question (see p. 23) and to make sure that all the provisions of your will dispose of your property completely and according to your wishes. Before making your final will, however, you need to consider the advantages of making some lifetime gifts—a procedure described later in this chapter. Other last-minute revisions of your will might include a change in your designation of personal representative, guardian of minor children, conservator, or trustee of any trust created in your will.

If all the revisions you plan to make are few and simple, there is no need to have the will entirely redrawn. Signing an amending codicil (see p. 27) will serve the purpose just as well.

Changing the beneficiaries in order to take account of changes in the membership of your survivor group (the death of a child who was childless, for example) is obviously sensible. But changing beneficiaries on an emotional basis can be risky indeed. True enough, people who know they are terminally ill often review their entire lives and achieve a more balanced perspective of their relationships with friends and relatives—a perspective that may lead to the forgiving of old injuries, real or imagined, and to a more rational view of old feuds and grudges. On the other hand, if the terminally ill person becomes embittered about his fate and reviews his life in terms of slights, feuds, and failed relationships, he may well express his unhappiness vindictively in his will, since this is now his only means of "getting back" at people. He may, for example, disinherit a child for failure to visit him in the hospital as frequently as he thinks is proper.

Perhaps the only counsel one can give the terminally ill person is to make any beneficiary changes from charitable rather than vindictive motives—but this advice may not prevent an impulsive and excessively generous gift to a nurse or other hospital employee for personal services that a more objective observer would consider entirely routine.

Holographic and Oral Wills

Revising your will or writing a codicil usually involves a lawyer, and the signing requires witnesses. If circumstances make this difficult or impossible, you might consider preparing a holographic will, which is recognized currently in twenty-seven states (see table 1). This informal will must be written entirely in your own handwriting. You must sign and date it, but your signature need not be witnessed.

If you live in a state that does not recognize holographic wills, don't prepare one with the thought that it might be "better than nothing." It will not be valid, and you will be regarded as having died intestate. Oral wills or deathbed statements have even weaker legal standing than holographic wills (see table 1).

Your Living Will

Now is the time, too, to sign or revoke a living will or medical power of attorney (see chapter 3). The approach of death may very well change whatever decision you might have made earlier with respect to the prolongation of your life by heroic measures or life-support systems. The pain you now suffer may be greater than you anticipated—although for most terminal patients it is apparently less. Or you may decide that the cost of your continued hospitalization may cause your survivors more deprivation than a few weeks or months of prolonged life are worth to you. On the other hand, if each day seems precious to you, you may decide to revoke the living will you made when you were in good health.

If your present circumstances persuade you to sign a living will, all you need do is copy the sample form shown in figure 8 and sign it in the presence of two witnesses. Whether or not your state recognizes the living will, the document communicates your wishes to your physician and your family. If, on the other hand, you decide to revoke an existing living will, the procedure is even easier: simply destroy the original and notify your physician and your family that you have done so.

Obviously, any such decisions need to be made carefully—over a period of weeks. For terminally ill people, the sudden discovery of a miracle cure—an argument often advanced by opponents of euthanasia—is too remote a possibility to deserve serious consideration. On the other hand, the decision to hasten your death should not be made during what may be a transitory condition of severe depression or pain.

Figure 13

HOLOGRAPHIC WILL

Will of John J. Jones

I, John J. Jones, declare this to be my last will. I revoke all previous wills.

First: I leave my art collection to my son, William B. Jones.

Second: I leave the rest of my property to my wife, Mary M. Jones, if she survives me. If she does not survive me, I leave the rest of my property to my children, in equal shares. If any of my children die before me, then that child's share shall go to that child's children by right of representation.

Third: If it cannot be determined if my wife died first, then it shall be presumed that my wife survived me.

Fourth: I nominate my wife as Personal Representative. If she does not act, I nominate my son, William in her place. My representative need not post bond.

Fifth: If my children need a guardian, I nominate my brother, Richard J. Jones.

Dated: January 15, 2001

John J. Jones

FUNERAL PLANNING

When death is imminent and the prospect of a funeral becomes a reality, people tend to react in widely different ways. Some find the notion of making specific plans even more grotesque than they might have when younger or in better health. Others, however, derive comfort from the opportunity to plan every detail of the disposal of their remains and the funeral service.

As death approaches, detailed planning becomes much more feasible than it was earlier in life. You are unlikely, at this time, to move to another community or to die far from home. You can now negotiate arrangements in terms of their dollar costs, since inflation is unlikely to change them appreciably. And you now know which of your survivors will take responsibility for the final arrangements and how much money will be available to pay for them. Hence, you can, if you like, call to your bedside your clergyman or other eulogist, a representative of the funeral home or memorial society, or anyone else involved in your plans and, with their advice, make plans covering every detail. (If you decide on this kind of prearrangement, you will find further information in chapter 8.)

If, on the other hand, you feel repelled by this procedure, there is no reason why you shouldn't leave it in the hands of whichever survivor will be ultimately responsible. This does not mean, however, that the subject should be regarded as taboo—never to be mentioned or discussed between you. If you ignore it entirely, your survivors are very likely to overspend on your funeral. A major reason that funeral directors are able to exploit their customers is that the customer is not only grief-stricken (and hence unable to make rational decisions) but also under enormous time pressures (and hence unable to do any comparison shopping). If, however, your approaching death is openly acknowledged, you can urge your survivors to begin making arrangements in a more leisurely and rational way.

If you have expressed your preferences in your letter of instruction, there is no need to do anything more than give it (or at least the part dealing with funeral arrangements) to your survivors along with the suggestion that the time has come for making definite plans. On the other hand, you may, since writing the original letter, have changed your mind about either the ritual or the method of body disposal. Now is the time to make your plans final.

You may also have changed your mind about anatomic gifts. Your own illness may have heightened your sympathy for people with illnesses that your anatomic gifts might alleviate or for the needs of scientists for anatomic materials in their research on certain diseases. Making an anatomic gift is a simple process that can be done at any time (see p. 110).

MATTERS OF MONEY

With respect to your estate, there are five steps you should consider taking as death draws near.

1. Revise your letter of instruction or make an inventory of your current assets—because both your assets and your liabilities may have changed significantly during the past few months.
2. Review the various probate-avoidance and tax-avoidance tactics described in chapter 2. If you have already utilized some of them, now is the time to consider transferring additional assets into such arrangements as joint ownership, pay-on-death bank accounts, transfer-on-death security registration and trusts or to shift assets from one to another to maximize the advantages each provides.
3. Consider the possibility of disposing of your estate, by giving away as much of it as possible before your death, including transfers to custodial accounts for minors—by an effective way of avoiding probate and federal estate taxes.
4. Take care of any administrative details that can be handled more easily while you are alive than by your survivors at a later date.
5. Review your will and your trust to see whether its provisions have been significantly changed by anything you may have done in steps 1–4.

The following pages describe steps 1–5 in detail. Although not every suggestion will be relevant to your situation, a careful reading is almost certain to uncover some simple, practicable measures that can save your survivors time and trouble, taxes, lawyer's fees, and court costs.

Inventory Your Current Assets

If you have never prepared a letter of instruction (see figure 10), now is the time to do it. If you already have one, it needs to be brought up to date—especially with respect to the listing of your current assets, debts, and insurance benefits. If your illness has been lengthy, some of your assets may have been used to pay medical bills or to meet household expenses if the illness interrupted your earnings. Perhaps your broker, if he has discretionary power, may have bought or sold securities since you became ill. You may also have some assets that you have hitherto concealed from your family or from the Internal Revenue Service—a secret bank account or perhaps a security bought abroad on which you have never paid income tax. Your list of assets is likely to change, too, if you follow some of the property-transfer procedures outlined later in this chapter.

Because your life insurance proceeds may represent a major portion of your total assets, you need to make certain that your survivors know where each of your policies is located and whether they are still in force. Sometimes survivors discard an old policy that looks as though it has lapsed, not realizing that the premiums paid earlier may have kept it in force (though at a reduced face value) or that the premiums were paid in full many years ago.

It is important, too, to make sure that your designation of beneficiaries—both primary and contingent—is up to date. If you would like to place some conditions or limitations on their access to the proceeds, there may still be time for you to set up a life insurance trust and name its trustee the beneficiary of all your life insurance proceeds. The trust can not only designate the beneficiaries but also set whatever conditions and timetables you choose with respect to their receiving the money. Be sure, however, not to name your own estate or personal representative as the beneficiary of your insurance, because this makes all insurance proceeds subject to probate (and to state inheritance tax, if applicable), whereas naming the trustee of a trust as the beneficiary does not.

If you live in a state that permits the sale of life insurance policies without medical examination or if you belong to a credit union that schedules open-enrollment periods for group life insurance, also without medical examination, you may be able to buy more coverage, even in your present condition. If this is possible, don't let your conscience trouble you on the grounds that you are committing fraud; you can be sure that the premiums are calculated to take your kind of situation into account.

Last-Minute Probate Avoidance and Tax Avoidance

Updating the inventory of your assets can help you determine whether they will require probate administration and whether your estate will be subject to federal estate tax. If you classify all your assets as either probatable or nonprobatable and if the total value of your probatable assets exceeds the maximum figure for "small estate" transfers in your state (see tables 5 and 6), now is the time to consider transferring these assets to forms of ownership that make them nonprobatable, such as the revocable living trust, which may take the simplified form of a bank account (Totten) trust. This device (described in detail in chapter 2) removes your assets from probate but does not remove them from your control—an important point if there is any possibility that you might yet recover from your present illness.

Although your inventory is very likely to disclose probatable assets, it is far less likely to tell you that your estate is subject to federal estate tax. To begin with, the current "unified gift and tax credit" (see p. 5) is so high that only 2 percent of all estates are currently exposed to the federal estate tax. Second, the unlimited marital deduction embodied in this federal tax permits you to transfer to your spouse your entire estate tax-free regardless of its value. If, however, you cannot or do not choose to take full advantage of the marital deduction, you should calculate the entire value of your taxable estate, which may *not* be the same as your probate estate, to determine whether this total, plus the total of all taxable gifts you have made during your lifetime, exceeds the maximums shown in table 3.

Giving Away Your Estate

If you discover that your estate may be subject to the federal estate tax, you can reduce its total below the taxable minimum by making lifetime gifts (within the $10,000 / $20,000 annual gift tax exclusion) or by transferring some of your assets to a custodial bank account for minors, an irrevocable trust, a family annuity, or some other form of irrevocable transfer described in chapter 2. These transfers (of $10,000 / $20,000 to *each* recipient) enable you to avoid both probate administration and federal estate taxes, but their great disadvantage is that they are irrevocable; hence, if you transfer your estate beyond your control and subsequently recover from what was thought to be a terminal condition, you could find yourself penniless. and financially dependent on the donees.

Giving away your assets removes them from probate, may reduce the value of your estate below the taxable minimum, and usually does not require the paperwork involved in setting up a trust. In addition, the recipients will be able to express their gratitude to you while you are still able to enjoy it, and you may derive additional pleasure from witnessing the uses to which they put your gifts.

Prior to 1981, any gift of more than $3,000 (or $6,000 if the donor's spouse consented to the gift) was taxable to the donor, and any taxable gifts made within three years of death were regarded by the IRS as having been made "in contemplation of death" and hence remained taxable as part of the donor's estate. These rules have been liberalized as follows:

The value of nontaxable gifts has been increased to $10,000 annually per donee ($20,000 if the donor's spouse consents to the gift), and gifts of unlimited value can be made to a spouse under the unlimited marital deduction.

You are entitled to make as many of these $10,000 / $20,000 gifts as you like, provided you make no more than one to any one individual per year. But since the IRS uses a calendar year in its calculations, you can make such a tax-free gift to the same person on December 31 and again on January 1.

Since there is no limit to the number of donees to whom you may annually make tax-free gifts of $10,000 / $20,000, there is no reason why you cannot make such a gift to one or more of your trusted friends with the understanding that they, in turn, will give it to one of your survivors—a tactic that is especially useful if you are not survived by a spouse and hence cannot take advantage of the unlimited marital deduction.

The "in contemplation of death" restriction has been removed on all gifts except the assignment of life insurance policies.

To be eligible for the annual $10,000 / $20,000 gift tax exclusion, a gift must be of a "present interest"—that is, it must be irrevocable and immediately usable by the recipient. Gifts to a revocable trust or gifts that cannot be enjoyed by the recipient until some future date are often fully taxable.

For gifts exceeding $10,000 / $20,000, you must file a gift-tax return and pay any gift tax on an annual basis. However, in computing the gift tax, you may first deduct the annual exclusion of $10,000 / $20,000 from the value of the gift to determine your "tentative tax"; unless the reduced taxable value of the gift exceeds your "unified gift and estate tax credit" (see p. 51), you need pay no tax. Upon your death, any unused portion of the unified credit will be applicable to reduce any federal estate tax.

There is no limit to the amount or number of tax-free gifts to charitable organizations.

All of these rules make it feasible for you to give away virtually everything you possess—not only to next of kin but also to friends, charitable institutions, and anyone else you choose. In fact, by "gifting off" your assets, you can carry out the provisions of your will while you are alive and at the same time avert any need for probate. True, these gifts will be irrevocable, but if your marriage is stable and your relationships with beneficiaries are good, there is little danger that you will be left destitute should you recover from your present illness.

Assets whose ownership is evidenced by written documents—securities, bank accounts, real estate, motor vehicles, for example—will require documentary evidence that reflects the new ownership: new signature cards in the case of bank accounts, new stock certificates in the name or names of the new owners, new property deeds that document the change in ownership of real estate, and new certificates of title reflecting new owners of motor vehicles. But even transfers of unregistered possessions—jewelry, a coin collection, a painting—should be documented in order to show transfer to the new owner. This can be done most conveniently by means of a bill of sale—a form available from stationery supply stores. Despite its name, the bill of sale need not indicate that any cash was involved in the transfer; it merely contains a description of the item and the names of the original and the new owner.

If you cannot conveniently obtain a printed bill of sale for transferring items of personal property, you may write or type out your own assignment form as long as you identify the property, the recipient, and your intent to make a gift, all followed by the date and your signature. An example of an acceptable assignment document is:

I hereby give and assign my coin collection and my 30-06 Remington deer rifle (serial # 0000) to my son, Joseph Jones.

Dated: 1/1/00
John Jones

Think Before You Give

The procedures we have described above can offer you a good deal of satisfaction from both an economic and a psychological point of view. In economic terms, they enable you to maximize the effectiveness of your estate planning for the benefit of your survivors by minimizing the erosion of your estate by probate costs and death taxes. But the psychological advantages may be even more substantial. When death is imminent, a review of one's life is almost inevitable—and the quality of one's life is measurable not only in terms of the personal relationships one has established but also (in our society, for better or for worse) by the real and personal property one has acquired. For many people on the verge of death, the revision of their wills and the making of lifetime gifts constitute a very real reassurance that their lives have been worthwhile.

On the other hand, as we have noted earlier, the prospect of death can easily distort one's perspective and precipitate a number of actions that are clearly ill-advised. Thus, the prospect of giving your possessions away while you are still alive and can experience the recipients' gratitude and pleasure may tempt you to reduce your estate to almost nothing. This may give you the additional pleasure of outwitting the taxing authorities, but bear in mind that it may be better for you to retain control of your estate and to preserve the opportunity to change your mind—even if this may result in your beneficiaries' eventually having to pay some probate costs and death taxes.

In addition, the recommendations in this chapter are based on the assumption that, when death is near, your family relationships are stable and your family structure is unlikely to change. But this may not always be the case. And so, before transferring ownership of the bulk of your assets to anyone, you must be totally confident that he or she will not use them in ways that would violate your wishes or your standards.

Lastly, as we pointed out at the beginning of this chapter, the doctor who predicted that you are to die shortly may just possibly be wrong. Lifetime gifts are legally irrevocable, and unless your beneficiaries are totally trustworthy, you may find yourself restored to good health but financially destitute as a consequence of your own generosity. For this very reason, you may be well-advised to use a revocable living trust or one of the other techniques discussed in chapter 2 as a means of avoiding probate while at the same time reserving your right to revoke or modify the entire arrangement at any time before you die.

Making Things Easier for Your Survivors

A number of matters that will become the responsibility of your survivors after your death can be attended to more easily and more flexibly while you are alive.

The ownership of your motor vehicles, for example, is more easily transferred by you than by your survivors. Most states permit the after-death transfer of the deceased's vehicles without probate, but these transfer procedures place a maximum limit on the value of the transferred vehicle, restrict the transfer to members of the deceased's family, and require an affidavit of heirship and a certified copy of the death certificate. If you make the transfer while you are alive, however, there is no limit on the value (other than gift-tax concerns) of the vehicle, nor is there any restriction on your relationship to the recipient. You can give the vehicle to anyone you please by signing the certificate of title and delivering it to the recipient.

The transfer of jointly owned property to the surviving joint owner also involves certain formalities if it is done after the death of one joint owner. If you make these transfers while you are alive, you may save your survivors time and trouble. If, for example, you own some stock certificates, whether in your own name alone or jointly, it would make sense to have a broker place them in a "street account." Once he does this, you need merely change the ownership of the account instead of having to go through a separate change-of-ownership procedure for each of the several securities.

If you rent a safe-deposit box, whether jointly or in your name alone, the bank, on hearing of your death, is sometimes required to seal the box and prevent further access to it until a representative of the state treasury arrives to inventory its contents for tax purposes. At that time, all the unregistered contents may be presumed to belong to you (and hence be subject to probate administration and estate tax) unless there is evidence to the contrary (see p. 194). For this reason, it may now be advisable for your corenter to empty the box of all contents not registered in your name and perhaps to rent another box under his or her name alone into which the valuables may be placed for safekeeping until they are disposed of. If the box you now have is rented in your name alone, a trusted friend can get access to it while you are alive if you provide him or her with a power of attorney or with an authorization form that some banks use for this purpose.

Although the avoidance of probate is generally advisable, there are some situations in which passing assets through probate has desirable tax consequences. If, for example, you own jointly with your daughter a hundred shares of a stock for which you paid $10 a share, the shares will pass to her automatically on your death, but when she sells these shares, her capital gain will have to be calculated on their original cost of $10 per share, regardless of their value at the time of your death. If, on the other hand, the shares were worth $20 each at the time of your death, this would be her "cost" if she acquired the shares through inheritance. In short, the value of any inherited asset is calculated, for tax purposes, as its value at the time of the owner's death rather than its value at the time he or she acquired it.

Alternatively, this "stepped up" tax basis can be achieved by transferring the securities by use of a revocable living trust or by a transfer-on-death securities account.

YOUR WILL—A FINAL REVIEW

If you have taken any of the actions suggested in the preceding pages, your will may no longer represent your intended disposition of your assets. If, for example, you have made a lifetime gift of your harpsichord to your elder daughter, there is no point in specifying this in the will as a bequest to her. Actually, this is of no great consequence, since a will cannot transfer property that the deceased did not own at the time of death. However, a final review and revision of your will to remove bequests that are no longer relevant may serve not only to prevent future disputes among beneficiaries but also to remind you of assets that you have overlooked or beneficiaries that you have neglected.

HOW IMPORTANT IS ALL THIS?

The suggestions and instructions in this chapter may well have given you the impression that the last days of your life should be spent with a calculator, tax tables, work sheets, and the company of your lawyer and accountant in a desperate effort to attain absolute perfection in your estate planning. This is not our intent.

To begin with, if you followed the suggestions offered in chapter 2, your last-minute adjustments should involve only trivial odds and ends, which, even if neglected or mishandled, should not make an enormous difference to your survivors. Furthermore, in our society it is the responsibility of survivors to take care of both the physical and financial remains of their parents and other relatives. Just as you or your siblings may have had to cope with the problems created by the deaths of your parents or other elderly relatives, so, too, your children or younger relatives can be expected to cope with yours. There is no need for you to be obsessively concerned with accounting for every last penny or every petty detail or to be conscience ridden by various bits of unfinished business.

The ending of life is a time for contemplation and for the repair or reinforcement of personal relationships. It would be unfortunate if you were to forego these important activities for the sake of a possible reduction in taxes or the costs of probate administration.

Part II

COPING WITH A DEATH IN THE FAMILY

A NOTE TO SURVIVORS

The burden is borne by those that mourn.

—Christiaan Barnard

Even if it was expected, the death of someone who was close to you not only evokes strong feelings of personal loss but may suddenly confront you with an overwhelming array of unfamiliar responsibilities, all of which seem equally pressing. Not only must you make funeral arrangements with an eye to the emotional needs of the survivors, but you must also deal with banks, lawyers, life insurance companies, courts, and other government agencies with an eye to their financial needs.

This burden, coupled with your own grief and bereavement, may throw you into a state of depression or apathy that prevents you from doing anything at all. But if you recognize that the most meaningful way of "paying your respects" to the deceased is to make life easier for the survivors, you are likely to find that taking care of the deceased's unfinished business does not interfere with your grieving but, on the contrary, helps the process run its normal course. And if you can list your various responsibilities in order of their urgency—so that you take care of first things first and postpone the postponable—you are likely to find that what appeared to be overwhelming turns out to be quite manageable.

To help you rank your responsibilities in order of their urgency, we have arranged the chapters that follow in a sequence that reflects their priority for most survivors. Typically, arranging for a funeral service and disposal of the body is the first order of business, and this is discussed in chapters 7 and 8. Finding and reviewing the will (chapter 9) is next in urgency—especially if the will names a guardian for minor children who have been orphaned by the death. And, lastly, the deceased's assets and liabilities must be assembled and evaluated (chapter 10) in order to determine whether the estate requires administration by the probate court before it can be distributed to the beneficiaries or heirs, a topic discussed in chapter 11.

Because every death is a unique event and because every family is different, we feel it would be presumptuous to offer advice on coping with grief, on handling condolence calls and social activities among mourners, or on dealing with the family disputes that are often triggered by the stress of a death. Hence, we have limited our discussion to matters of fact and matters of law.

Two pieces of advice, however, are so universally applicable that we cannot refrain from offering them. First, don't be in a hurry, and don't let anyone press you for time. In making funeral arrangements, you can rest assured that nothing terrible will happen to the deceased or to you if you take all the time you need for a thoughtful decision, preferably in consultation with other survivors. The same holds true for financial matters. No matter how urgent the survivors' need for money, take as much time as you need to ensure that you are making the best possible decisions with respect to each of the deceased's assets.

Second, bear in mind that many of the tasks you face—especially those that are immediately pressing—can be delegated to relatives, friends, neighbors, even children. If you ask a neighbor, for example, to take responsibility for reserving accommodations for out-of-town mourners, he can use his own telephone and avoid tying up yours. Perhaps you can post an older child or a relative at your own telephone to handle the inevitable condolence calls and to give callers information about the funeral service. Someone not closely related to the deceased should be asked to remain at the house during the funeral and burial to receive deliveries of flowers and to protect the premises against burglars, some of whom schedule their activities by reading the obituaries to find out when survivors are likely to be away from home.

Above all, if you possibly can, ask a relative or a close friend for help in making funeral arrangements. Such a person can not only give you emotional support but can double your efforts to compare the services of several funeral homes and can restrain you from impulsive and costly decisions.

Help of this kind is easy to enlist, because many mourners—and even neighbors who knew the deceased only casually—are very eager to "do something to help out." Give them an opportunity and you are likely to find that their cooperation and competence make short work of what at the outset seemed almost insuperable.

7

BODY DISPOSAL AND FUNERAL RITES

The first task facing you as a survivor—planning for the funeral ritual and the disposal of the body—is almost inevitably painful and difficult. Grief, inexperience, and the pressure of time may combine to impair your judgment and lead to a number of decisions you might not otherwise make.

Grief, especially if it is compounded with guilt and remorse—the feeling that "now it's too late" to do for the dead person all that you might have done—can cause you to compensate for your earlier failings, real or imagined, by overspending for a needlessly elaborate funeral.

Inexperience—because a death in the family is, after all, a very infrequent event—can result in mistakes in buying funeral services that you would not make in buying something equally expensive but more familiar.

Time pressure, often exerted by a hospital or nursing home in its eagerness to get rid of the body, can lead you to make hasty arrangements with the first funeral home that comes to mind without considering alternative arrangements that might be less expensive or more satisfactory.

The stress you feel and the mistakes that result from it are to some extent unavoidable, but they can be reduced to a minimum if you follow the two basic principles we have mentioned earlier. First, don't allow yourself to be pressured into hasty decisions. Second, even if the major responsibility seems to be yours, try to involve other survivors or family friends in your planning. Decisions arrived at jointly are likely to be more objective and more rational and—perhaps more important—they can avert the arguments and long-term alienation among family members that often stem from disagreements over what should or should not have been done.

RESISTING THE PRESSURES

If the death has occurred in a hospital or a nursing home, that institution is likely to show indecent haste in urging you to remove the body. Indeed, the same telephone call that informed you of the death may have included a request that you "make arrangements" before the end of the day.

This urgency is understandable from the institution's point of view. Bodies, if they are awaiting autopsy or if they are to remain in an embalmable condition, must be refrigerated, and most hospitals, especially those that do autopsies for the county medical examiner as well as on their own patients, suffer a chronic shortage of refrigerator space.

But from your point of view this urgency is important only if the person who died left his body or specific organs as an anatomic gift or if you, as a survivor, are making the gift yourself in the dead person's behalf. In such circumstances, time is of the essence. The donated organs must be collected within a few hours of death, or the entire body must be promptly transported to the recipient. In the absence of an anatomic gift, however, there is no need to feel pressed for time, because the institution is not permitted by law to dispose of the body without the consent of the next of kin. Keeping the body for a reasonable length of time may inconvenience the institution, but yielding to the pressure and, as a result, making arrangements that you have not thought out and discussed with others is a worse alternative.

Occasionally, nursing home or hospital personnel will suggest to you the name of a funeral home that can remove the body promptly. Although such a suggestion may be well-intentioned, you would not be paranoid if you suspected a financial arrangement between the funeral home and the "helpful" hospital employee. In most cases, you would do better to make your own choice.

In years past, it was not uncommon for hospital personnel to call a favored funeral home and instruct it to pick up the body without any authorization from the survivors—on the pretext that it had to be embalmed. This practice has presumably disappeared, because it is now strictly illegal. A funeral director who claims or embalms a body without authorization from the next of kin or who refuses to release a body to the next of kin faces immediate loss of license as well as a possible lawsuit brought by the survivors.

DEATH AT HOME

If a death occurs in a hospital or nursing home, the death certificate (which must be executed before the body can be moved to a funeral home) can be signed either by the deceased's attending physician or by any physician on the staff of the institution. If the death occurs at home, however, the certificate must be signed by the deceased's physician or by the county medical examiner (sometimes called the coroner).

In two sets of circumstances, involvement of the medical examiner is required by law. First, he must be notified if the deceased was not under the care of a physician. (The definition of "under the care of a physician" varies from state to state; in some it means having been seen by a physician during the forty-eight hours preceding death; in others the time limit is two weeks or more.) In most such situations the death is likely to have been sudden and the cause unclear. Second, the medical examiner must be notified of any death resulting from violence—not only possible suicide or homicide but also accidents of all kinds.

In some such situations the medical examiner may waive his examination, but the death should always be reported by a telephone call to his office.

SOME LEGAL CONSTRAINTS

Before making any plans or decisions, you need to be aware of the state laws that relate to anatomic gifts and autopsies and that specify who has the final say about funeral arrangements and responsibility for the funeral bill. Although some of these laws are often violated and rarely enforced, a general understanding of them can help you avoid problems.

ANATOMIC GIFTS

Under the Uniform Anatomical Gift Act, currently the law in all states, any gifts of organs or the entire body made by the deceased must be honored by the survivors. After the donor's death, the person in possession of the gift document, usually a donor card (see figure 12) but sometimes a will, is legally obligated to carry out the instructions it contains. However, the deceased's intent may be frustrated, deliberately or otherwise, by several circumstances.

To begin with, unless the body or any donated organs are in medically usable condition, the gift will not be accepted. Although the gift may be rendered unusable by disease or mutilation, the more common problem is delay: the body or organs must be transferred to the recipient within a very few hours of death. If the anatomic gift is made by means of a will and if the will is not found or read until a day or two after the death, neither the organs nor the body will be medically usable, and the donee is likely to reject the gift.

The gift of a body may also be refused if, at the time it is offered, there is an adequate supply of bodies or if transportation from the place of death to the donee institution turns out to be impracticable or too expensive. The donee always has the right to refuse a gift for any reason, or for no reason at all.

In all such situations, the survivors, having made good-faith efforts to comply with the deceased's wishes, are free to choose any alternative method of body disposal.

Even if the anatomical gift is made by means of a properly witnessed donor card, it may be frustrated by a reluctant survivor who conceals or destroys the card, refuses to sign the consent form that most donor institutions require, or fails to notify the donee. Although destruction of such a donor card is a clear violation of the law, it is altogether unlikely to result in court action, because the monetary value of the gift is too low to induce the prospective recipient to file suit.

THE DECEASED'S WISHES

Aside from making an anatomic gift, the only other legally binding way in which a person can specify the disposition of his or her body is through a will. (Wishes expressed in a letter of instruction or in any other informal way, orally or in writing, have no legal standing.) But the instructions specified in a will are not always carried out—either because survivors ignore the will or the will is not discovered or produced before the disposal has taken place or because the survivors go to court to have the instructions set aside as unreasonable or unduly burdensome on them.

The person who has died may, of course, have negotiated a pre-need contract with a funeral home, specifying the kind of funeral wanted, stipulating the price to be paid, and setting aside a sum of money to pay for it. But even legal contracts of this kind have been successfully contested in court by survivors claiming that the money was more urgently needed for their own welfare.

Who Has the Right to Decide?

One major problem, experienced by survivors and by funeral directors alike, stems from uncertainty as to who has the final say on all details of the ritual service and the disposal of the body. Survivors report that such issues as cremation versus burial or open versus closed casket have generated not only angry arguments at the time of the death but, occasionally, lifelong enmities within the family group. Funeral directors, in turn, complain that after they have set up painstakingly detailed arrangements with one member of the family, another arrives to countermand them and demand something entirely different.

Family conflicts of this kind often stem from intergenerational differences. At the death of a young man, for example, his widow may prefer a simple secular service followed by cremation, because both she and her husband had long ago abandoned formal religious observances. The husband's parents, on the other hand, still adhering to traditional religious practices, may insist on an elaborate religious service, a luxurious casket, grave burial, and an expensive grave marker—even though they have neither the intention nor the ability to pay the funeral costs, which may have to be paid from a pitifully small estate left to the widow.

Actually, the laws of your state specify, in priority sequence, the persons who have the right to make decisions about funeral arrangements. But, as we shall see, these laws are relatively easy to evade and difficult to enforce.

In general, the following people, in order of precedence, have the right to decide on all arrangements: the surviving spouse (if not estranged), an adult child, a parent, an adult sibling, a guardian of the deceased, or "any other person authorized or obligated to dispose of the body"—presumably a coroner or the administrator of a hospital or nursing home. But although the order of priority is clear and although it may be useful to cite in an attempt to settle family disagreements, it very rarely becomes the basis for a lawsuit—in part because disposition of the body usually must take place before court action is possible and because very few judges will order a body exhumed so that it can undergo an alternative method of disposal or be buried in a different place.

Who Pays the Funeral Bill?

Under state law, all "reasonable" funeral expenses are chargeable against the estate of the deceased, even if the arrangements are made by a surviving relative rather than the personal representative. A relative who actually makes any payment for funeral services is entitled to reimbursement from the estate.

Often, however, there may be no estate, or it may be too small to cover the funeral bill, or the funeral director may have no idea of the financial situation of the person who has died. In such cases, the funeral director is likely to require the relative making the arrangements to cosign for the bill or to guarantee payment if the estate should prove unable to pay. For this reason, you should read very carefully any papers you are asked to sign in connection with funeral arrangements. In some cases, you will be asked to sign an order authorizing certain services; in other cases, your signature also signifies your acceptance of responsibility for paying the bill. If you accept such responsibility, you will be legally liable for the entire bill or for whatever part of it the estate is unable to pay.

One way of reducing the direct charges against the estate (or against the cosigning survivor) is to sign over to the funeral director any Social Security or veterans' death benefits to which the deceased is entitled (see p. 168). Taken together, these may cover the funeral director's basic costs and thus persuade him that cosigning is unnecessary. In addition, he, rather than you, will have to do the paperwork involved in applying for these benefits and endure the delay until they are paid. Most funeral directors are quite willing to do this because it assures them of at least some cash payment.

Under the law, the funeral director enjoys a preferred status among the estate's creditors; his bill must be paid by the estate before any other debts except administrative expenses (court costs, attorney fees, and personal representative fees) are paid, even though his charges may deplete the estate entirely. In return for this preferred status, the funeral director is expected to behave more ethically and more professionally toward his customers than are most other suppliers of goods and services, and the courts have frequently disapproved or reduced funeral bills that seemed exorbitant—not merely in absolute terms but in relation to the income level of the bereaved family. If a distraught widow is exploited by an unethical funeral director or even if the funeral director permits her to order an excessively expensive funeral, she may seek relief in the courts. Many, if not most, funeral directors are aware of this and govern their behavior accordingly.

AUTOPSIES

In all cases of violent death and in most cases of death under unknown or unusual circumstances, an autopsy to determine the cause of death is required by law. In such situations there is nothing that you can do except modify whatever arrangements you made to allow time for the autopsy to be completed.

Often, however, when the cause of death is known, the attending physician or the hospital will ask permission of the survivors to conduct an autopsy in order to learn more about the deceased's condition at the time of death or about the disease from which the patient died. There is no charge for this work.

Although the prospect of having the deceased's body mutilated and the organs removed and examined may be repugnant, you should carefully consider the possible benefits to society or to you personally. In addition to its usefulness to doctors, an autopsy can offer you considerable comfort if the results indicate that a death that seems sudden and inexplicable was, in fact, inevitable within days or weeks of its unexpected occurrence.

Autopsies do not, of course, preclude an open-casket funeral. Cosmetic restoration by the funeral director removes any indications that an autopsy has been performed.

WHOSE FUNERAL IS IT?

As our review of the legal situation indicates, the law is both specific and enforceable with respect to autopsies in certain cases and with respect to the payment of funeral bills. Most of the other legal provisions—those governing anatomic gifts, compliance with instructions expressed in the will, the priority of persons making funeral decisions, and the validity of preneed contracts—can often be disregarded, circumvented, or contested. Thus, although you may wish to honor the deceased by carrying out his wishes, you can feel reasonably comfortable about disregarding them if they seem capricious, unduly burdensome to the survivors, or otherwise unreasonable.

Fundamentally, a funeral is for the benefit not of the deceased but of the survivors. It should, within the financial limits of the estate, be as satisfying as possible to all of them—emotionally, aesthetically, and socially. A young widow may be entirely justified in disregarding the expensive preferences of her in-laws if satisfying them would threaten the future welfare of herself and her children. On the other hand, you may feel that disregarding or rejecting a close relative's strong preferences isn't worth jeopardizing your relationship for a lifetime.

For all these reasons, even though the responsibility for choice of the arrangements and for payment of their cost is clearly specified by law, the most satisfactory funeral arrangements usually represent a compromise among the preferences of various family members. To achieve this compromise, your best plan is to arrange a meeting (or a long-distance conference call) among the next of kin in order to achieve some consensus on the following alternatives.

SOME BASIC ALTERNATIVES

As you begin formulating specific arrangements, you need to bear in mind that two separate procedures are involved: a ritual service of some sort and the physical disposal of the body. Although they are not entirely independent of one another—for example, the anatomic gift of an entire body precludes an open-casket ritual service—they can be put together in a large number of combinations. For this reason, you may want to make separate decisions about them.

In a few situations, simply following the wishes of the person who has died—whether or not they are legally binding—may relieve you of all responsibility, or at least the responsibility for disposal of the body. If, for example, a preneed arrangement was negotiated by the deceased with a funeral home, and if this arrangement strikes you as reasonable and appropriate, you need merely set it in motion by notifying the funeral home that the death has occurred. In such circumstances it is likely that the ritual service as well as the disposal method has been specified.

TABLE 7

Funeral Alternatives

Ritual	*Body Disposal*	*Essential Costs**	*Optional Costs**
Service with body present			
With casket open for viewing	Burial	1-10	11, 14, 15
	Cremation	1–4, 6–8, 12	9–11, 13–15
With closed casket	Burial	1, 3, 4,[a] 5–10	11, 14, 15
	Cremation	1, 3, 4,[b] 6–8, 12	9–11, 13–15
Graveside service only Closed casket	Burial	4, 5, 8–10	3, 11, 14, 15
Memorial service, body not present			
	Burial	[c]	14, 15
	Cremation	[c]	14, 15
	Body donation[d]	None[e]	14, 15

* Key to Costs

1. Transportation of body from place of death.
2. Embalming and cosmetic restoration.
3. Other professional services by funeral home staff.
4. Casket.
5. Vault or grave liner (not required by law but often required by cemeteries).
6. Viewing and/or visitation facilities at funeral home.
7. Chapel facilities at funeral home (or additional transportation charges to move body to house of worship).
8. Transportation of body to grave or crematory.
9. Cost of cemetery plot.
10. Opening and closing of grave.
11. Transportation of mourners by limousine to and from committal.
12. Crematory charge.
13. Columbarium charge for urn committal.
14. Clergy fee.
15. Classified obituary notices.

[a]A less expensive casket can be used, because it is not the center of attention and can be covered with flowers or a pall.

[b]Casket can be replaced by a much less expensive crematory container.

[c]One all-inclusive charge covers all costs of body disposal, but memorial service and claiming of death benefits remain responsibility of survivors.

[d]For research or teaching and eventual cremation.

[e]The body (in a sealed casket) or the cremated ashes may be returned for disposal by the survivors, but this is rarely done.

If either the deceased or you, on his behalf, make an anatomic gift of the entire body, you are relieved of the problem of body disposal but not of the ritual service. If, however, the anatomic gift involves only one or more organs and not the entire body, you are faced with the responsibility of planning both the ritual service and disposal of the body.

One way to review and evaluate the alternatives available to you is to consult table 7, which presents the entire array of rituals and methods of disposal. The table is necessarily somewhat oversimplified, and it is not intended as a guide to detailed funeral arrangements, but a thoughtful reading of it can (1) make you aware of some alternatives you may not have considered, (2) give you a general notion of the procedures involved in—and relative costs of—the various alternatives, and thereby (3) immunize you against suggestions offered by a possibly greedy or unethical funeral director.

Although the table emphasizes costs, both the disposal of the body and the ritual service have not only economic consequences for the survivors but also profound social and psychological significance. It is important, therefore, that any decisions you make should not be based on cost alone. If, for example, direct disposal with cremation appalls you aesthetically or threatens the religious beliefs of close kin, the fact that it is the cheapest method—or even the fact that it represents the expressed preference of the person who has died—probably should not sway your decision. On the other hand, it may be irresponsible to spend on unessential funeral services money that could make a significant difference in the survivors' standard of living.

The social and psychological significance of the various styles of ritual and the several methods of body disposal is so individual and personal a matter that little can be said about it in a book of this kind. Perhaps the most effective way for you to reach a satisfying compromise between the economic and the other considerations is to answer, together with the other involved survivors, the following questions. Although your answers will be determined largely by your collective feelings, the economic implications will be inescapable.

A Body-Centered or a Person-Centered Funeral?

If you focus strongly on the body of the person who has died, you will probably choose (as most Americans do) a service with an open casket, visitation and viewing of the body for several days, a cortege to the cemetery, grave burial, and a highly visible grave marker. Because an open casket funeral requires embalming and cosmetic restoration, an above-minimum-price casket, and a number of other goods and services provided by a funeral home (see table 7), this is by far the most expensive form of funeral.

If, on the other hand, you feel (as do an increasing number of Americans) that the body is less significant and that you want to focus on the individual's character and social relationships, then you may prefer direct disposal by cremation and a scattering of the ashes, followed by a memorial service at a later time. With this choice, many of the most expensive components of the traditional funeral service—embalming, cosmetic restoration, the casket, the use of a funeral home for visitation, the cemetery plot, and grave marker—are eliminated.

Although the cost differences between the two alternatives are obvious, the psychological differences are not. Some psychologists (and virtually all funeral directors) firmly believe that it is only after viewing the body that survivors accept the reality and finality of the death and that such viewing actually facilitates the grieving process. Some of them believe that even young children should view the body.

Other psychologists (and many clergymen), however, argue the opposite point of view with equal conviction. They do not feel that viewing a highly cosmeticized corpse helps the survivors accept the death, and they feel that in some circumstances viewing the corpse may be a traumatic experience. They point out that concern with the physical body may divert attention from the quality of the person's relationships, accomplishments, and personality.

There are, of course, no scientific data to support either position, but it is doubtful that such data would change people's convictions. Whatever your personal view, it is important that the choice resulting from it be acceptable to other survivors who may have been as close to the deceased as you were.

Largely Public or Largely Private?

If the deceased was a public figure or simply a person with a vast number of friends and acquaintances, you may be obligated to give them an opportunity to mark his or her death, and this may require turning the funeral into a public event, complete with visitation and viewing, a large and elaborate ritual service, a cortege, and other features that you personally might prefer to avoid.

In such circumstances, you can, of course, make compromises. Even if the ritual service is likely to attract large numbers of people, there is no need for the casket to be open, and it is quite possible for the committal (whether by burial or cremation) to be restricted to members of the immediate family. It is also feasible to keep the entire funeral simple and private and to hold a larger, more public memorial service at a later date. In general, the more public the funeral, the more expensive it is likely to be.

In thinking about the funeral in relation to people outside the immediate family, it is useful to distinguish between people with whom the dead person was socially *involved* and those whom the survivors would like to *impress*. As we've noted, your social obligation to the deceased's friends and acquaintances is both real and largely unavoidable. On the other hand, some survivors arrange expensive and elaborate funerals merely to impress neighbors with whom they have had no relationship. A funeral seems a rather futile occasion for keeping up with the Joneses.

CREMATION OR EARTH BURIAL?

Because the aesthetic and philosophical aspects of cremation have been dealt with elsewhere (see p. 107), we shall restrict our discussion here to comparative costs. If you bear in mind that cremation is simply a method of body disposal that can be used with any style of ritual service—from a simple postcremation memorial service to the most elaborate open-casket-with-visitation service—you will realize that its actual cost requires a rather careful comparison with earth burial (see table 7).

Cremation would seem to be cheaper than earth burial because, although ashes may be buried in a cemetery, this is not necessary. If no cemetery plot is used, there are no costs for a grave liner, a grave marker, or for opening and closing the grave. But this obvious saving will be reduced by the charge the crematorium makes for its service and possibly by additional charges if you want the ashes "inurned" and kept permanently in a columbarium, an urn repository usually operated by the crematorium.

Cremation can be cheaper because it requires, instead of a casket, only an inexpensive corrugated cardboard container—but this saving will not be realized if you choose an open-casket ritual service. Similarly, cremation does not require embalming or cosmetic restoration—but neither does earth burial if you decide on a closed casket or a graveside service.

It is likely that the cost difference between cremation and earth burial will increase as the prices of cemetery plots and caskets continue to rise. At the time of this writing, however, cremation is not as much cheaper than earth burial as many people believe, and the fact that it is chosen more often by people who are well-to-do suggests that the choice is made on other than economic grounds.

OBTAINING THE SERVICES YOU'VE CHOSEN

Once you and the other survivors have decided on the method of body disposal and the style of ritual service you prefer, you are ready to get in touch with one of the following organizations.

A Direct-Disposal Firm

Direct-disposal firms operate at present in only two or three states, largely because the funeral-industry lobby has successfully opposed them in the others. These firms provide a minimal one-price service that includes removal of the body from the place of death and either burial (in a grave provided by the survivors) or cremation. The disposal is carried out so promptly that no embalming is required, and since there is no viewing of the body, neither is cosmetic restoration. Survivors who use this service usually plan a memorial service some time after the death. They take responsibility, also, for applying for death benefits and for other services normally rendered by the conventional funeral home.

Whether these firms appeal primarily to people seeking low-cost services or to people who take the person-centered rather than the body-centered approach to death is unclear, but the fact is that these firms are flourishing despite the persistent efforts of the funeral industry to place legislative or regulatory obstacles in their path.

If your state does not license direct-disposal firms, there is no reason why you should not ask for similar direct-disposal service from a conventional funeral home. Because the Federal Trade Commission (FTC) requires funeral homes to publish an itemized price list of services, you should be able to order only those services that are absolutely necessary for prompt, direct disposal. You may meet with some resistance or downright refusals, but it is likely that at least one funeral home will quote you a price for exactly what you want.

A Memorial Society

Even if neither you nor the person who has died has a current membership, a local memorial society (see p. 117) may be willing to offer you immediate membership or refer you to a funeral home with which it has a contractual arrangement or an informal relationship based on satisfactory service and prices. Once in touch with a recommended firm, you can usually make whatever arrangements you prefer with reasonable confidence that you will be treated fairly.

A Funeral Home

If your state does not license direct-disposal firms, if your community does not have a memorial society, or if you prefer services that are not available from either, you will need to deal with a funeral home. Because this is the situation in which most survivors find themselves, we have devoted almost all of the next chapter to this subject.

8

NEGOTIATING WITH FUNERAL DIRECTORS

Although most of this chapter is devoted to a discussion of the goods and services you will be offered when you shop for a funeral, you are likely to be in a stronger position to negotiate with a funeral director if you have some understanding of the current situation in the funeral industry as a whole.

During the past two decades, the rise of consumer activism generated an increasingly critical public attitude toward the suppliers of a vast array of goods and services, but few of them were attacked as sharply and persistently as the funeral industry. Responses to abuses perpetrated by funeral directors ranged from such exposés as Nancy Mitford's *American Way of Death* to the proliferation of memorial societies, whose fundamental purpose is to help funeral purchasers avoid exploitation. Although a number of states produced legislation intended to curb abuses, the major consumer victory occurred in 1984, when the Federal Trade Commission implemented a set of regulations that offer survivors effective protection.

Because the Federal Trade Commission regulations (see p. 158) are relatively recent, however, and because their memories of earlier abuses are still vivid, many people regard funeral directors as only slightly less devious or dishonest than used-car salesmen.

Although serious abuses do occur, there is no evidence that the funeral industry attracts practitioners of poor moral character or that buyers of funerals are deceived or exploited more frequently than buyers of other goods and services. It is important, therefore, that you understand the relationship between the funeral director and the customer and something about the structure of the industry, because this understanding can help you avoid being exploited—or feeling convinced that you have been exploited, whether you have been or not.

To begin with, all of us share a fear of and a revulsion toward death. But since death itself is too abstract and remote to serve as a target for our feelings, we tend to shift our hostilities and anxieties to the people who deal with it, and thus the funeral director becomes a convenient scapegoat. Moreover, the funeral director sells us goods and services that we don't want to buy and that give us no joy and little satisfaction. And, lastly, the funeral director sells us goods and services with which we have had little experience and which, therefore, we are unable to evaluate critically. By virtue of our ignorance and inexperience, he is in a position to tell us what to buy and then to sell it to us—all this at a time when we are especially vulnerable. Given these circumstances, the funeral director, no matter what his ethical standards, is likely to be regarded with suspicion and hostility.

The structure of the industry also produces practices that disadvantage the consumer. Critics of the industry agree that it is overpopulated, that it could serve the public just as effectively if some 25 percent of funeral homes were to go out of business tomorrow—as indeed they might if they were to compete aggressively with one another on a price basis. It is for self-protective reasons, therefore, that the industry discourages (where it cannot prohibit) itemization of exact charges, price advertising, quotation of prices over the telephone, or any other practice that would encourage competition.

Price competition would, of course, threaten the existence of the small funeral home, because the home that handles one hundred funerals a week does not have fifty times the overhead—in land costs, payroll, preparation facilities, visitation areas, or casket inventory—of the small firm that handles only two. But in the absence of price advertising, the customer who is unwilling or unable to do some comparison shopping has no way of knowing whether the price charged by the large firm reflects its relative efficiency or its maximization of profit or whether the price charged by the small firm reflects its inefficiency or the willingness of its owners to subsist on a minimal profit margin in order to survive. This is why you cannot assume that the larger firm will necessarily quote you a lower price.

On the other hand, many funeral directors urge expensive and elaborate goods and services on their customers not merely to maximize profits but, rather, because they genuinely believe that an elaborate funeral is "better"—just as an automobile salesman genuinely believes that an Audi is better than a Volkswagen or as a university professor believes that a four-year degree is better than a two-year degree and that a doctorate is better yet.

Funeral directors point out in their own defense, moreover, that expensive and elaborate funerals often turn out to be "exactly what the customer wanted." Although this argument may often be disingenuous, there is evidence to indicate that some survivors do prefer to buy an expensive funeral.

Because the goods and services that make up a funeral are highly variable both in number and in price, funeral directors have been accused of sizing up each customer—in terms of severity of grief, level of affluence, and sophistication about funeral practices—and then adjusting services and costs to the maximum that each customer will be willing to pay. Funeral directors readily admit that they size up each customer, but their motive, they claim, is self-protection and not exploitation. They point out, quite correctly, that very few funerals are paid for in advance, that time does not permit a check on the size of the deceased's estate or the creditworthiness of the customer, and that payments are slow and often difficult to collect. Hence, they argue, a quick assessment of the customer is essential, and many of them pride themselves on their skill in making it.

Whatever its motivation, you can protect yourself against this assessment in several ways. First, if you are acutely grief-stricken—so much so that your normal good judgment and your usual consumer skills have deteriorated—have a friend who is emotionally less involved than you are accompany you and monitor all your discussions, decisions, and transactions. And, if you possibly can, give the friend veto power.

Your level of affluence cannot be entirely concealed from the funeral director, because it will be revealed in your clothing, your style of speaking, the car in which you arrive, and your address. But you can reduce the potential for exploitation by demonstrating, at the earliest possible moment in the negotiations, that you are aware of the provisions of the Federal Trade Commission regulations as well as any additional regulations that may be in force in your state.

THE FEDERAL TRADE COMMISSION FUNERAL RULE

The FTC Funeral Rule, adopted in 1984 after several years of opposition from the funeral industry, governs three aspects of a funeral transaction: prices, misleading or deceptive statements or behavior, and charges for the provision of optional services.

PRICES

Perhaps the most important provision—because it facilitates comparison shopping—is the requirement that in response to a telephone call the funeral director must (1) inform you that prices for individual components of a funeral are available by telephone and (2) answer any reasonable questions you raise in the course of your call. This requirement enables you to decide in advance precisely what you want and to telephone (or ask a friend to telephone) a number of funeral homes for information that will permit reasonably accurate price comparisons.

When you visit a funeral home in person, the funeral director is required to provide you with—and let you keep—a price list that itemizes the cost of every product and service offered. This price list must include the entire range of caskets available—from the most expensive to the cheapest—and if the funeral home offers cremation services, the list must include a plain wood box or a corrugated container (both of them much less expensive than a traditional casket).

Once you have chosen the casket and specified the services you want, the funeral director must give you an itemized statement with each of your choices priced separately and must offer you the option of adding or deleting items before making a final decision. Bear in mind that you are not obligated to buy anything you don't want unless state law or cemetery regulations require it. A particular cemetery may, for example, require you to provide a grave liner, or state law may require embalming under certain exceptional circumstances, but in these situations the requirement must be cited specifically on the statement.

MISLEADING OR DECEPTIVE STATEMENTS

It is illegal for a funeral director to state or imply that any product or service—a special casket, for example, or embalming—will retard or prevent decay of the body or that a more expensive casket or a grave vault will protect the body from water seepage. Similarly, he may not state that embalming is required by state law. In fact, he must inform you that embalming is not mandatory in any state except in special circumstances, although it is usually essential if the casket is to be open for viewing. If the funeral home offers cremation service, it must not insist that a conventional casket is mandatory and must offer you a less expensive container.

OPTIONAL SERVICES

Some of the details connected with a death—application for death certificates, purchase of obituary notices and flowers, provision of music, pallbearers, or a eulogist—can be carried out by the survivors, but they are often delegated to the funeral director. If these involve out-of-pocket disbursement by the funeral home and subsequent reimbursement by the survivors, the funeral home must inform you whether it adds a service charge to its cash disbursements or whether it receives a discount or rebate from the providers. Where the actual costs of some of these items cannot be precisely determined in advance, the funeral director must provide a reasonably accurate estimate.

DOES THE FEDERAL TRADE COMMISSION PROTECT YOU?

This summary of the FTC rule may reassure you, but during the years since its adoption, it has proved to be something of a paper tiger. As with other federal regulations, its effectiveness depends less on the stringency of the rule itself than on the resources devoted to its enforcement, and thus far there is no evidence that the FTC has mustered a police force. And even if you recognize that the funeral director with whom you are dealing has overcharged you through a clear violation of part of the rule, the FTC will not help you seek redress. In fact, the FTC's Consumer Protection Bureau states that it "does not resolve consumer or private disputes" but merely invites complaints that "may show a pattern of conduct or practice that the Commission may investigate to determine if any action is warranted."

This does not mean, however, that the FTC rule is valueless. Many laws that are poorly enforced (state seat-belt laws, for example) achieve a fair degree of compliance simply because people feel uncomfortable about breaking them. This is likely to be true of funeral directors—especially if you give them evidence, in the early stages of negotiation, that you are fully aware of the FTC requirements. Furthermore, should you decide to take a funeral director to court over a dispute, evidence that he has violated the FTC rule will weigh heavily in your favor.

STATE REGULATIONS

Until the adoption of the FTC Funeral Rule, a number of states had adopted regulations governing funeral-home pricing practices and funeral and burial procedures. Many of these regulations have been superseded by the FTC Funeral Rule, but those governing matters that are not covered by the FTC rule remain in force.

These regulations are far too heterogeneous and complex to be dealt with on a state-by-state basis, but we can note that some states provide the consumer with significantly stronger protection than others. Oddly enough, the "good" states cannot be distinguished from the "bad" ones on the basis of their geographic location or the characteristics of their populations. Among the most protective states are such very different ones as Arizona, California, Colorado, Florida, New York, and Texas. The states least protective of the consumer—among them Iowa, Kentucky, Maryland, Massachusetts, and Tennessee—also appear to have little in common except, perhaps, a politically powerful funeral lobby. But survivors living in a "bad" state may need to be more cautious than those who are better protected by state law.

USING THE FEDERAL AND STATE REGULATIONS

As we have noted, the most effective way of using federal and state regulations to protect yourself against exploitation is to communicate to the funeral director—subtly if possible but emphatically if necessary—that you are aware of the several obligations that the regulations impose on him.

In addition, however, there are tactics and behaviors not prohibited by the regulations that can offer you some clue as to the funeral director's integrity. Does his showroom display of caskets, for example, feature the low-priced caskets as prominently as the deluxe models, or are the latter prominently floodlighted and the former tucked away in a dim corner? Tentatively select his lowest-priced model and note whether he disparages your choice, verbally or by facial expression. Ask to see his suppliers' catalogs and check whether the price range of caskets displayed in his showroom reflects the full price range of caskets available to him or only the more expensive models. Inquire about the lowest-priced model shown in the catalog and note his response about delivery problems—which in fact arise very rarely.

HOW FUNERALS ARE PRICED

The goods and services offered by the typical funeral home generally include the following:

Casket
Vault (unless a grave liner is purchased from the cemetery)

Professional services:
- embalming
- cosmetic restoration

Use of funeral home and facilities:
- for visitation and viewing
- for ritual service

Transportation:
- for body, from place of death to funeral home
- for body, from funeral home to disposal site (via house of worship if desired)
- for mourners and pallbearers, to and from disposal site
- for flowers, to disposal site (via house of worship if desired)

Other services:
- professional pallbearers
- visitors' register
- acknowledgment cards
- application for death benefits

Outlays on behalf of survivors:
- crematorium charges or cemetery costs—grave, and opening and closing charges

copies of death certificate
newspaper obituary notices
flowers for casket
clothing for body (if not provided by survivors)
clergy fee
fee for music provided

Some of these services are, of course, optional, and not all of them are included in what is called, in the language of the trade, a "standard adult funeral." They are listed here simply to provide the context for the several pricing methods used by funeral homes.

More than half of all funeral homes currently use the *unit pricing system:* they quote a single price, which includes the casket and some of the services listed above, for a "standard adult funeral." Under this system, the price of the funeral depends on the price of the casket selected by the customer, but the services provided remain the same in number and quality regardless of the casket price. Outlays on behalf of the survivors—for cemetery plot, obituary notices, etc.—are not included.

Some funeral homes have adopted a *two-unit pricing system:* they quote one price for professional services and a separate price for the casket. Under this system, the various services provided are specified but are not itemized separately.

A third system (advocated by the Federal Trade Commission and currently used by a minority of funeral homes) involves *item pricing:* each component of the funeral, whether essential or optional, is priced separately, and the price list is offered to the customer before any arrangements are made.

Item pricing would seem to be the best system from your point of view. It enables you to compare prices not only among funeral homes offering item pricing but also with those using the unit or two-unit system. Armed with a printed list of item prices, you may be able to negotiate both services and prices with funeral homes offering the "standard adult funeral."

But item pricing is not widely used. Some funeral homes offer an itemized list but insert prices only after discussion with the customer. In such a situation, you can't know whether the prices are standard, whether the funeral director has adjusted them to what he perceives to be your income level, or whether he has raised them to compensate for your choice of a low-priced casket. Moreover, if you reject one of the items (embalming, for example), you may be forced to accept another item (refrigeration of the body).

If you are not overwhelmed by grief or by time pressures, the most effective way to buy funeral services is to decide in advance—at least tentatively—which services you want and to try to get itemized or comparable quotations from two or more funeral homes. You may be able to do this without going from one home to another by yourself. Once you have the itemized list in hand, you may be able to get price information by telephone, even if your state law does not require the funeral home to provide it.

Most funeral directors are reluctant to quote prices by telephone because, they argue, misunderstandings are inevitable when customers do not know which services they want, which services are essential, and which services are included in the quoted price. Critics of the industry, on the other hand, maintain that this resistance to telephone quotation stems from the funeral director's desire to "get hold of the body" or at least the customer before discussing prices. But if you can communicate to the funeral director that you know precisely what you want and if you can imply that you plan to compare his quotations with those of his competitors, you may get results. If not, perhaps you can furnish one or two friends or relatives with your tentative list and have them visit several funeral homes to compare prices on everything except the casket, since this is a choice you probably want to make personally.

To help you prepare this tentative list, we shall describe briefly the goods and services offered by the typical funeral home.

CASKET

The casket—usually the most expensive component of the funeral and the most profitable for the funeral director—can range in price from less than two hundred to several thousand dollars. Prices are likely to rise sharply, because both wood and skilled labor are becoming more costly and because the rapid disappearance of small manufacturers will leave the market (and hence the control of prices) to a small number of large firms.

A casket is generally bought—or, more accurately, sold—on the basis of three kinds of appeal. The first of these fosters the illusion that the corpse is somehow alive and is therefore sensitive to physical discomfort and to the attitudes of the survivors. This explains the sale of luxuriously upholstered caskets based on the implication that they are more comfortable. It also justifies the argument that "this is the last thing you will ever be able to do for your father," the implication being that your dead father's feelings will be hurt if you choose a casket that is something less than luxurious.

A second appeal capitalizes on the survivors' fantasies about decay of the corpse. Expensive one-piece or hermetically sealed metal caskets are often urged on the survivors with the implication that they will postpone decay. Exhumations have provided fairly conclusive evidence, however, that the construction of the casket has little or no effect on the rate of decay—even if this were a desirable goal. Casket manufacturers who offer a ten-year or twenty-year guarantee that their product will remain intact are quite safe in doing so because they are altogether unlikely to be presented with claims by unsatisfied customers. Both the Federal Trade Commission regulations and some state regulations prohibit any claims that caskets postpone or prevent decay, and most funeral directors don't make them, but a good deal of casket salesmanship relies on this claim, which is usually subtly suggested rather than explicitly stated.

A third appeal implies that because it is the most conspicuous element in the funeral, the casket is an important indicator of social status—that a "quality" casket advertises the socioeconomic level of both the deceased and the survivors as well as the survivors' love and respect for the deceased. In actual practice, however, the price of the casket is often related inversely to the affluence of the deceased.

Your choice of casket may be influenced not only by your susceptibility to these appeals but also by your preferences for other elements of the funeral. If you plan to choose an open casket for viewing of the body, you may feel that the casket will be the focus of considerable attention. A closed casket, on the other hand, plays a less prominent part in any ritual, and an inexpensive model can be covered with a pall or with flowers. If you choose cremation, you will need only an inexpensive container; if cremation is to be preceded by a ritual service with the body present, it can, in some states, be placed in a rented casket; in others, the cremation container can be inserted in a rentable casketlike enclosure.

Entering the casket display room to make a selection is, for many survivors, the most traumatic episode of the entire bereavement process, and their emotional state makes a rational selection difficult. Compounding the difficulty is the practice of some funeral directors of placing the less expensive caskets in inconspicuous, poorly lighted corners of the display room and, by subtle arrangements of lighting and room arrangement, focusing the customer's attention on the medium-priced and more expensive models. This wordless "bait and switch" strategy is sometimes reinforced by a display of the least attractive versions of the cheaper models (even though more attractive models are readily available) or by gestures, facial expressions, or even remarks of disapproval when the customer shows interest in the less expensive models.

The Federal Trade Commission regulations, as well as some existing state laws, require that a certain number of caskets in the lowest price range be displayed in every funeral home, but even in the absence of such regulations your persistent inquiry about minimum-priced models should yield results. If you don't like those that are on display, ask to see the manufacturer's catalog; any model it lists can usually be delivered promptly. If the style of the casket doesn't matter to you, inquire about the price of the Orthodox Jewish casket. Because religious law requires that this be a plain wooden box with no ornamentation whatever, it is likely to be inexpensive, and it is available almost everywhere. Many people like its simplicity and austerity.

VAULT OR GRAVE LINER

Once you have chosen a casket and decided on grave burial rather than cremation, you are likely to be offered a vault—a container in which the casket is enclosed in the grave. Although you may be told that the vault serves to "protect" the casket (and hence, presumably the body), its actual purpose is to prevent the ground level of the grave from sinking as the casket decays with the passage of time. This purpose is served just as effectively by a cast-concrete grave liner, which can be bought from the cemetery at a substantially lower price.

Neither vaults nor liners are required by any state law, and you should be suspicious of any funeral director who implies that they are. Some states, however, give the individual cemetery the right to require a liner as a condition of burial. If you are concerned with the long-term condition of the grave, the liner may provide some protection against future maintenance problems.

Embalming

Embalming involves the replacement of the blood and other body fluids by a preservative solution in order to retard decay. If it is to be effective in preserving the body for purposes of viewing in an open-casket ritual, it must be done within about eight hours of death, by which time some deterioration has already begun. If the body is intended as an anatomic gift, however, embalming will render it unacceptable unless it is done under the supervision of the medical school or other recipient.

No state requires embalming in all cases, and some states (as well as the Federal Trade Commission regulations) prohibit it without the consent of a survivor, but all states require it in certain circumstances, such as death from a communicable disease, delay in body disposal, or interstate transportation of the body.

Embalming is not necessary if you choose direct disposal, and it is usually unnecessary if you choose cremation followed by a memorial service—although one state, presumably under pressure from the funeral industry, requires embalming if the body is held more than twenty-four hours but prohibits cremation sooner than forty-eight hours after death.

In some circumstances, deterioration of the body can be retarded by refrigeration instead of embalming, but refrigerator space is not always available, and the process is not inexpensive. If the body is to be viewed, it will require intermittent periods of refrigeration, and its low temperature is likely to shock mourners who want to touch or kiss it.

Cosmetic Restoration

Cosmetic restoration is unnecessary if a closed casket is used or, of course, if you choose direct disposal. But when an open casket is used, most survivors insist on it. An unrestored corpse is gray in color (because blood has left the surface capillaries), with open mouth and staring eyes, but these inescapable facts of death are likely to be traumatic to the survivors and other mourners who would like to see the deceased "as we remember him."

On the other hand, the quality of the restoration is always something of a gamble. Some funeral directors do a remarkable job of producing a likeness but, in the process, reduce the patient's apparent age by ten to twenty years. Others produce a gross caricature that is a source of severe distress to the survivors and cannot be corrected to their satisfaction once the body is ready for viewing.

Clothing

For open-casket viewing, the body will, of course, have to be clothed, and many funeral homes offer a wide array of styles and colors. There is no reason whatsoever to buy this merchandise if you have access to a favorite dress or suit that belonged to the dead person.

Viewing, Visitation, and Ritual Facilities

If you choose an open casket, you will probably want to use the funeral home for visitation and viewing, and you will recognize that charges for the use of these facilities are legitimate. If you choose a closed casket, however, you may prefer to invite mourners to visit you at home, in which case the casket can be stored in the funeral home until committal, and the funeral-home charges are reduced accordingly.

The same holds true for the use of the funeral home for any kind of ritual service. If you plan to hold a memorial service at home or elsewhere after the body has been disposed of, or if you plan a service at a house of worship, there is no justification for a funeral-home charge for use of its chapel (although there will be a charge for transporting the body to and from the house of worship).

One alternative, which represents a compromise between direct disposal and a traditional funeral, is a graveside service with a closed casket. Although the funeral home may make a charge for the additional time involved at the graveside, this should be more than offset by elimination of the charges for use of the chapel, for viewing, and possibly for embalming and restoration. The graveside service is commonly used when death has occurred elsewhere and the casket is brought directly from the airport to the cemetery.

Transportation Charges

The "standard adult funeral" usually includes charges for transporting the body from the place of death to the funeral home, and thence to the cemetery or crematorium, and for one limousine to transport the principal mourners to and from the disposal site. Your decision to order additional limousines will be based, of course, on the number and the emotional states of the mourners, but usually such a decision can be made at the last minute—during the ritual service, if necessary. Generally, most mourners can be relied upon to drive their own cars and to provide space in them for those who don't.

If flowers are involved, there is likely to be an extra charge for the vehicle that transports them from the funeral home to the church or the cemetery but not for arranging them in the funeral home.

Other Services

The traditional funeral home provides a number of miscellaneous services that should be specified when you make arrangements, whether or not their cost is itemized.

Death Certificates

In settling the estate, you will need a certified copy of the death certificate in order to transfer ownership of *each* piece of real estate, *each* stock certificate, and *each* motor vehicle; to collect the benefits payable under *each* insurance policy; to collect *each* death benefit; as well as for a variety of other purposes, such as gaining access to the deceased's safe-deposit box.

Virtually all funeral homes will offer to get these certificates for you from the local county clerk or the state health department. But there are two problems connected with this offer. First, although some funeral homes provide this service at actual cost—the nominal fee charged by the county clerk or the health department—others add a surcharge, which you can easily avoid by the simple process of getting the copies yourself. Second, it is almost impossible for you to know, at the time you are making arrangements, precisely how many certified copies of the death certificate will be necessary in settling the estate, and consequently you are likely to order either too many or too few. The best solution may be to order only the minimum number that is needed immediately and to obtain additional copies yourself as the need arises.

Death Benefits

Funeral homes may offer to file applications in your behalf for any Social Security or Veterans Administration death or burial benefits to which the survivors are entitled, but often they will do this only if the benefits are applied to the funeral bill. Although this service may relieve you of responsibility for some or all of the funeral bill (see p. 146), and although it eliminates your having to file the applications yourself and waiting for payment, it has one disadvantage. If the funeral bill is presented to the personal representative with the death benefits already credited, the personal representative may regard the bill as reasonable, whereas the total bill may in fact be unreasonably high and hence challengeable. On the other hand, payment of the entire bill from the estate's assets reduces the net value of the estate and thus may eliminate the need for probate or reduce estate or inheritance taxes.

Pallbearers

Unless the funeral service takes place in a house of worship, pallbearers are unnecessary, because funeral-home employees will move the casket into and out of the hearse. If they are necessary, you can choose them from among the friends of the deceased, bearing in mind that carrying part of the combined weight of casket and body is not a task for the physically frail. An alternative is to ask the funeral home to provide professional pallbearers and to designate the deceased's friends as honorary pallbearers. You will, of course, be charged for the services of the professional pallbearers.

Crematorium or Cemetery Arrangements

If you do not own a cemetery plot and if you have not already made arrangements for disposal of the body, the funeral director can help you choose a cemetery or a crematorium and will add the charges to his bill. In some circumstances, this service can be very helpful, because funeral directors are usually well acquainted with all cemeteries and crematoriums within a reasonable radius of the community. As we shall see shortly, however, problems can arise when the funeral home advances substantial sums of money in your behalf.

Obituary Notices

The funeral director will usually offer to place paid obituary notices in the appropriate local newspapers and to help you with the wording of the notice. His experience can be useful, because grief-stricken survivors tend either to omit essential information from the notice or to overload it with unnecessary detail.

Cash Outlays by the Funeral Director

A number of the services described above—obtaining the death certificates, placing the obituary notices, buying a grave plot, or paying the charges for opening and closing the grave—involve cash disbursements by the funeral director in your behalf. In addition, the funeral director will also add to the bill gratuities for the hearse and limousine drivers and for the grave diggers.

At first glance, it would appear that the funeral director's willingness to take care of all these transactions spares you a good deal of effort and inconvenience at a time when you are under stress—and often this is the case. But critics of the funeral industry point out that this convenience is not always free of charge. Some funeral directors add to the bill an amount greater than the sum of the separate disbursements; others obtain discounts (for obituary notices, for example) that they fail to pass on to the customer. Worse yet, in many instances, clergymen complain that they never receive the honorarium for which the funeral director has billed the customer.

There is something to be said, therefore, in favor of your handling some of these matters personally. Since you are not likely to select a grave or a crematorium sight unseen, you may as well make the financial arrangements at the same time that you inspect the site. You may want to see to it, also, that your honorarium for the clergyman reaches its intended destination, especially since, if you make your check payable to the church or synagogue rather than to the individual, the amount becomes tax deductible as a charitable contribution.

When Two Funeral Homes Are Involved

When a death occurs away from home—perhaps as the result of an automobile accident or a heart attack during travel—your best plan is to get in touch with a funeral director in your own community. He will make arrangements with a funeral director near the scene of death, and the two will collaborate on the services required to produce a complete funeral. You should not be charged more than the price of a "standard adult funeral" for their combined services, but you can expect to be billed for certain services you might not have required had the death occurred at home. Embalming, for example, is almost universally required if a body is to be shipped interstate, and airfreight charges for a casketed body are substantial. You can avoid the former and significantly reduce the latter by deciding on cremation where the death occurred and holding a memorial service locally at some later date.

SPECIFYING THE FINAL DETAILS

As we have noted, the funeral director is in the ethically difficult position of having to *advise* the customer which goods and services to buy and, at the same time, having to *sell* them to the customer. This is why customers who don't know what they want and put themselves into the hands of a funeral director whose entrepreneurial role requires him to maximize profit are rather likely to be exploited. After reading this chapter, however, you should have developed a reasonably clear idea of what you want and, more important, what you don't want. And just as you have learned to disregard or reject the suggestions of the automobile salesman who tries to sell you optional extras, so you should feel quite comfortable about rejecting funeral goods and services that strike you as inappropriate or unnecessary.

The funeral industry is, as we have noted, highly competitive, despite the absence of price competition in public advertisements. Every funeral director knows that an inexpensive funeral is more profitable than no funeral at all, and some may feel forced to forego any profit merely to pay their continuing overhead costs. Consequently, if you come to the funeral home with a set of clearly defined specifications, and if you can convey the impression that you are there to buy a funeral, not to be sold one, you are likely to get exactly what you want, and at a competitive price.

Although the funeral industry is, on the whole, probably no more dishonest than any other retail business, it has lobbied vigorously and successfully against regulation by both federal and state governments. Since regulation is often proposed in response to widespread or severe consumer abuse or exploitation, it is important that you be on your guard.

If you use our summary of FTC rules as a guide during your negotiations, bear in mind that no funeral director is likely to comply with every one of its requirements. But if the funeral director with whom you are dealing violates a significant number of the more important provisions, you should probably try one or more of his competitors.

DEALING WITH A CREMATORIUM

Unlike the funeral home industry, the crematorium industry is not overcrowded, and you are unlikely to have much choice among competing firms unless you live in a metropolitan area. And, again unlike funeral homes, crematoriums do not offer an essentially identical range of services. Some firms, catering mainly to survivors who choose direct disposal, provide only crematory service, which includes delivery of the ashes in a sealed canister to the survivors. Others provide, in addition, viewing and visitation facilities and a chapel for ritual services. Still others include facilities for the disposal of the ashes: a garden in which the ashes may be scattered or a columbarium, a building containing tiers of niches in which the ashes may be permanently inurned. All these differences in the range of services offered make price comparisons difficult.

In general, however, your guiding principle probably should be simplicity. The choice of cremation instead of grave burial is made more often by the deceased than by the survivors, and if the survivors disagree with it they can, as we have noted (see p. 145), disregard it. Hence, those survivors who comply with the deceased's wishes presumably share the philosophy underlying the decision: a lack of concern for the physical remains. With this in mind, they are less likely to seek preservation of the ashes in a decorative urn set permanently in a columbarium niche and more likely to see cremation as a method of swiftly returning the body to its basic elements.

SEEKING REDRESS

Because funeral negotiations usually take place under severe emotional stress and time pressure, you may, despite your best efforts, be misled, overcharged, or cheated. Although the FTC will not investigate or resolve individual complaints, you are not completely without resources.

Your first step (and the easiest to take) is to discuss the issue with the funeral director in the hope that the difficulty stemmed from a misunderstanding rather than any intent to defraud you. If this fails, the Better Business Bureau of your community may be helpful. But don't despair if the Better Business Bureau is of no use.

Although in recent years this organization has strengthened its efforts on behalf of the public, some of its branches tend to retain their original function: protecting their merchant members from customers who feel that they have been victimized or treated unfairly.

Another possible resource is your state "mortuary board"—the administrative body that controls the licensing of funeral directors. As in the case of the Better Business Bureau, the degree of cooperation and support you'll receive depends on the state in which you live. Some states include on their mortuary boards not only licensed funeral directors but also "public" members, whose explicit function is to represent and protect the interests of the consumer; other state boards consist entirely of funeral directors. Some boards are concerned with professional ethics; others are concerned primarily with restricting entry to the industry and thus protecting current practitioners against newcomers and other competitors.

The National Funeral Directors Association (135 West Wells St., Milwaukee, WI 53203) sponsors an independent organization known as ThanaCAP that arbitrates consumer complaints against funeral directors, whether or not they are members of the association.

But before you take any action, you need to be as certain as you can that you are not directing against a perfectly honorable funeral director your very understandable anger or resentment over the death itself.

9

THE WILL: GUARDIANSHIPS AND OTHER FIRST STEPS

Although detective novels may have left you with the impression that an urgent search for the will immediately after a death is a mark of villainous greed, the fact is that a will should be located and read promptly because it is likely to contain information that may be needed immediately. Disposing of the deceased's property is only one function of a will, and often not the most important one. In addition, the will may:

Make anatomic gifts of the deceased's organs or entire body.

Express the deceased's preferences as to funeral rites or body disposal.

Nominate a guardian for minor children, and possibly a conservator for any assets left to them in the will.

Nominate a personal representative (formerly called an executor) to manage the deceased's assets and to settle the estate.

Identify specific assets owned by the deceased.

Not every will, of course, is likely to deal with all these matters, but most wills contain some instructions that require very prompt action as well as some that can, or must, be delayed. Anatomic gifts, for example, or funeral preferences must receive immediate attention. And the appointment of a guardian for minor children may be at least as urgent. The identification and disposition of the deceased's assets, on the other hand, may be a long-drawn-out process extending over several months at the very least. But since the survivors cannot be certain just what the will specifies, they should find it and read it without delay.

FINDING THE WILL

If the deceased was a person of orderly habits, he probably told one or more members of his family (or specified in his letter of instruction) that he had signed a will and had deposited it in the local probate court or left it for safekeeping in his lawyer's office or at his bank. In such cases, a telephone call to the court, the lawyer, or the bank can confirm the existence and whereabouts of the will and arrange for obtaining copies.

But because some people are not orderly and some die unexpectedly, it is not uncommon for survivors to be uncertain about the existence of a will and totally ignorant of its location if, indeed, one exists at all. In such circumstances the survivors may be tempted to conclude that the deceased left no will, since three out of every four people die without one, but this statistic is misleading because it covers people of all levels of education and income. If the deceased was reasonably well educated and had even a moderate net worth, or left minor children, a search for a will should begin at once.

One common storage place for a will is a safe-deposit box rented by the deceased. Although, as we shall see (p. 194), access to the deceased's safe-deposit box may be restricted by state law, the probate courts of most states will permit access to the box for the express purpose of searching for a will and filing it with the court. Permission usually requires the filing of a petition with the court—a process that is simple but too slow to make anatomic gifts feasible.

If the safe-deposit box fails to yield a will or information as to its whereabouts, your next step is to find out from the deceased's bank whether he had nominated the bank as personal representative of the estate or as trustee of a trust. Often, in such cases, the lawyer who prepared the will sends a copy to the bank, along with information as to the whereabouts of the original. Indeed, some banks and trust companies provide safekeeping services for original wills, trusts, and related documents.

Another source of clues is the deceased's file of canceled checks, which may yield the name of a lawyer who prepared a will. And in some cases it may be advisable to publish in a local newspaper a notice inquiring about the possible existence and whereabouts of a will executed by the deceased.

If these sources yield nothing, you will need to search the deceased's home, especially those places where he habitually kept personal papers—a desk, a strongbox, perhaps even a shoe box stored in a closet or dresser drawer. However, although you ought to search conscientiously, there is no need to turn the house upside down. Most Americans, even some with considerable assets, *do* fail to make a will—or they sign an informal do-it-yourself document that has no legal standing in states that do not recognize holographic wills. In either case, the deceased will be regarded as having died intestate.

Intestacy can be inconvenient and sometimes expensive, but it should not be regarded as a disaster. In most cases, the probate court will comply with the wishes of the survivors with respect to the appointment of a personal representative or a guardian for minor children. It is only in connection with the disposition of the deceased's assets that the court is bound by state law rather than by the preferences of the survivors—and this becomes significant only if the deceased's probatable assets are substantial.

Once you have found a will, open it and read it. Although movies and novels tend to depict the reading of a will as a formal and legalistic procedure, no formalities whatever are required by law. Some states require that the original will be promptly filed with the probate court—and this may be advisable for its protection even if it is not compulsory—but there is no reason why you should not make one or more photocopies for yourself and for any other interested party.

Your first reading of the will should enable you to classify its instructions into three categories: (1) matters that can be taken care of immediately by you or other survivors, (2) matters that involve the probate court but require prompt attention, and (3) matters that either can or must be delayed. The rest of this chapter will deal with the first two of these categories, because those in the third category cannot be attended to until you have read the next chapter.

STEPS YOU CAN TAKE BY YOURSELF

Anatomic Gifts

If the will makes an anatomic gift of one or more of the deceased's organs or of the entire body, time is of the essence, but fortunately you often do not need prior court approval of the will or any other legal authorization in order to carry out the deceased's wishes. Simply get in touch with the donee specified in the will and make arrangements for the transfer, with a clear understanding as to who is responsible for any transportation costs. If no donee has been specified, you can usually find one by getting in touch with a local hospital or organ bank.

Don't blame yourself, however, if you discover the will too late to make such gifts possible. As we have noted, anatomic gifts should be made by means of a uniform donor card and not a will—because they must be carried out within hours of the death and wills are all too often not found and read in time, especially by survivors who worry about showing indecent haste.

Funeral Arrangements

The deceased's preferences for funeral rites and body disposal may also be found in the will, although the will is as inappropriate a vehicle for these preferences as it is for anatomic gifts—and for the same reasons. If the will is found in time, most survivors attempt to satisfy the wishes of the deceased, but it is doubtful that the will is legally binding on them if the deceased's preferences will seriously deplete the estate. If, for example, the estate amounts to $20,000 and the will specifies a funeral that is likely to cost $6,000, no court will fault the widow for disregarding her husband's wishes, arranging a more modest funeral, and conserving as much of her husband's estate as she feels is necessary for her own continued support.

Identification of Assets

As we noted in chapter 1, a properly drawn will should refer to assets in general terms rather than make a complete itemization, which would require revision each time the assets change. In the absence of a letter of instruction, however, the will may provide you with clues as to the existence of certain assets—as, for example, in the sentence "I give my one hundred shares of AT&T common stock to my nephew, James Brown." This should alert you to look for the stock certificate and, if you fail to find it, to get in touch with AT&T to find out whether the deceased still owned the stock at the time of death.

STEPS INVOLVING THE PROBATE COURT

Although in the minds of most people the primary function of the probate court is the administration of the deceased's estate, an equally important function is the protection of the person and property of minor children orphaned by the deceased. If the deceased was a sole surviving parent of minor children or if both parents of minor children died simultaneously, your first—and perhaps only—contact with the probate court may be in connection with the appointment of a guardian, a conservator, or both. The probate court having jurisdiction over minor children is located in the courthouse of the county in which the children reside and is listed in the phone book under the name of the county.

Guardians of the Persons of Minor Children

Unmarried minor children—in most states individuals under eighteen years of age—not only need to be provided with food, clothing, shelter, discipline, supervision, and guidance, but, in addition, they are legally incapable of enrolling in school, consenting to medical or dental treatment, marrying, enlisting in the armed services, and engaging in a number of other activities without the consent of a parent or legal guardian. Obviously, then, the appointment of a guardian for orphaned minors is a matter of real urgency.

If the will has nominated a guardian and if the guardian consents to undertake the responsibilities, the court will almost invariably approve the appointment. Some states permit the nomination to be made in a writing separate from the will. Once the nomination is approved by the court and the guardian notifies the court in writing that he or she is willing to accept the appointment, the court issues letters of guardianship certifying that the guardian is entitled to act, in all respects, in place of the deceased parent or parents.

In some situations there may be conflict or confusion over the appointment of a guardian, but most of these are resolved by law. If, for example, the minor's natural father and mother name different guardians in their respective wills, the guardian named in the will of the parent last to die takes precedence. If parents are divorced and the mother has custody of the children, the guardian nominated in her will is not likely to be appointed as long as the children's natural father is willing to serve and not found unsuitable. And if the natural father dies after his divorced wife, his nomination of guardian will take precedence over hers, even though she has custody of the children.

In all such situations, however, the court is, by law, required to be concerned primarily with "the best interests of the child," and hence any interested party—grandparents, aunts, uncles—can challenge the appointment of any person they regard as manifestly unsuitable or unfit. In all states, in fact, a minor fourteen years of age or older may challenge the appointment of his or her guardian either before or after the appointment is made by the court. The objections must be submitted to the court in writing, and the child may nominate another person as his or her guardian.

If the guardian nominated in a will or other writing is unable or unwilling to serve or if the minor's parents died without nominating one, the court is empowered to appoint anyone it chooses. This is usually done after a hearing, which all interested parties may attend. Again, the overriding concern is "the best interests of the child," and priority will be given to a nomination by a minor fourteen years of age or older if the nominee seems suitable to the probate judge.

Guardianship is a responsibility that should not be undertaken lightly. To begin with, it is a long-term involvement that does not terminate until the child marries, reaches the age of majority, or is adopted by others. Second, any money bequeathed by the parents or others to the child must be used exclusively for the child's benefit and must be accounted for, and any excess must be carefully preserved for the child's future needs. On the other hand, although the guardian cannot be held *legally* responsible for the expenses involved in rearing a child, there is a *moral* responsibility that may be burdensome if the deceased parents did not leave enough money to cover the child's expenses—a very common situation. The guardian can, of course, resign by petitioning the court, but this is practicable only if someone else is available and willing to assume the guardianship.

Protecting the Property of Minor Children

Because minor children are by law incapable of owning, managing, or selling any kind of property, some provision must be made for the management of any assets they inherit.

If the estate planning was thoughtful and the value of the child's inheritance is substantial, the deceased probably established a trust, to be managed by a trustee for the benefit of the minor children. If the trust was created and funded before the death, whatever assets it owned are immediately available to the trustee without any need for administration by the probate court. If, on the other hand, the trust was created by the will and thus did not become effective until the death, any assets destined for the trust other than life insurance will most likely need to undergo probate administration. In either case, there is nothing that you as a survivor can do to alter the trust arrangement established by the deceased.

In the overwhelming majority of cases, however, no trust of any kind is established by the deceased, and in such cases the procedure to be followed depends largely on the value of the assets and the laws of your state. In some states, if the value is less than a specified maximum (for example, $5,000), the personal representative may turn the management of the child's inheritance over to the child's legal guardian (or to the child's parents if, for example, the bequest was made by someone other than the parents). If, on the other hand, the assets exceed the state limit, the probate court will appoint a conservator, or guardian of the child's estate, to receive, hold, and manage them until the child reaches the age of majority.

If the will has nominated a conservator, the court will usually appoint the nominee. In the absence of such a nomination, or if there is no will, the court may appoint either an individual or a bank or other financial institution.

There is no legal reason, of course, why the person appointed as guardian of the child's person should not petition the court for appointment as conservator, as well, because unless the assets are complex and substantial, no great financial acumen is required. In fact, in most states the role of the conservator is highly restricted: he is charged solely with responsibility for protecting the assets and for ensuring that they are used exclusively for the support of the minor. Selling the assets in order to reinvest the money for higher yield usually requires the permission of the probate court, and in some states even the court is restricted to authorizing only a narrow range of ultraconservative investments.

Given these restrictions, a conservator who is highly sophisticated in financial matters is more likely to suffer personal frustration than he is to increase the value of the assets for which he is responsible. The conservator may also be frustrated by the fact that his responsibility ends when the child attains majority. At that time, the assets, whatever their value, are turned over to the child, whether or not he or she is mature enough to use them wisely.

Appointment of the Personal Representative

Whether or not it nominates a guardian or a conservator, every properly drawn will nominates a personal representative, but whether this appointment should be formalized by the probate court immediately requires careful judgment. To begin with, if the deceased followed some of the suggestions offered in chapter 2, there may be no probatable assets and hence no need for a personal representative. Even if probatable assets exist, they may, if they do not exceed a specified amount, be transferable by simplified "small estate" procedures that avoid or significantly minimize probate-court administration.

In many states, however, these simplified transfer procedures are not available if a petition for the appointment of a personal representative is pending or has been granted (see tables 8 and 9). If you are premature in petitioning the court to appoint a personal representative, you may be disqualifying the survivors from taking full advantage of the "small estate" transfer procedures, which are invariably simpler, quicker, and less expensive.

On the other hand, there are many circumstances that require the appointment of a personal representative at the earliest possible moment. If the deceased left a business that is still operating, he presumably designated in his will someone who is competent either to manage or to liquidate it. If the deceased left real estate, an investment portfolio, or even a savings account with a balance of more than $5,000 titled in his own name, you can be quite certain that a personal representative will have to be appointed to manage such assets and to distribute them according to the terms of the will.

If the appointment of a personal representative seems inevitable at the outset, you may as well proceed with the court formalities immediately, because until he is appointed, none of the assets can be managed or disposed of. Furthermore, the appointment of a personal representative does not in itself obligate the estate to go through formal probate administration.

On the other hand, the appointment may involve the estate in expenses that may ultimately prove unnecessary if an inventory of the assets reveals that nothing requires probate or that the probatable assets do not exceed the maximum value allowed by your state's "small estate" transfer procedures. In most cases, then, the most sensible plan may be to postpone the appointment of a personal representative until your inventory of the assets, as explained in chapter 11, determines whether the appointment is necessary.

PROBATE ADMINISTRATION OF THE ESTATE

Thus far, we have dealt with the preliminary functions of the probate court—essentially the protection of minor children and possibly the appointment of a personal representative. In the eyes of many people, the more important function of the court is to oversee the distribution of the deceased's assets—either to the beneficiaries named in the will or to the heirs specified by state law in the absence of a will.

In reality, however, only a very small percentage of estates require full administration by the probate court. Moreover, the need for probate is not necessarily related to the size of the estate. Indeed, it is likely that very large estates are those most likely to be planned so that probate administration is successfully avoided. You can be certain, of course, that if the deceased died without leaving a will, the probate court will be involved, even if the assets amounted to only a few thousand dollars. But if the deceased left a will and an estate valued at several hundred thousand dollars, you cannot be sure that probate-court administration will be necessary until you have separated the probatable from the nonprobatable assets. This procedure is explained in the next chapter.

10

SORTING OUT THE ASSETS

After almost every death remains some unfinished business that becomes the responsibility of the survivors. Any property owned by the deceased, for example, must be identified, perhaps appraised, and protected until it can be disposed of. Often there are moneys coming to the deceased: salary or pension checks, for example, or stock dividends and tax refunds. Usually there are bills or other debts that the deceased incurred but did not pay. In addition, there may be insurance proceeds to collect, tax returns to file, death benefits to claim, and other financial matters to be attended to.

Your first task as a survivor, then, is to make a complete inventory of the deceased's assets and liabilities as promptly as possible. This inventory will serve two purposes. First, it will give you and the other survivors a realistic picture of what you can expect in the way of inheritance. Second, it will tell you whether the deceased's estate will require lengthy (and often expensive) administration by the probate court or whether it can be distributed to the survivors through much simpler "small estate" transfer procedures or without any probate action at all.

If the estate is large and complex, the deceased is likely to have nominated in his will a professionally qualified personal representative—a bank, trust company, or lawyer—to handle the inventory and settlement processes. If this is the case, your personal responsibilities may be few, but this chapter can help you ensure that the personal representative does the job competently and overlooks nothing.

In the vast majority of cases, however, responsibility for handling the estate falls into the hands of a surviving spouse or an adult child who has never before had such an experience. For such survivors, this chapter is intended as a fairly specific "how to do it" guide.

If you find yourself in this position, there are to reasons why you may be tempted to skip or merely skim this chapter. On the one hand, you may have participated so actively in the deceased's financial affairs that you feel you know everything you need to and that the procedures described in this chapter are "obvious." Experience shows, however, that such survivors often make serious mistakes, because handling the affairs of someone who has died is different in many respects from participating in them while he or she was alive.

On the other hand, you may shun this chapter for the opposite reason—because you know nothing at all about the deceased's financial affairs other than that the estate amounts to little or nothing. In such a situation, you are likely to overlook available death benefits that are all the more important if, in fact, the estate is small or insolvent and if the survivors need every cent that can be recovered.

The handling of an estate, even a modest one, can involve so many seemingly urgent matters that you may either "freeze up" and do nothing because you don't know what to do first or, feeling the pressure of time, you may make hasty and unwise decisions. Actually, a priority sequence is fairly simple to establish: your first task is to get into the hands of the survivors whatever money and other possessions they need immediately in order to continue their normal lives; second, you need to attend to those of the deceased's assets that may depreciate (or fail to appreciate) in value until their ownership has been transferred. All other matters can be safely postponed, and some of them may take weeks or months to conclude despite your best efforts. In fact, you are likely to conclude, after reading this chapter, that handling a deceased's estate requires patience and persistence rather than financial sophistication and experience.

WILL THE ESTATE REQUIRE PROBATE ADMINISTRATION?

As we have noted, sorting out the assets will help you determinate whether or not the estate will require administration by the probate court. This is important to know because your responsibilities as a survivor will be largely governed by the answer to this question, but the answer will depend both on the nature of the assets and on your understanding of why, and under what circumstances, probate administration is necessary.

The basic purpose of the probate process is to ensure that all assets belonging to the deceased are distributed properly—that the persons named in the will (or the heirs designated by law if there is no will) receive what they are entitled to, that all death taxes are paid, and that the deceased's creditors collect their lawful debts. The key phrase in this definition is "belonging to the deceased," because this means that any property owned jointly by the deceased and another person (who survived the deceased), or any property owned by a living trust established by the deceased (see p. 38), or life insurance and financial accounts having designated beneficiaries, is *not* part of the probatable estate. Thus, for example, stock certificates or bank accounts in the name of the deceased alone at the time of death are subject to probate administration, but those jointly owned with a surviving spouse simply pass to the survivor without any form of probate-court administration. Life insurance proceeds are not probatable assets unless the estate of the deceased has been designated as beneficiary; otherwise they pass directly to whichever survivors are named as beneficiaries, as do the proceeds of pension plans and retirement accounts, including IRA, SEP, Keogh, and 401k accounts. Pay-on-death bank accounts and transfer-on-death securities accounts pass directly to the designated beneficiaries, without probate administration.

The same principle holds true for debts: charge accounts, loans, or other debts in the name of the deceased alone are subject to probate, and this means that the creditors can collect what is owed them only from the estate. But debts on which another person has cosigned remain the responsibility of the surviving cosigner as well as the estate.

As you can see, the need for probate administration is not necessarily related to the value of the assets that the deceased left for the survivors. If the deceased followed the advice offered in chapter 2, he may have reduced the value of his *probatable* assets to a few hundred dollars or to nothing at all, even though he left to the survivors assets worth millions. On the other hand, some people leave assets of very modest value that, because of their form of ownership, require full-fledged administration by the probate court.

Unless you have participated actively in the affairs of the deceased, you may not know at the outset whether or not the estate includes probatable assets or what the current value of these assets amounts to. By the time you have concluded your inventory, however, you will know which of the following four situations you face and precisely what you have to do:

1. *You may discover that there are no assets whatever that require probate*—because all of the deceased's assets were owned jointly, were held in a living trust, or consisted of life insurance or financial accounts that designate beneficiaries. In this situation the will does not need to be probated because, in fact, there *is* no probate estate; the deceased left nothing that belonged exclusively to him and did not automatically pass to survivors by operation or law. Hence, your only responsibility is to be of whatever help you can in seeing that jointly owned or trust-owned assets and any life insurance or other financial benefits actually pass to the appropriate survivors. You may, of course, discover a long-forgotten bank account in the deceased's name alone with a balance of perhaps only $50, but you may decide that it is easier to abandon this account and let it ultimately pass to the state treasury than to go through the formalities of probate-court administration. Before abandoning such an account or, for that matter, any other asset, however, you should read p. 217 to determine whether it can be assigned to the survivors by utilizing one of the "small estate" transfer procedures that obviate full probate-court administration.
2. *You may need to petition the probate court to appoint you as personal representative.* This may be necessary if you discover assets owned exclusively by the deceased that will have to be liquidated or transferred to another owner. As personal representative, you will be authorized by the court to manage or liquidate the deceased's property, have access to his safe-deposit box, and conduct most of the transactions that the deceased could have conducted had he not died.

   Petitioning the court for appointment as personal representative is in itself neither expensive nor time-consuming (see p. 227), and it does not commit you to full probate administration of the estate. You should consider it, therefore, just as soon as you discover any asset that requires the action of a personal representative—an individually owned piece of rental property, for example—because if you find one such asset, you are likely to find more as you continue your inventory.

3. *You may be able to take advantage of two swift and simple procedures known as transfer by affidavit or "small estate" probate administration.* Because the probatable assets and liabilities that most people leave when they die are relatively low in value and simple in nature, all states have adopted various simplified transfer procedures that are inexpensive, informal, and relatively speedy. The legally specified maximums vary from one state to another, from a low of $500 to a high of $140,000, usually exclusive of the value of any motor vehicles (see p. 218). Your county probate court or a lawyer can provide you with the details.
4. *The estate may have to undergo the full probate-administration process* if the value of the probatable assets exceeds the state maximum for affidavit transfer or "small estate" transfer procedures. Probate court administration of an estate is described in detail in chapter 11, but because it is lengthy as well as expensive, it should be initiated just as soon as your inventory proves it to be necessary. As we point out on p. 227, serving as the deceased's personal representative throughout the full probate process is not insuperably difficult, but since you will inevitably need the help of a lawyer, getting in touch with one in the early stage of your inventory gives you the advantage of his advice and help in the later stages, even before the formal probate process begins.

   It is important that the lawyer you select be experienced in probate administration. If you cannot find one by word of mouth through trustworthy friends, you might ask the clerk of your probate court, your banker, or the lawyer-referral service of your local or state bar association for the names of several lawyers who specialize in probate law.

IDENTIFYING AND LOCATING THE ASSETS

The difficulty you experience in identifying and making an inventory of the assets will depend, of course, on your relationship with the deceased. If you are an adult child who has lived at a distance from a deceased parent, you are very likely to be less familiar with his or her financial affairs than if you are a widow or widower who took a strong interest in your deceased spouse's every transaction. No matter what your situation, however, you would do well to read the next few pages carefully, because experience shows that even those survivors who participated actively in the deceased's affairs tend to overlook some assets, benefits, or opportunities to increase one or the other.

The Letter of Instruction

If the deceased left a letter of instruction for his survivors (see chapter 4), your task will be vastly simplified. The letter, if it is reasonably up to date, will specify in full detail the nature, location, and current value of most, if not all, of the assets and liabilities. In addition, the letter will probably specify the whereabouts of a will. This is why locating the letter of instruction promptly is a matter of the highest priority.

Your search, however, should not become a frantic and time-consuming process, because most people who prepare a letter of instruction tell their survivors about its existence and whereabouts. Actually, the letter is a relatively recent innovation, and some lawyers who routinely prepare wills and trusts fail to advise their clients about its usefulness. As a consequence, the vast majority of people die without having prepared one. If you don't find one after searching the deceased's safe-deposit box, his desk drawers, or any other place where personal papers are kept, you can safely assume that one doesn't exist.

Checking Accounts

In the absence of a letter of instruction, your most useful "map" of the deceased's financial situation is likely to be his checkbook, his bank statements, his file of canceled checks, and his computer files, if any. A careful review of every check issued during the year immediately preceding death should give you reasonably reliable information on the following:

Insurance policies—checks for premium payments will identify the insurance company and possibly each current life, accident, or health policy.

Land contracts and mortgages—payment checks can help you identify the properties subject to these liens.

Investment accounts—checks will identify brokerage accounts, money market or mutual funds, recent specific securities purchases, and IRA, SEP, Keogh, and 401k accounts.

Charge accounts and loans—checks should help you determine the current level of indebtedness.

Federal, state, and local income taxes—checks will indicate payments and, hence, accounts still payable.

Property taxes—payments can identify owned property.

Utility payments—bills paid can identify owned property not revealed by tax or mortgage payments.

Hospital and medical expenses—payments should be checked against recent health-care bills and against health-care insurance policies for possible reimbursement.

Payments for goods and services not actually used—airline tickets, for example, which can be refunded in full if they were not used.

License fees for cars and other vehicles—checks can identify vehicles owned by the deceased.

Charitable contributions—if you will be responsible for filing an income-tax return on behalf of the deceased.

Safe-deposit box or post-office box rental—so that you can locate the box.

Similarly, a careful review of each deposit noted in the checkbook or ledger may help you identify such sources of assets or future income as:

Rents on income property

Stock dividends and bond interest payments

Payments on mortgages, land contracts, or promissory notes held by the deceased

Royalties on patents, mineral rights, or books

Insurance dividends—a clue to paid-up policies

Tax refunds

Social Security, Veterans Administration, and pension benefits

Fees for consultation or other services

Deposits for electricity, telephone, and other services

This review is not likely to unearth every single asset. The deceased may have had some stock dividends that were paid directly into a savings account or a money market fund. Similarly, he may have made some regular payments by means of money market fund checks. And paid-up insurance policies that do not pay dividends will not appear in the bank record. Nevertheless, tedious though it may be, your examination of the deceased's banking activities will save you a great deal of time and trouble in the later stages, especially if you take responsibility for filing the deceased's last income-tax return.

The Deceased's Mail

A second source of information about assets and liabilities is the mail that will continue to arrive for the deceased, because, in addition to advertising matter and social correspondence, it is likely to contain dividend and pension checks, bank and brokerage statements, payments on debts owed to the deceased, utility bills, and bills or notices about insurance premiums, charge accounts, and other liabilities.

The postal regulations governing delivery of the deceased's mail are reasonably clear. When the local post office hears of the death of a mail recipient (either through notification by a survivor or, informally, through the letter carrier, who may notice mail accumulating at the address), it will hold the mail for fifteen days and then return it to the sender. Most of the deceased's mail can be claimed at the post office or readdressed through the usual change-of-address form either by an adult family member or an heir who can provide the postmaster with satisfactory identification and a copy of the death certificate or by a formally appointed personal representative, who must show the postmaster his letters of authority (see p. 228).

But not all the deceased's mail will be available to you through these procedures. Most U.S. Treasury checks—for Social Security or Veterans Administration benefits, for example, but not income-tax refunds—must be returned by the postmaster to the sending agency. Other government checks—state, county, or municipal—must be handled in accordance with instructions printed on their envelopes, as must mail containing driver's licenses, credit cards, and other documents intended for the exclusive use of the deceased.

If the deceased rented a post-office box, a survivor who has the key or the combination can continue to collect all mail but is legally obligated to return to sender U.S. Treasury checks and other materials mentioned in the preceding paragraph. Usually, however, the survivor will find it more convenient to execute a change-of-address form than to make periodic visits to the post office to monitor the box.

Normally the mail-collection procedure works smoothly, but occasionally problems arise: the postmaster may, for example, receive two different change-of-address forms, each signed by a different person, either because the survivors are in conflict or because they did not communicate adequately with one another. In such circumstances the postmaster will honor the change form signed by the personal representative; otherwise the deceased's spouse will have priority. If family conflict persists, the postmaster is authorized to deliver the mail to a third party agreed upon by the family members or to refer the dispute to the U.S. Postal Service regional counsel, whose decision as to who may receive the mail is final.

If you become responsible for the deceased's mail, you should immediately sort out all mail addressed to joint owners (bank statements, dividend checks, bills, etc.) and send it on to the surviving owner, because none of it constitutes part of the deceased's assets or liabilities. The rest of the mail should be separated into five categories:

1. Assets—dividend checks and other items payable to the deceased alone
2. Liabilities—credit card and charge-account statements, utility bills, premium notices, tax bills, and other notices of payments due
3. Social correspondence
4. Magazine subscriptions
5. Advertising and other "junk mail."

The handling of assets and liabilities will be dealt with later in this chapter and in the chapter that follows. Social correspondence can be answered personally by you or another survivor or by means of a simple printed announcement of death. Magazine subscriptions, if they are of no interest to the survivors, may be transferred to a friend or a local library or, if relatively recent, can be canceled along with a request for a refund for future issues. Advertising mail can, of course, be discarded when received.

Although the volume of mail addressed to the deceased is likely to diminish rapidly, it should be monitored conscientiously for at least six months and preferably for a year. Some banks, money market funds, IRA, Keogh, and 401k account managers, and other investment facilities issue statements only annually; most bond interest is payable only semiannually; and many certificates of deposit have terms of one year or more. Similarly, some insurance premiums are payable semiannually or annually. Unless you watch the mail over a long period of time, you may overlook both assets and liabilities.

There is no need, however, to delay settling the estate in the hope that such assets may turn up later. It is always possible to reopen the probate estate after closure for the purpose of settling and distributing newly discovered assets.

The Safe-Deposit Box

Like the deceased's mail, his safe-deposit box may contain actual assets (such as cash, collectibles, jewelry, or unregistered bonds) or documentary evidence of assets (such as insurance policies, property deeds and land contracts, stock certificates, bills of sale, receipts, vehicle titles and registrations, savings passbooks, money market certificates, promissory notes, mortgages, and the like). In addition, the box may contain a will, a trust agreement, a letter of instruction, a property inventory or other documents identifying the whereabouts and ownership of certain assets. It may also contain a military-service record.

Unless you are a surviving joint lessee of the box, you may not be aware that the deceased rented one, but it is a mistake to assume that he didn't. If your review of the checking account did not turn up any evidence of box-rental payments, look among the deceased's personal belongings for a flat, multinotched key, often enclosed in a small envelope, or inquire at the banks at which the deceased maintained accounts or conducted business.

Access to the box and its contents may present problems. Unless you have been appointed personal representative or unless you can enlist the cooperation of a surviving co-lessee, the bank will not give you permission to open the box. Even if you are a surviving co-lessee, the bank, on hearing of the death, will often "seal" the box and allow you to open it only in the presence of a representative of the state treasury department, who will inventory its contents for tax purposes.

In those states that require it, requesting a state treasury representative to make the inventory is quite simple, and any bank officer should be able to arrange it without delay or tell you how to do it. Although its primary purpose is to protect the state against possible tax evasion, it can also protect you in case disputes arise among the interested parties as to what was or was not in the box at the moment it was opened. Even if you are a surviving co-lessee or the deceased's personal representative, you should not open the box unaccompanied, because this leaves you vulnerable to all sorts of accusations with respect to its contents. If several beneficiaries are available, have them go with you and sign or initial a dated inventory of the contents.

Joint rental of a box does not in itself constitute conclusive evidence that its contents are owned jointly. Unless there is solid evidence to the contrary, the contents may be presumed to be the sole property of the deceased and hence probatable as part of the deceased's estate. Stock certificates and bonds registered in joint ownership become, of course, the property of the surviving joint owner, but unregistered bonds and untitled assets (cash, for example) and such items as coin collections, precious stones or metals, and other valuables are considered the sole property of the deceased unless there is documentary evidence to prove joint ownership. Women's jewelry found in a box leased jointly by husband and wife will be presumed to belong to the wife, but the ownership of such jewelry found in a box leased jointly by two brothers will depend upon such evidence as receipts, bills of sale, canceled checks, or written statements of ownership.

Once the contents of the box have been inventoried by the representative of the state treasury, those assets that are jointly owned should be distributed to the surviving owner. Those that represent probatable assets must be protected against theft, loss, or damage until they are transferred to the entitled beneficiaries by one of the procedures described in the next chapter. One way to do this is to store them in a safe-deposit box leased in your own name so that you will have access to the contents at any time.

PROTECTING THE ASSETS

Your review of the deceased's checking account, your monitoring of his mail, and your inventory of his safe-deposit box should give you not only a fairly clear picture of the assets and liabilities but also an answer to the question of whether the deceased's assets will require probate-court administration. But whether or not the estate must eventually pass through probate, you are likely to have some immediate responsibilities. You may have to consolidate—and in some cases manage—the assets and protect them until they are disposed of. And you may have to decide which of the liabilities must be settled immediately and which can be postponed or ignored. To help you do this effectively, we will deal, in the pages that follow, with those assets and liabilities that comprise the typical estate.

House and Contents

In many, if not most, cases, the house and its contents constitute the largest part of the deceased's assets and, consequently, are extremely important to the survivors.

If the house was owned jointly (usually with a surviving spouse), its ownership passes automatically to the surviving joint owner without any need for probate administration. The surviving joint owner need only record a certified copy of the death certificate with the register of deeds in the county in which the house is located to establish, as a matter of public record, that he or she is now the sole owner and is therefore exclusively entitled to occupy, rent, mortgage, sell, or otherwise control the property.

This new sole ownership by the survivor, however, makes the house part of the survivor's probatable estate when he or she eventually dies. You may want to advise the surviving owner, therefore, to make a new will and to consider some of the strategies for probate avoidance described in chapter 2.

If the deceased's house was titled in the name of the trustee of a living trust (see p. 38), the procedure is just as simple: the trustee or successor trustee named in the trust will either hold the house in trust, sell it, or deed it to the beneficiary or beneficiaries designated in the trust, and record the new deed with the register of deeds for the county in which the property is located—again without the need for any administration by the probate court.

If, however, the house (or other real estate) was owned solely by the deceased, it becomes part of the probatable assets, and it will eventually have to be disposed of by a court-appointed personal representative under the supervision of the probate court. Meanwhile, it is critically important that both the house and its contents be protected against any kind of loss or damage. This means that you should make mortgage payments if failure to make them may result in foreclosure; you should pay utility bills if termination of service might damage the house or its contents; and you should pay premiums to maintain insurance protection against fire, burglary, vandalism, and personal liability.

If you have been designated as personal representative, you are authorized to pay these expenses out of the estate assets (see p. 233). But even if you make these payments out of your own pocket before the probate court has appointed a personal representative, you are entitled to be reimbursed from the estate's assets.

The general procedures described above apply also to second homes, summer cottages, vacant land, and all other real property. If they are not owned jointly or by the trustee of a living trust, they should be carefully protected until they are disposed of by the transfer procedures described in the next chapter.

The fact that a house was owned jointly does not mean, strictly speaking, that its contents were also owned jointly. In practice, however, joint ownership is often presumed, and the contents pass to the surviving joint owner of the house, except for items specifically willed to other people—a stamp collection, for example, or a piece of antique furniture. Such items may be effectively willed, however, only if they can be proved (by receipt or bill of sale) to have been the exclusive property of the deceased. If, for example, the deceased bequeathed a prized shotgun to a hunting companion, his wife might refuse to let him have it on the grounds that it was jointly owned with her, having been purchased with money contributed by both spouses or by use of a credit card that was issued to both of them, or that the deceased left written evidence specifying that the shotgun was jointly owned with the spouse or another person.

If an asset is proven to be solely owned by the deceased, it is a probate asset and passes according to the deceased's will, and if none, according to state intestacy laws. If the asset is proven to be the subject of a lifetime gift, the donee keeps it even if the will purports to bequeath it to someone else.

Motor Vehicles

Many motor vehicles are not owned jointly—and there are good reasons why they should not be—but this does not mean that their transfer to survivors necessarily requires formal probate administration. Many states have adopted swift and simple procedures for transferring titles of the deceased's vehicles to a surviving spouse, adult child, or other next of kin (see p. 218). Only if there are no interested or eligible survivors is a motor vehicle likely to require formal probate court administration.

Pending its final disposition, however, whether by transfer to a survivor, by gift to a beneficiary, or by liquidation, the motor vehicle belongs to the deceased's estate. Hence, you have a responsibility to protect it from deterioration and from involvement in accidents, because in the event of an accident the estate, as well as the driver, may be responsible for any liability exceeding the existing insurance coverage. Insurance premiums should be paid when due. Storage of the vehicle can protect it against both deterioration and accident. If possible, you should refuse requests by survivors to borrow the vehicle as long as it remains registered in the name of the deceased, because studies show that accidents frequently occur to drivers who are stressed by a recent bereavement.

Bank and Brokerage Accounts

Like all other jointly owned property, bank accounts, securities, and other investments become the property of the surviving joint owner. To transfer title on a joint bank account, the surviving owner merely files with the bank a new signature card identifying him or her as the sole owner, although some banks may require a copy of the death certificate. To avoid the need for probate administration when he or she dies, however, the surviving joint owner may want to create a new joint account—perhaps with an adult child or with a trusted younger friend—or to use one of the other probate avoidance measures described in chapter 2.

Funds in the deceased's pay-on-death bank accounts are also easily collected without any need for probate administration. The person designated as beneficiary on the P.O.D. account need only present identification plus a copy of the deceased's death certificate, after which the bank will pay the account balance to the beneficiary.

Jointly owned brokerage accounts are handled in much the same way as joint bank accounts. If securities have been held in the broker's "street name" in a joint account, the broker need only be instructed to change the name on the account to that of the survivor as sole owner. To carry out this change, the broker will require a certified copy of the death certificate, certain other forms that he can prepare for the signature of the surviving owner, and, in some states, a waiver from the state treasury department certifying that inheritance tax has been paid or is not payable.

If, on the other hand, the securities are registered in the names of the joint owners rather than in the broker's "street name," this same procedure will have to be done for each of the securities through the corporation's transfer agent. Any stock broker can assist in this process. The deceased's securities that are held in a transfer-on-death securities account are immediately transferable to the designated beneficiary, likewise without probate administration.

The transfer of jointly held assets is not a pressing matter, because the surviving owner enjoys full control of them and of their dividends or interest even before formal transfer takes place. Assets that are held solely in the name of the deceased, however, need prompt attention, and usually their management requires that a personal representative be appointed. As soon as you encounter such individually owned assets, therefore, you should read the next chapter to determine whether their transfer requires the appointment of a personal representative. If it does, a petition for appointment should be filed promptly so that the personal representative will be able to collect, manage, and ultimately dispose of those assets.

In the case of individually owned bank accounts, both savings and checking, the personal representative may need to provide each bank with a copy of his letters of authority and direct that the accounts be closed and that a check for the account balances be delivered to him. With respect to IRA, SEP, Keogh, 401k and other retirement accounts *on which the deceased had named a beneficiary*, nothing more need be done than to see to it that the balances are paid to the beneficiary. Such accounts, like insurance policies, are not considered probatable assets. If, however, the deceased failed to name a beneficiary, the personal representative should handle them in the same way as other individually owned bank accounts.

MANAGING THE ASSETS

Moneys collected by the personal representative should be deposited in one or more bank accounts under the name "John Jones, Personal Representative of the Estate of Mary Smith, Deceased," but the type of account chosen involves careful judgment. Since the personal representative will use this money to pay the funeral bill and other debts of the deceased and to transfer assets to the beneficiaries, a checking account will obviously be essential. On the other hand, until the checks are written, the personal representative should try to protect the money against erosion from inflation by depositing it into an interest-bearing account.

Any account that is federally insured (an account in a bank or a savings and loan association) offers high security but a relatively low yield. The conscientious personal representative may therefore feel that he should seek a higher yield through some sort of short-term investment such as a money market fund. But because most such funds are not insured, the personal representative should not use them unless he is authorized to do so by the will, by the probate court, or by all the estate's beneficiaries and creditors.

Any checks payable solely to the deceased that arrive after the death can legally be deposited in an account in the deceased's name or in the personal representative's account. But because all such deposits become probatable assets, salary checks and checks representing other employee benefits should not be deposited until it is determined whether they can be distributed to the survivors by the simplified procedure described on page 219.

Income tax refunds on a jointly filed return may be turned over to a surviving spouse. Refunds on the deceased's individual returns are an asset of his estate.

Solely owned brokerage accounts require prompt action. Any margin accounts should be liquidated and closed immediately, because a sudden drop in share prices will result either in a call for more margin (for which the estate is liable) or the sale of the shares at unfavorable prices. At the same time, the personal representative should cancel any open orders to the broker to buy or sell shares.

Securities owned solely by the deceased, whether in his own name or in a broker's street account, should be left in the deceased's name until you have determined whether they can be transferred to the survivors by one of the "small estate" procedures described on pp. 223–225. If this is not feasible, they should be disposed of promptly unless you have good reason to believe that their value is likely to appreciate in the foreseeable future. A cautious and conscientious personal representative who feels that stock prices are low at the moment may be tempted to hold the securities until they can fetch higher prices. Because nobody can consistently predict the behavior of the stock market, however, this tactic is risky and should be used only with the consent of all interested parties. In general, the personal representative is expected to manage all estate assets prudently, and it is probably safer to err on the side of conservatism.

Promissory Notes, Land Contracts, and Other "Accounts Receivable"

Your review of the assets may disclose "accounts receivable" that will remain owed to the deceased for a long time into the future, often in indeterminable amounts: a ten-year promissory note or land contract, for example, royalties from a book, or leases of mineral rights that may go on indefinitely in irregular amounts.

In order to avoid keeping the estate open indefinitely for the sole purpose of receiving these payments, the personal representative can arrange an assignment of the accounts to the entitled beneficiaries so that all future payments are made directly to them. If there are several beneficiaries, each entitled to a share of the payments, they can designate a bank as their collection agent. The bank, in return for a fee, will collect each payment and distribute it among them.

Claims for "Wrongful Death" Benefits

A possible source of assets sometimes overlooked by survivors is money damages that may be recoverable if the deceased's death was caused, in whole or in part, by the intentional or negligent behavior of someone else. Although such damage claims are probably most common when death results from an automobile accident, it is also possible to sue physicians, hospitals, and other health-care providers for failure to make a correct diagnosis or provide appropriate medical care. Similarly, suit can be brought against building owners for structural defects or inadequate maintenance, against manufacturers and retailers of unsafe or defective products, against employers for failure to maintain a safe work environment, and against police departments for use of excessive force resulting in death.

Some commentators, citing the recent rise in medical malpractice claims, conclude that we are becoming an increasingly litigious society, but the proliferation of such claims can also be explained by the fact that more people are receiving medical treatment and are better informed about their legal rights and remedies. Other commentators argue that many justifiable damage claims are never pursued simply because the survivors fail to recognize that they have a viable claim or because they feel that filing a lawsuit is not worth the time, effort, psychological stress, and possible costs.

If the deceased's death can be linked in any way to someone's intentional or negligent behavior, you should make every effort to identify the person or persons involved and discuss promptly with a skilled personal injury lawyer the possibilities of pursuing a claim for money damages. In considering such a claim you should bear in mind two well-established legal principles. First, the death need not occur immediately after the negligence; the recovery of money damages may be justified even if death occurred many months after the precipitating event. Second, under the laws of many states, it is not necessary that the wrongdoer's negligence be 100 percent responsible for the death. Even if the wrongdoer's behavior is found by the judge or jury to have been only 25 percent responsible, the other 75 percent having been caused by the deceased's contributory negligence, 25 percent of the claimed damages may be awarded to the deceased's estate or the survivors.

Examples of successful negligence suits are not hard to find, and those presented here should help you understand that the underlying negligence need not always be clearly apparent or immediately present. In cases of death by fire, building owners have been sued for maintaining unsafe premises or violating fire codes even though the victim had been smoking in bed. Owners of swimming pools have been held responsible for leaving open a gate through which a child wandered in and subsequently drowned even though the child's parents may have been negligent in their supervision of their child. And, of course, automobile manufacturers have been sued as a result of deaths attributed to faulty vehicle design or manufacture even though the victim's driving behavior may have precipitated the accident in whole or in part. It is a mistake, therefore, to assume that a wrongful-death claim will necessarily be unsuccessful simply because the victim's behavior contributed in part to his own injury and consequent death.

Two further considerations often discourage survivors from making damage claims. First, there is the notion that the negligent party is not worth suing "because he obviously hasn't enough money to pay a judgment of any size." This conclusion is, of course, premature until the possibilities of insurance coverage have been investigated—especially in states with compulsory automobile liability insurance. Second, many people believe that a lawsuit is simply too expensive to initiate even if the prospect of an eventual recovery seems favorable.

Actually, the cost of pursuing a claim need not be a deterrent because most lawyers who take such cases are willing to do so on a "contingent fee" basis: if the lawyer recovers money damages, he is entitled to keep a specified portion (usually one-third of the net recovery) as his fee for services. If he loses the case and recovers nothing, he receives no fee at all.

Although the contingent-fee arrangement has been called "the poor man's key to the courthouse" and although it would appear to make damage claims affordable by anyone, it is not without its problems. The processing of a claim typically requires the lawyer to incur out-of-pocket expenses—for purchasing transcripts and other records, for hiring expert witnesses, for taking depositions and conducting investigations, and for the payment of court costs—and these expenses, though normally advanced by the lawyer, are ultimately chargeable to the client whether the case is won or lost. Thus, if you fail to win a suit, either you or the deceased's estate (depending on who hired the lawyer) may face legal costs of several thousand dollars. If you approach a lawyer about bringing suit, therefore, be sure to discuss not only the contingent fee but also the anticipated amount of and responsibility for the out-of-pocket expenses.

Although many survivors neglect to initiate a viable claim, there are others who are all too eager to bring suit. This occurs not necessarily because they are naturally litigious but because they are trying to find an outlet for the frustration and grief caused by the death. If a close relative dies after surgery, for example, the survivors may allege faulty work by the surgeon or improper care by the hospital staff even though both may have been performed in exemplary fashion. One might think that a lawyer's negative opinion would deter such people from bringing suit, since few lawyers are likely to reject the pursuit of a claim that has merit; but because the motivations for bringing such suits are largely psychological, an objective opinion from the lawyer to the effect that the claim is without merit may lead only to a search for a lawyer with a different opinion.

If you believe that you have grounds for a claim, you should consult a lawyer immediately, because such claims must be filed within one to three years following the deceased's death and because critical evidence—for example, autopsy results, medical records, accident-scene photos, preservation of a wrecked auto or its parts—must be gathered and preserved while it is still fresh. Finding a competent personal-injury lawyer may be as difficult as finding one experienced in estate planning, because this is a field crowded with lawyers seeking such often lucrative cases. The state bar association's lawyer-referral service is a far more reliable source than the Yellow Pages or television and internet commercials. Once the lawyer and you sign a contingent-fee agreement, he will investigate the merits of the claim and the financial condition or insurance coverage of the alleged wrongdoer. He will then submit a written claim to the wrongdoer or his insurance company setting forth the claim's factual and legal basis and demanding money compensation for some or all of the following items of damage:

- Conscious pain and suffering experienced by the deceased
- Ambulance, hospital, and medical expenses
- Funeral and burial expenses
- Loss of income or support that the deceased would have provided to his dependents had he enjoyed his full life expectancy
- Loss of the society and companionship that the deceased would have provided to his family

If the claim has merit and if the wrongdoer has sufficient funds or insurance coverage, the response to your lawyer's letter is likely to be an offer of an out-of-court settlement, for an amount somewhat less than you initially demanded. Your lawyer may or may not be able to negotiate an increase in this settlement offer, but acceptance of a settlement will provide the beneficiaries with immediate cash, avoid the delay, expense, and uncertainties of a trial, and eliminate your anxiety about a procedure with which you and the other survivors are likely to be unfamiliar.

You may explore the possibility of a damage claim without having been formally appointed as personal representative, although if you have not been appointed, the lawyer's out-of-pocket expenses may be your own responsibility rather than the estate's. If, however, you receive a settlement offer or if the case must go to trial, a personal representative may have to be appointed. Acceptance of a settlement check requires a release that can be signed only by someone who legally represents the estate, and the initiation of a lawsuit requires the same kind of representation. In some states, monies recovered either through a settlement offer or as the result of a court judgment accrue to the estate and become probatable assets, ultimately to be distributed to the beneficiaries or to the heirs designated by law. In other states, however, wrongful death proceeds are payable directly to certain survivors specified by law.

REVIEWING THE LIABILITIES

As you continue to monitor the deceased's mail, you will almost certainly find bills, statements, premium notices, and other evidence of debts. Bills for goods and services that have been bought jointly (or through a joint charge account) remain the responsibility of the estate as well as the surviving joint debtor. If the estate has sufficient assets, the surviving co-debtor may prefer that the estate take care of the debt in due course. But if the estate's assets are insufficient and the surviving debtor wants to preserve a good credit rating and avoid continuing interest charges, the debts should be paid promptly. Bills or statements addressed to the deceased alone but which involve jointly owned property (utility, oil, and telephone bills for a jointly owned home, for example) should also be paid by the surviving owner, especially if he or she intends to continue to own and occupy the property.

Debts incurred by the deceased alone, however, confront the personal representative with a dilemma. Strictly speaking, these bills are payable by the estate, and hence the personal representative should not pay them until he has determined (1) that they are legitimate and (2) that the estate has enough money to pay them, because if the estate has insufficient assets, some of the creditors need not be paid in full. Furthermore, the "small estate" procedures in some states (see p. 217) permit the transfer of the deceased's assets to the survivors without regard to the claims of creditors. All these considerations should lead you to postpone paying any such bills until you have a clear idea of the value of the probatable assets and the type of probate procedure, if any, they will require.

On the other hand, failure to pay certain kinds of bills—mortgage payments, charge accounts, taxes, or utility bills—may, as we have noted, harm the estate in one way or another. In such situations, whether or not you have been appointed personal representative, you must use your best judgment. If you are convinced that the charges are legitimate and that the bills must be paid promptly, you can pay them out of your own pocket and claim reimbursement from the estate. But doing this entails two risks. First, the estate may have insufficient assets to reimburse you, or the estate may have such low value that it is not required to pay any of its creditors, as we shall see in the next chapter. Second, the creditors of an estate are ranked by law in a specified order of priority (see p. 233). If you have paid a low-priority creditor, you may be held personally responsible for the high-priority creditor's unpaid claim. For these reasons, you should probably postpone the payment of any bill that is reasonably postponable—at least until you have read the next chapter.

Whether or not you decide to pay charge accounts promptly, the charge card should be either destroyed or, in the case of cards issued by banks, returned to the bank that issued it. Destroying it will prevent unauthorized use, but it will not terminate the annual fee that many banks charge for the use of the card. Returning it to the bank will avert further use charges and may produce a refund of the unused annual fee.

Because many survivors apparently feel that they are paying their respects to the deceased by settling all his outstanding debts regardless of their nature, it is important to recognize that in many cases they are under no legal obligation to do so. The Uniform Probate Code provides that under certain circumstances (see p. 223) the deceased's debts may be ignored. The intention here was to discourage survivors from depleting small estates because they felt morally obligated to prevent the deceased from "having died a debtor." Every creditor makes provision for a certain percentage of "bad debts," and there is no reason why survivors should not recognize this reality.

Of course, if the deceased left no assets whatever, there is no reason for the survivors to pay his debts, because no law requires anyone to assume the debts of another, no matter what their relationship.

COLLECTING NONPROBATABLE ASSETS

Once you have taken care of the chores enumerated above, you should have a fairly clear notion about the value of the probatable assets and the amount of the estate's liabilities. You should also know whether any kind of probate procedure will be necessary—although you may not know what kind of probate is involved until you read the next chapter.

There are, however, several other types of assets to be collected that, although they are not part of the probate estate, nevertheless belong to the beneficiaries. Because these assets are not involved in the probate process or in the settlement of the estate, collecting them may not strike you as urgent. They may, however, amount to a considerable sum of money that is urgently needed by the survivors, and it is likely that they are earning little or no interest at the moment. Consequently, you should not postpone collecting them any longer than is absolutely necessary.

LIFE INSURANCE

The proceeds of a life insurance policy, if the designated beneficiary is one or more living persons, a charitable institution, or any kind of existing organization, are payable directly to the named beneficiary without the need for any probate procedures. Only if the designated beneficiary is the deceased's estate or the personal representative of the estate, or if there is no surviving designated beneficiary, do the proceeds become probatable. Because policies with a designated beneficiary other than the "estate" need not be used to pay any of the deceased's debts, they often constitute the most important asset left to the survivors, and hence the proceeds should be collected promptly.

If the deceased left a letter of instruction, it will almost certainly list and describe any current life insurance policies. If, however, you find no policies in the various places where you looked for a will—a safe-deposit box, desk drawers, etc.—don't conclude that none exist. Review the deceased's canceled checks for the preceding twelve months for a check payable to an insurance company or agency, review the deposit record for evidence of a dividend check on a paid-up policy, and question the agent who handled the deceased's other insurance coverages. Also, be sure to ask the deceased's employer whether the company has provided any life insurance on the deceased's life, as this is a common fringe benefit available in both private and public employment. Lastly, check the deceased's automobile insurance policy for possible death benefits.

Once you have discovered a policy, obtain from the local agent or from the insurance company a claim form, which you will have to submit to the company along with a certified copy of the death certificate. The application form need not be signed by a formally appointed personal representative unless the beneficiary is the deceased's estate, in which case the personal representative must submit a copy of his letters of authority along with the claim form.

If the insurance company requires you to surrender the original policy along with the claim form and any supporting documents, be sure to photocopy the face sheet of the policy as well as the application form and your covering letter, which should list and describe all the enclosures. If you cannot find the original policy, ask the insurance company for an affidavit form on which you can indicate that the policy has been lost. Your letter should also request the return of any unearned premiums (because the deceased may have died only a month or two after having paid an annual premium) as well as any dividends due if the policy normally earned dividends. The entire packet should be sent by registered or certified mail so that you will have a receipt in case the company later asserts that it never received your claim.

Because insurance companies occasionally are reluctant to pay life insurance proceeds, you need to be prepared to act aggressively in response to the following tactics, which have been used to delay or avoid payment:

The Claim Was Not Submitted Promptly

Some policies contain a clause specifying that the claim must be submitted within a certain time after the death—usually 90 or 180 days. Although it is doubtful that this restriction would be upheld by the courts today, you can avoid expensive litigation by submitting the claim promptly.

Fraud in the Original Application

The company may claim that the insured, in making the initial application for coverage, misrepresented or omitted parts of his medical history that might have led the company to reject him as uninsurable. This pretext is sometimes used, because virtually nobody, in filling out an insurance application, can list *every* detail of his medical history. Some beneficiaries, however, are so intimidated by the mention of "fraud" that they fail to pursue the claim.

It is important to note that an insurance company that alleges fraud must assume the burden of proof: it must demonstrate that the insured's misstatements or omissions were intentional rather than the result of a memory lapse, that the misstated or omitted condition was related to the insured's death, and that the company relied and had a right to rely on the insured's misstatements in deciding to issue the policy. Generally the fraud defense cannot be successfully raised by the insurer after two years beyond the issue date of the policy.

Suicide

Most policies provide coverage for death by suicide if it occurs more than two years after the issue date of the policy. When such coverage is excluded, however, insurance companies occasionally claim that an accidental death was in fact a suicide. Again, it is important to recognize that the burden of proof lies with the insurer and that suicide is often difficult to prove. In such circumstances an autopsy may be critical in determining the cause of death. Some apparent suicides can be proven by autopsy to have been accidental. Furthermore, what appears to be a suicide may be authoritatively characterized otherwise by the attending physician or the medical examiner if the deceased was mentally ill at the time of death.

Lapse for Nonpayment of Premiums

Insurance companies sometimes reject a claim on the grounds that the policy had lapsed for nonpayment of premiums. This refusal should not be accepted without a careful scrutiny of the policy. Many policies specify that if premiums are not paid, a certain amount of coverage nevertheless remains in effect or that the policy's accumulated cash value can be used to maintain some level of coverage. Moreover, the insurer may be legally barred from raising a lapse defense if it fails to prove that it gave the insured adequate notice of the lapse.

If you sense any recalcitrance on the part of the insurance company or if your claim is flatly rejected for any reason, your first step is to file a complaint with the state insurance commission or similar regulatory agency. If this fails—or if your state regulatory agencies have a poor record of consumer advocacy—consult a lawyer. Often the mere threat of legal action gets results from large insurers who may be reluctant to have a jury decide a dispute between a multimillion-dollar corporation and a widow whose survival depends entirely on the modest proceeds from her husband's life insurance policy.

In such a situation, however, avoid the contingent-fee basis for paying the lawyer. Because the lawyer is likely to get results by writing two or three letters, he is not entitled to a substantial share of the insurance proceeds for this minimal investment of time. You would be better advised to pay him on an hourly fee basis. Only if the claim involves a lawsuit should you consider a contingent-fee arrangement—and only provided that the lawyer agrees to a lower proportion than the customary one-third charged for handling wrongful-death claims. Don't hesitate to try negotiating a fee lower than the percentage initially quoted by the lawyer.

Social Security Benefits

If the deceased was covered by Social Security long enough to be eligible, he is entitled to two kinds of benefits: a death benefit, which is intended to help defray funeral expenses, and survivors' benefits to help support his children and, in some cases, his spouse.

The death benefit (currently $255) may be paid to a surviving spouse or, if there is none, to the deceased's dependent children.

The children of the deceased may be entitled to survivors' benefits to the age of eighteen, or to the age of twenty-two if they are full-time students, or, if they are disabled, for as long as the disability persists. A surviving spouse who is responsible for the care of children under eighteen or disabled may also be entitled to benefits. If there are no children who qualify for benefits, the surviving spouse may begin drawing benefits at age sixty, although the amount of the benefits may be reduced if the spouse's earnings exceed a specified limit. A divorced spouse of the deceased may begin drawing benefits at age sixty, provided the marriage lasted ten years or longer.

If the deceased had been receiving Social Security retirement checks, he is not entitled to benefits for the month in which he died. Thus, if the death occurred at any time in July, the check dated August 3 (representing the payment for July) must be returned unless it is made out jointly to husband and wife, in which case the surviving spouse should consult the local Social Security office before cashing it. If Social Security checks were deposited directly in the deceased's bank account, the bank should be instructed to return any payments received after the death.

An application for benefits can be obtained (usually by telephone) from the nearest Social Security Administration office. The documents that must accompany the application include the deceased's Social Security card, certified copies of both birth and death certificates, and copies of the deceased's most recent W-2 or 1099 form and federal income tax return.

Veterans' Benefits

If a veteran's death is not service-connected, up to $300 may be paid toward the veteran's funeral and burial expenses, $150 is payable as a plot or interment allowance if the survivors do not exercise their right to free burial in a military cemetery. Also eligible are the survivors of members of the armed forces who served during peacetime but who received disability benefits or who were retired for service-connected disabilities. If the veteran's death resulted from a service-connected disability or injuries, these death benefits are increased. Application for these benefits can be made by the creditor who provided the services, the person who paid the expenses, or the personal representative of the deceased's estate.

The surviving spouse and minor children of veterans who received benefits for service-connected disabilities are entitled also to monthly payments from the Veterans Administration, the exact amount of which will be based on the veteran's earning record during military service or on his or her occupation at time of death. Application for these benefits should be made to the Veterans Administration at the address (or through the toll-free telephone number) listed in your local telephone directory.

Despite some improvement in recent years, the Veterans Administration has been repeatedly charged with inefficiency and inaccuracy in handling claims. If you encounter either delay or rejection of your claims, you may find it necessary to enlist the help of a lawyer. Before doing so, however, you should write a detailed letter to your congressman or your U.S. senator, who often can straighten matters out at no cost to you.

Employee Benefits

If the deceased was employed (or on sick leave) at the time of death, you should get in touch with the employer to collect any wages (including vacation and sick-leave pay) that were due at the time of death. Under many state laws, the employer can pay such sums directly to the spouse or next of kin (see p. 219), and hence they are not considered probatable assets.

Group life insurance, pension plans, profit-sharing plans, health insurance, accidental death insurance, and any other fringe benefits provided by the employer should also be investigated for possible payments. Many labor unions, professional associations, and fraternal societies also provide special death benefits for their members.

Another potential source of assets, if the death occurred at, during the course of, or as a consequence of the deceased's employment, is the worker's compensation disability benefit system. This often mandatory form of worker protection, which functions on a "no fault" basis, provides a wide range of benefits to the surviving spouse and children of anyone who dies of work-connected injuries or occupational diseases.

One might expect employers to be cooperative in paying worker's compensation claims in full, but there are several reasons why they may not be. Those employers who are self-insured are naturally reluctant to pay claims. Those who are protected by private or public insurers may fear a rise in their premiums if they have numerous claims. And some employers fear that a worker's compensation claim may disclose working conditions that violate state or federal occupational safety codes. If an employer denies a claim or offers a settlement short of full payment, you would do well to consult a lawyer experienced in handling such claims. In such circumstances a contingent-fee arrangement may be appropriate because the fee is sometimes regulated by the state and is usually less than the one-third charged in the typical personal-injury or wrongful-death claim.

Credit-Union Benefits

Many credit unions offer one of two kinds of death benefit to their members: a life insurance policy whose value equals the member's balance at the time of death or a so-called credit life insurance that pays off any loans outstanding at the time of death. Before making any payments on credit-union loans, therefore, be sure to rule out the possibility that the balances have been paid off by this form of insurance or that the life insurance policy has doubled the balance in the deceased's savings account.

BENEFICIARY BEWARE

Statistics indicate that women are likely to outlive their husbands by about three years. When all the deceased's assets have been assembled, it is possible that the surviving spouse (most often the widow) may find herself in control of a larger sum of money than she is accustomed to dealing with. If she is inexperienced in the handling of money, she will need to think carefully about possible investments. Well-meaning relatives may suggest business ventures or other investments. Brokers' representatives, mutual-fund salespeople, and others may offer financial advice that is neither prudent nor altogether disinterested. And feelings of bereavement, isolation, and helplessness may increase her vulnerability to a variety of "sure things" or get-rich-quick schemes.

Although no investment offers complete immunity against the ravages of inflation or fluctuations in the economy, it is important that the surviving spouse err on the side of conservatism. If the survivor is in fact a woman, who is likely to outlive her spouse for a considerable period of time, careful conservation of her assets is essential if she does not relish the prospect of becoming dependent on others.

11

SETTLING AND CLOSING THE ESTATE

Once you have assembled and evaluated all the assets listed in chapter 10, you are ready to settle and close the deceased's estate. Your separation of the assets into probatable and nonprobatable categories should give you a fairly clear notion as to what, if any, formal probate procedures are necessary, because the value of the probatable assets is a major factor in determining whether they must be administered by the probate court.

Actually, the vast majority of estates are settled and closed without any intervention by the probate court. If your own situation is typical, a reading of the next few pages should relieve you of any anxieties you may have concerning the probate process.

IS PROBATE NECESSARY?

The basic purposes of probate administration, as we have noted, are to determine whether a will is valid, to provide protection to minor children and their property, to see that the deceased's creditors receive their lawful claims and taxes are paid, and to distribute the remaining assets to the beneficiaries named in the will or to the heirs specified by state intestacy laws if the deceased left no will.

Obviously, if the deceased left no orphaned minor children and no property—because he owned nothing or because everything he possessed was given away before death, was owned jointly, was in a trust, or consisted of life insurance or some other account or contract right that specified a designated beneficiary—there are no probatable assets and hence nothing to probate. If this describes the situation confronting you, there is no need for you to read the rest of this chapter. Once you have seen to the transfer of jointly held and trust-held assets and the collection of insurance proceeds, financial accounts, and other benefits as described in chapter 10, your responsibilities are at an end. Although some states permit creditors to file claims against a trust or its assets, creditors' claims against the deceased can be ignored, although it would be courteous (though not legally necessary) to notify creditors that the deceased left no assets with which to pay their bills.

Some form of probate court action, however, will be necessary in each of the following circumstances, although in most cases the estate can be settled by procedures that are simpler, quicker, and cheaper than full probate-court administration.

If the deceased left minor orphans—a not uncommon occurrence when husband and wife die simultaneously in an accident—the probate court must be involved so as to appoint a guardian for the children and, if their inheritance is substantial, a conservator to manage each minor child's inheritance until the child reaches adulthood. This type of mandatory probate action is dealt with in chapter 9, and it may not necessarily involve the court in the administration of the deceased's estate. The estate itself, depending on its value, may be eligible for one of the informal small-estate transfer procedures described below.

If the deceased died in circumstances giving rise to a wrongful-death claim (see p. 201), the probate court may be required to appoint a personal representative to investigate the claim, to initiate a lawsuit, to sign settlement and release papers if money damages are recovered, and to distribute the proceeds to survivors specified by state law.

If the deceased carried life insurance but was not survived by the policy-designated beneficiary or if the beneficiary he designated was his own estate or its personal representative, the distribution of the insurance proceeds may require some probate-court action, the precise procedure depending on the amount involved.

If the deceased left probate assets, the probate court may be required to appoint a personal representative to consolidate, protect, and manage the assets; to pay the deceased's debts; and to distribute the balance to the entitled beneficiaries. You need not, however, take this requirement too literally, because it depends on both the amount and the nature of the assets. For example, household furnishings and appliances, stamp collections, and other contents of a jointly owned home may technically be regarded by law as the sole property of the deceased, but in everyday practice their ownership will pass informally to the surviving joint owner of the house unless some other person raises a claim. Thus, a surviving spouse will automatically take possession of the deceased's personal effects unless adult children or some other interested person lays claim to some of them—in which case the conflict may have to be resolved by the probate court.

More important, if the value of the deceased's probate assets is low, you may still be able to avoid lengthy probate administration. In response to public criticism of the probate process as antiquated, time-consuming, expensive, and designed to protect the job security of lawyers and judges rather than the interests of widows and orphans, most states have adopted streamlined, simplified, and relatively informal procedures for the settlement of so-called "small estates." Many of these procedures do not require a lawyer, and most of them can be completed in a matter of days, whereas full probate court administration takes at least several months and may drag on for years.

"SMALL ESTATE" AND OTHER INFORMAL TRANSFER PROCEDURES

Once you identify the deceased's probate assets, your first step is to find out—by consulting tables 8 and 9 and inquiring of the local probate court, a local law library, or a lawyer skilled in probate law—precisely what the requirements are for "small estate" transfers in the deceased's state of residence. If, instead, you simply approach a lawyer and tell him to "probate the estate," he may, knowingly or unknowingly, involve you in the full process of formal probate-court administration at a substantial cost to you in both time and money.

As tables 8 and 9 indicate, the eligibility of an estate for settlement through one of the "small estate" transfer procedures varies from one state to another, but generally it hinges on (1) the value of the assets, (2) the nature of the assets, (3) the relationship of the survivors to the deceased, and (4) whether or not the funeral bill has been paid. The "small estate" transfer procedures described below are sufficiently typical, however, to serve as guidelines, although the precise requirements and procedures in your state may differ in some respects from the general model.

Motor Vehicles

If the deceased's assets included motor vehicles (not only passenger automobiles but also trucks, motor homes, recreational vehicles, and motorcycles), they may have been registered in his name alone. If their total value does not exceed a specified amount—usually between $25,000 and $50,000—ownership of these vehicles can be transferred to a surviving spouse or next of kin without any intervention by the probate court or help from a lawyer.

The local branch of your state motor vehicle bureau can tell you whether the simplified transfer procedure is available and what it involves. Usually all the surviving spouse or next of kin need do is present the vehicle title (which in some states is the current registration certificate) and a certified copy of the owner's death certificate. Once the applicant has signed an affidavit of heirship (provided by the motor vehicle bureau), title can be transferred into his or her name on payment of a nominal fee. The applicant's estimate of the vehicle's current value is not likely to be questioned, but reliable figures are available in several used-car pricing guides found at banks, libraries, and auto dealerships.

If neither the spouse nor any eligible next of kin transfers ownership of the deceased's vehicle, it becomes a probatable asset and hence may require action of the probate court. To avoid this—especially if there are no other probate assets—it might be advisable for the spouse or next of kin to have ownership of the vehicle transferred to his or her name and to sell it immediately. If there are other probate assets, this tactic will have the effect of reducing their total value. In some states, however, this transfer procedure is not available if probate administration is pending.

Of course, if the vehicle was registered jointly, its ownership passes automatically to the surviving joint owner, as is the case with any other jointly owned property. Similarly, if the vehicle's title is held in trust, it remains in the trustee's name for disposition according to the terms of the trust document.

WAGES AND FRINGE BENEFITS

Any salary, wages, accumulated vacation and sick pay, and other fringe benefits owing to the deceased may, according to the laws of many states, be paid by the deceased's employer directly to a surviving spouse, children, or other next of kin without the need for any probate proceedings. The employer may, in order to protect his interests, require the claimant to produce a death certificate and to sign an affidavit that identifies the claimant and specifies his or her priority right to receive the deceased employee's money.

TABLE 8

State Requirements for "Small Estate" Transfer by Affidavit

State	*Dollar Limitation ($)*	*Waiting Period Following Death*	*Applicable to Real Estate*	*Creditors Must First Be Paid*
Alabama		Not available		
Alaska[1]	15,000	30 days	No	No
Arizona[1]	50,000	30	No	No
Arkansas[1]	50,000	45	No	Yes
California	100,000	40	No	No
Colorado[1]	27,000	10	No	No
Connecticut[1]	20,000	30	No	No[6]
Delaware[1]	20,000	30	No	Yes
District of Columbia	2 cars	No	No	Yes
Florida		Not available		
Georgia		Not available		
Hawaii[1]	20,000	30	No	No
Idaho[1]	25,000	30	No	No
Illinois	25,000	No	No	Yes
Indiana[1]	25,000	45	No	No[6]
Iowa		Not available		
Kansas		Not available		
Kentucky		Not available		
Louisiana[3]	50,000	No	No	Yes
Maine[1]	10,000	30	No	No
Maryland	Formula[4]	No	No	No

TABLE 8

State Requirements for "Small Estate" Transfer by Affidavit *(continued)*

State	*Dollar Limitation ($)*	*Waiting Period Following Death*	*Applicable to Real Estate*	*Creditors Must First Be Paid*
Massachusetts	Formula[5]	60	No	No
Michigan[1]	15,000	28	No	No
Minnesota	20,000	30	No	No
Mississippi	20,000	30	No	No
Missouri	15,000	No	Yes	Yes
Montana[1]	7,500	30	No	No
Nebraska	25,000	30	No	No
Nevada	10,000	30	No	No
New Hampshire[2, 7]	500	No	No	No
New Jersey[2, 3]	10,000	No	Yes	No
New Mexico[1]	20,000	30	No	No
New York	10,000	30	No	No
North Carolina[3]	20,000	30	No	Yes
North Dakota[1]	15,000	30	No	No
Ohio[7]	2,500	No	No	No
Oklahoma[1]	10,000	10	No	No
Oregon[3]	140,000	30	Yes	Yes
Pennsylvania		Not available		
Rhode Island		Not available		
South Carolina[1]	10,000	30	No	No
South Dakota	25,000	No	No	Yes
Tennessee	1,000	30	No	No[6]
Texas	50,000	30	Yes	No
Utah[1]	25,000	30	No	No
Vermont		Not available		
Virginia[1]	10,000	60	No	No
Washington[1]	60,000	40	No	Yes
West Virginia[1, 7]	1,000	120	No	No
Wisconsin	10,000	No	No	No
Wyoming[1]	70,000	30	No	Yes

[1] Not available if petition for appointment of personal representative has been granted or is pending.

[2] Available only if deceased is survived by a spouse.

[3] Available only if deceased left no will.

[4] Not more than two vehicles plus a boat (maximum value of $5,000) plus life insurance (maximum value of $1,000).

[5] Life insurance up to $10,000 plus bank accounts up to $3,000 plus wages up to $100.

[6] Funeral expenses must first be paid.

[7] Available only for wages, salaries, and commissions.

TABLE 9

State Requirements for "Small Estate" Summary Probate Procedures

State	*Dollar Limitation ($)*	*Waiting Period Following Death*	*Applicable to Real Estate*	*Creditors Must First Be Paid*
Alabama	3,000	No	No	Yes
Alaska	Formula[2]	No	Yes	No
Arizona	Formula[2]	No	Yes	No
Arkansas	Formula[3]	No	No	No
California	100,000	No	Yes	No
Colorado	Formula[2]	No	Yes	No
Connecticut	Formula[2]	No	Yes	No
Delaware		Not available		
District of Columbia	15,000	No	Yes	No
Florida	60,000	No	Yes	Yes
Georgia		Not available		
Hawaii	20,000	No	Yes	No
Idaho	Formula[2]	No	Yes	No
Illinois[5]	50,000[4]	No	Yes	Yes
Indiana	Formula[2]	No	Yes	No
Iowa[6,8]	50,000	No	Yes	Yes
Kansas	Formula[2]	6 mos.	Yes	Yes
Kentucky[5 or 7]	7,500	No	Yes	Yes
Louisiana		Not available		
Maine	Formula[2]	No	Yes	No
Maryland	20,000	No	No	No
Massachusetts	15,000	30	No	No

TABLE 9

State Requirements for "Small Estate" Summary Probate Procedures *(continued)*

State	*Dollar Limitation ($)*	*Waiting Period Following Death*	*Applicable to Real Estate*	*Creditors Must First Be Paid*
Michigan	Formula[2]	No	Yes	No
Minnesota[1, 8]	30,000	No	Yes	No
Mississippi	500	No	No	No
Missouri	40,000	30	Yes	No
Montana	Formula[2]	No	Yes	No
Nebraska	Formula[2]	No	Yes	No
Nevada	200,000	60	Yes	Yes
New Hampshire	5,000	No	Yes	Yes
New Jersey		Not available		
New Mexico	Formula[2]	No	Yes	Yes
New York[8]	20,000	No	Yes	No
North Carolina		Not available		
North Dakota	Formula[2]	No	Yes	No
Ohio	35,000	No	Yes	Yes
Oklahoma	60,000	No	Yes	Yes
Oregon	Formula[2]	No	Yes	Yes
Pennsylvania	25,000	No	No	No
Rhode Island	15,000	No	No	Yes
South Carolina[8]	10,000	No	Yes	No
South Dakota	60,000	No	Yes	Yes
Tennessee	10,000	45	Yes	Yes
Texas	Formula[2]	No	Yes	Yes
Utah	Formula[2]	No	Yes	No
Vermont	10,000	No	No	Yes
Virginia	10,000	60	No	No
Washington		Not available		
West Virginia	100,000	No	Yes	No
Wisconsin[6]	30,000	No	Yes	Yes
Wyoming	70,000	No	Yes	Yes

[1] Not available if petition for appointment of personal representative has been granted or is pending.

[2] Available where entire estate, less liens and encumbrances, does not exceed certain statutory allowances plus expenses or last illness, funeral, and administration . . . all of which may approximate $25,000 in some cases.

[3] If personal property is less than statutory dower and allowances to widow or minors, court may immediately assign estate to them.

[4] Includes deceased's probate and nonprobate assets.

[5] Available only if all beneficiaries consent in writing.

[6] Available only if deceased is survived by a spouse, children, or a parent.

[7] Available only if deceased is survived by a spouse.

[8] Available only if deceased left no will.

[9] Exclusive of statutory family allowances or exempt property.

The personnel departments of most large corporations are quite familiar with this procedure, but small employers may not be. If you encounter problems, ask your local probate court or your state's department of labor for information. You should be able to collect the money without hiring a lawyer. If you feel that the employer is withholding payment or delaying it unreasonably, however, you might consider filing a complaint with the state department of labor, filing a suit in your local small-claims court or, if the amount is substantial, retaining a lawyer.

TRANSFER BY AFFIDAVIT

For the transfer and settlement of "small estates"—usually defined as personal property not exceeding a specified maximum ($500 to $140,000)—many states offer an affidavit transfer procedure that eliminates the need for a personal representative, any probate-court action, or any notification of the deceased's creditors. The transfer affidavit, usually a printed form available from the financial institution holding the deceased's money or other assets, must state that (1) the claimant is legally entitled to inherit the deceased's assets, (2) the value of the entire estate, less liens, does not exceed the maximum specified by state law, (3) that a minimum number of days (usually 30 to 45) have elapsed since the death, and (4) no petition for the appointment of a personal representative is pending or has been granted by the probate court.

Under the Uniform Probate Code (adopted by fifteen states as of this writing), anyone indebted to or holding personal property of the deceased is required, upon receipt of the transfer affidavit, to pay the debt or deliver the property to the person who claims to be an entitled beneficiary of the deceased. In simpler language, this means that the affidavit procedure can be used to collect and transfer the deceased's bank accounts, insurance policies, money market accounts, promissory notes, various securities, and the contents of safe-deposit boxes—provided their total value falls within the state-specified monetary limit. Under this procedure, the deceased's creditors need not be notified or paid.

Other states, even though they have not adopted the Uniform Probate Code, provide similar procedures for the swift and informal transfer of "small estates" by affidavit. You may or may not need the help of a lawyer to take advantage of this shortcut. Before obligating yourself to legal expenses, find out what you can about your own state's "small estate" affidavit transfer procedures by reviewing table 8, by calling the local probate court, or doing some research in a law library.

Summary Probate Administration

If the deceased's probate assets exceed the maximum values specified by state law or do not consist of the types eligible for transfer by affidavit, or if the assets include real estate, most states offer an abbreviated form of probate procedure, sometimes called "summary" or "small estate" probate administration. This procedure is usually available (1) if assets do not exceed a specified value, (2) if no interested party (such as a creditor) objects to it, and (3) if the will does not direct otherwise.

In California, for example, you may petition the probate court to issue an order specifying the survivors' right to acquire the property without the need for full probate administration. The petition must include an inventory and appraisal by a probate referee of the deceased's probatable real and personal property, showing its gross value. The petition is scheduled for a hearing, and notice must be given to all interested parties. If the petition is granted the probate court will issue an order specifying who acquires the title to the property. A certified copy of this order is then delivered to the person or entity holding personal property and is recorded in the county in which any real property is located.

The Uniform Probate Code also provides for summary probate administration if the survivors include a spouse and minor children. As the nominated personal representative, you may file an application for informal appointment and thereby obtain letters of authority. If, after you have filed an inventory and appraisal, it appears that the value of the probate estate does not exceed the aggregate value of (1) the statutory "family protection allowances" (approximately $25,000 but varying among states), (2) funeral expenses, (3) necessary expenses for the deceased's final health care, and (4) costs of administration, you may immediately distribute the estate to the spouse and minor children without giving the normally required notice to the deceased's creditors and an opportunity for presentation of their claims.

After the assets have been distributed, you can immediately close the estate by filing a sworn statement that to the best of your knowledge the value of the estate did not exceed the sum of items 1 through 4 above, that the distribution of assets is complete, and that a copy of the final statement was sent to all beneficiaries and to known unpaid creditors. Under this procedure, creditors need not be paid.

FORMAL PROBATE ADMINISTRATION

If the value of the deceased's probate assets exceeds the maximum for your state's "small estate" transfer procedures or if a lawsuit for wrongful-death benefits seems likely, the estate must undergo formal probate-court administration. Depending on the complexity of the probate assets, claim disputes, will contests, arguments among beneficiaries, and whether there is delay in obtaining tax clearances, this process can take from six months to several years, and it can be rather expensive, because the personal representative is entitled to be paid for his services and because his bonding fee as well as attorney fees and court costs must be paid by the estate before it can be closed. Although formal probate administration might have been avoided had the deceased adopted some of the probate-avoidance strategies suggested in chapter 2, it is, unfortunately, inevitable at this juncture.

The basic purposes of probate administration help to explain why the process can be lengthy and costly. The court must appoint a personal representative to identify, collect, manage, and settle the estate; it must determine the validity of any purported will; it must identify and notify the beneficiaries named in the will as well as the heirs designated by law; it must notify the deceased's creditors and determine the legitimacy of their claims; and it must ensure that the remaining assets, after the payment of debts, taxes, and administration expenses, are properly distributed to the will-designated beneficiaries or the heirs at law if the deceased left no will.

Initiation of Probate Proceedings

Even if the deceased's will has been filed with the local probate court, probate proceedings do not begin automatically upon his death. To initiate probate administration, some "interested party" must petition the court to appoint a personal representative. If the probate assets are substantial, there will be no dearth of "interested parties": beneficiaries or heirs eager to get possession of the deceased's assets or even creditors to whom the deceased owed large sums. Because the deceased's probate assets can be transferred only by a personal representative, his appointment by the court is the first order of business.

If you have been named in the will as the personal representative or if, in the absence of a will, you seem to be the logical choice, you may feel daunted by the responsibilities that confront you. Bear in mind, however, that as personal representative you have the right to hire lawyers, accountants, and other professionals to help you and that their fees are chargeable against the estate. In addition, unless the will specifies otherwise, you are entitled to reasonable compensation for your work and reimbursement for your expenses.

You can, of course, refuse to serve, in which case the probate court will appoint someone else, usually observing the following priority sequence:

Priority Rank	*Description of Candidates*
1.	Persons named in will as personal representative and successor personal representative.
2.	Surviving spouse who is a will-designated beneficiary (or spouse's nominee).
3.	Other will-designated beneficiaries (or their nominee).
4.	Surviving spouse (or his/her nominee).
5.	Other heirs at law by degree of kinship (or their nominee).
6.	Any creditor 45 days after death.

If none of these people is willing to petition for the appointment, the court may request that anyone file a petition, and in such circumstances the court may appoint a bank, a lawyer (sometimes a political friend), or some other stranger.

Your decision to undertake the responsibility, then, may depend on your own status as a beneficiary and your relationship to other beneficiaries. If you are concerned with conserving the assets, you are likely, despite your "amateur" standing, to do a more conscientious job than a bank or a professional who takes on the task solely for financial gain. If you decide to serve, your first step is to have your lawyer prepare and file a petition requesting your formal appointment and the commencement of probate proceedings. If your petition is approved, the probate court will formalize your appointment and issue you the necessary letters of authority (see figure 14)—often immediately.

The Personal Representative

Once appointed, the personal representative has much the same powers over the assets as the deceased had during his lifetime. Armed with the letters of authority, he can sell property owned by the estate, continue to manage an existing business, make investments with estate capital, mortgage estate property, and do anything else that is necessary to preserve or increase the value of the estate. In brief, he may be regarded, for all intents and purposes, as the ghost or the alter ego of the deceased, empowered to manage all of the deceased's financial affairs that were interrupted by death.

The personal representative's activities are, however, subject to three limitations. First, unlike the deceased, who could do absolutely whatever he wished with his property, the personal representative must always act "prudently" so as not to jeopardize the value of the estate—through speculative investments, for example. Second, he must do everything he can to settle the estate—pay its debts and distribute the residue to the beneficiaries or heirs—as promptly as possible. Third, he must do nothing with respect to the estate that works to his personal advantage—for example, buying for himself at an unreasonably low price a boat or other probate asset belonging to the estate.

The deceased's will may stipulate that the nominated personal representative is to serve without bond. But if this is not specified, the estate is chargeable for the personal representative's bond premium. In some states, the personal representative's annual compensation is specified as a percentage of the value of the estate; in California, for example, the personal representative is entitled to 4 percent of the first $15,000, 3 percent of the next $85,000, 2 per-

Figure 14

LETTERS OF AUTHORITY

STATE OF MICHIGAN PROBATE COURT COUNTY OF	LETTERS OF AUTHORITY FOR PERSONAL REPRESENTATIVE	FILE NO.

Estate of ____

TO: *Name, address, and telephone no.*

You have been appointed and qualified as personal representative of the estate on ____________________ . You are authorized to do and perform all
Date

acts authorized by law except as to the following:

❑ Real estate or ownership interests in a business entity excluded from your responsibilities in your acceptance of appointment

❑ Restrictions:

❑ These letters expire: ____________________
Date

__________ ____
Date *Judge (formal proceedings)/Register (informal proceedings)* *Bar no.*

SEE OTHER SIDE FOR NOTICE OF DUTIES.

____
Attorney name (type or print) *Bar no.*

____
Address

____
City, state, zip *Telephone no.*

I certify that I have compared this copy with the original on file and that it is a correct copy of the original and that these letters are in full force and effect as of the date on the letters.

__________ ____
Date *Deputy register*

Do not write below this line - For court use only

cent of the next $900,000, and 1 percent of the next $9,000,000; and 0.5% of the next $15,000,000; plus a reasonable fee for the balance. Even when it is not regulated, however, compensation is expected to be "reasonable" and is subject to challenge in the probate court by any beneficiary, heir, or creditor. For a state-by-state listing of fees chargeable by a personal representative, see table 10.

TABLE 10

PERSONAL REPRESENTATIVES' FEES, BY STATE

State	*Fee*
Alabama	Just and fair amount up to 2.5% of receipts and disbursements.
Alaska	Reasonable compensation.
Arizona	Reasonable compensation.[1]
Arkansas	Up to 10% of first $1,000 of personal property; 5% of next $4,000; 3% of balance plus reasonable additional fee for services involving real estate.
California	Up to 4% of first $15,000; 3% of next $85,000; 2% of next $900,000; 1% of next $9,000,000; 0.5% of next $15,000,000; plus reasonable fee for the balance.
Colorado	Reasonable compensation.[1]
Connecticut	Reasonable compensation.
Delaware	Combined executor's and attorney's fees up to $250 plus 11.3% of amount over $2,000 for estates under $5,000; $565 plus 6.8% of amount over $5,000 for estates under $10,000; $905 plus 5.6% of amount over $10,000 for estates under $20,000; $1,465 plus 5.1% of amount over $20,000 for estates under $30,000; $1,975 plus 4.5% of amount over $30,000 for estates under $40,000; $2,425 plus 3.9% of amount over $40,000 for estates under $60,000; $3,205 plus 3.7% of amount over $60,000 for estates under $80,000. For fees on larger estates, see court rules.[2]
District of Columbia	Reasonable compensation.
Florida	Reasonable compensation.[1]
Georgia	2.5% of money received and paid out plus additional for extraordinary services.

TABLE 10

PERSONAL REPRESENTATIVES' FEES, BY STATE (continued)

State	*Fee*
Hawaii	Reasonable compensation.[1]
Idaho	Reasonable compensation.[1]
Illinois	Reasonable compensation.
Indiana	Reasonable compensation.[1]
Iowa	Reasonable compensation not to exceed 6% of first $1,000; 4% of next $4,000; 2% over $5,000.
Kansas	Reasonable compensation.[1]
Kentucky	Up to 5% of personal property plus 5% of income collected.[2]
Louisiana	2% of value of estate.
Maine	Reasonable compensation.
Maryland	Up to 10% of first 20,000; $2,000 plus 4% of amount over $20,000; limit of 10% of real estate sold by executor[2].
Massachusetts	Reasonable compensation; customarily 6 to 7% on income; on principal, 5% of first $100,000, 4% on next $200,000, and diminishing percentages on balance.
Michigan	Reasonable compensation.
Minnesota	Reasonable compensation.
Mississippi	Up to 7% of estate.[2]
Missouri	Up to 5% of first $5,000; 4% of next $20,000; 3% of next $75,000; 2.75% of next $300,000; 2.5% of next $600,000; 2% of amount over $1,000,000.[2]
Montana	Up to 3% of first $40,000; 2% of amount over $40,000.
Nebraska	Reasonable compensation.
Nevada	4% of first $15,000; 3% of next $85,000; 2% on excess over $100,000.[2]
New Hampshire	Reasonable compensation.
New Jersey	5% of first $200,000; 3% of excess up to $1,000,000; 2% on balance.[2]
New Mexico	Reasonable compensation.[1]

TABLE 10

PERSONAL REPRESENTATIVES' FEES, BY STATE *(continued)*

State	*Fee*
New York	5% of first $100,000 received and paid out; 4% of next $200,000; 3% of next $700,000; 2.5% of next $4,000,000; 2% of amounts over $5,000,000.
North Carolina	Up to 5% of receipts and expenditures. On estates of less than $2,000, clerk sets fee.
North Dakota	Reasonable compensation.
Ohio	4% of first $100,000; 3% of next $300,000; 2% of balance, determined with reference to personal property, income received, and proceeds of real estate.[2]
Oklahoma	5% of first $1,000; 4% of next $5,500; 2.5% of excess over $6,000.[1, 2]
Oregon	7% of first $1,000; 4% of next $9,000; 3% of next $40,000; 2% on amount over $50,000; plus 1% of property subject to inheritance or estate tax.[1, 2]
Pennsylvania	Reasonable compensation.
Rhode Island	Reasonable compensation.
South Carolina	Up to 5% of personal property plus 5% of proceeds of sold real estate plus 5% of income earned by the estate.[2]
South Dakota	Reasonable compensation.[1]
Tennessee	Reasonable compensation.
Texas	5% of incoming and outgoing cash.
Utah	Reasonable compensation.[1]
Vermont	$4 per day while performing duties of office.[2]
Virginia	Reasonable compensation.
Washington	Reasonable compensation.[1]
West Virginia	Reasonable compensation (usually 5% of receipts).
Wisconsin	2% of estate, less mortgage and liens, plus higher fee if approved by majority of beneficiaries.
Wyoming	10% of first $1,000; 5% of next $4,000; 3% of next $15,000; 2% of amount over $20,000.[2]

1 Personal representative may renounce fee limits in will and collect higher fee allowed by law unless compensation is set by contract

2 Court may award higher fee.

The purpose of the bond is to protect all interested parties against possible fraud, embezzlement, or negligence on the part of the personal representative in his management and disposal of the estate's assets. Like the personal representative's compensation, the annual premium for the bond is based on the total value of the probatable assets plus any income they are expected to produce. The annual premium costs range from $2.00 to $9.00 per $1,000 of this value, depending upon the amount of the bond.

Although the will may specify that the personal representative is to serve without bond, the probate judge may override this aspect of the will and require bonding if he believes it necessary for the protection of the beneficiaries and the creditors. On the other hand, if the will does not make this specification and if the personal representative is the sole heir or beneficiary, the judge may waive the bonding requirement.

Bonding is extremely easy to arrange through almost any insurance agent, but despite the pressure of time, some shopping around is advisable—as it is in the purchase of any other kind of insurance. If the value of the assets is substantial, the personal representative can sometimes negotiate a discount on the premium from an insurance agent who is particularly eager to sell this coverage.

Bonding premiums are payable annually until the probate process is completed. Because they are renewed automatically, the personal representative should cancel his bond as soon as the estate is closed by sending the insurance company a copy of the probate court's final "Order Closing Estate and Discharging Personal Representative" (see p. 238) and request a refund of any unearned premium.

"Proving" the Will

The initial petition for appointment as personal representative typically includes a request that the court approve the will or, if there is no will, to determine which of the heirs listed in the petition are entitled, according to state law, to share in the estate. In response, the court schedules a hearing and sends a notification of its time and place to all parties who may have an interest in the estate: creditors, beneficiaries named in the will, and heirs who, under state law, would inherit if there is no valid will.

At this hearing, the will may be contested by any interested party who contends that the deceased signed it in a state of diminished capacity or was unduly influenced or under duress, that he made errors in executing the will, or that he subsequently revoked it. If any of these claims are proved, the court will not "admit" the will to probate, with the result that the deceased is regarded as having died intestate unless there is an earlier will that is valid.

If, on the other hand, the will is not successfully contested, the court will admit it to probate or, if there was no will, identify the heirs entitled to share the estate.

NOTIFICATION OF INTERESTED PARTIES

Once appointed, the personal representative must send to each interested party (creditors, beneficiaries, and heirs) written notification of his appointment, including his name and address and the location of the probate court where the will and all other documents relating to the estate are filed. The basic purpose of this notice is to inform all interested persons about the appointment and to offer them an opportunity to challenge it if grounds for a challenge exist. In addition, however, it invites the interested parties to ascertain the value of the estate by consulting an inventory, which the personal representative must file with the probate court, listing the current value of each of the estate's assets as well as any mortgages or liens against them. By consulting this inventory, beneficiaries can estimate what they may expect to receive, and creditors can determine whether they are likely to collect their debts.

DEALING WITH CREDITORS

Upon his appointment, the personal representative must send written notice to each of the deceased's known creditors inviting them to submit in writing all claims against the estate within a specified time. In addition, he must publish a copy of this notice in a newspaper distributed within the county in which the deceased lived so as to inform possible creditors of whom he is unaware (see figure 15). Both the number of times the notice must be published and the period of time during which they must appear are governed by state law, as is the deadline for the submission of claims. Typically, the creditor must submit a copy to the court. In all states, claims submitted after the deadline are barred.

Although the personal representative may pay legitimate claims in the order in which he receives them, he should be cautious about doing this if the possibility exists that the assets will not be suffi-

Figure 15

NOTICE TO CREDITORS

STATE OF MICHIGAN PROBATE COURT COUNTY OF	NOTICE TO CREDITORS Decedent's Estate	FILE NO.

Estate of ______________________________ Date of birth:

TO ALL CREDITORS:*

NOTICE TO CREDITORS: The decedent,____________________, who lived at ____, Michigan died
Street address *City*

______________.
Date

Creditors of the decedent are notified that all claims against the estate will be forever barred unless presented to __________________________, named personal representative or proposed personal representative, or to both the probate court at ____
Address *City*
and the named/proposed personal representative within 4 months after the date of publication of this notice.

____
Date

______________________________ ____________
Attorney name (type or print) *Bar no.*

____
Personal representative name (type or print)

______________________ ______________________
Address *Address*

______________________ ______________________
City, state, zip *Telephone no.* *City, state, zip* *Telephone no.*

PUBLISH ABOVE INFORMATION ONLY

Publish ____ time(s) in________________________ in _________ County
Name of publication

Furnish ____ copies to __________________________________

Furnish affidavit of publication to the probate court with copy to _________
____

Forward statement for publication charges to ____________________

*NOTE TO PREPARER: If there is a known creditor whose address is unknown and cannot be ascertained after diligent inquiry, insert "including [name of creditor] whose address and whereabouts are unknown:"

Do not write below this line - For court use only

cient to cover all claims. In such circumstances, claims must be paid according to the priority sequence established by state law, which is typically as follows:

1. Costs of administering the estate, including the personal representative's and lawyers' fees, court costs, and bond premiums
2. Reasonable funeral charges and medical and hospital charges incurred by the deceased immediately before death
3. Taxes and those debts that state law specifies as having priority
4. All other legitimate debts

In this priority system, high-priority claims are paid in full, and if no assets remain, low-priority creditors get nothing.

For example, if, after paying all debts in priorities 1, 2, and 3, the estate remains with $500 in assets and $1,000 in debts, each class-4 creditor will receive 50 percent of his claim.

Income Taxes

The personal representative is responsible for preparing and filing the deceased's final federal, state, and local income-tax returns, as well as tax returns on behalf of the estate itself.

If the deceased left a surviving spouse and it was their custom to file a joint return, the final return may also be joint even if the death occurred during the first few days of the tax year. On the other hand, there is no obligation to file a joint return if the surviving spouse finds it advantageous to file an individual return.

If the estate itself has received income of more than $600 during any year—from the operation of a business, for example, or from yields on investments—the personal representative must file a return on its behalf.

Federal Estate Tax

The federal estate tax is an excise tax levied against all property (both probatable and nonprobatable) that is controlled by the deceased at the time of death, and it must be paid by the personal representative within nine months of the death. The tax rates, deductions, and credits, however, have been so liberalized in recent years that only 2 percent of all estates are liable for any tax payment at all. Because the chances are very high that the estate with which you are dealing will not be subject to this tax, we will not attempt here to provide you with complete instructions for calculating the tax and filing the return. This is a task you should not undertake unassisted unless you are an experienced tax lawyer or accountant. Instead, we shall offer you a relatively simple formula by which you can determine whether the estate is likely to be subject to tax.

The formula for calculating estate federal tax liability is:

VALUE OF THE GROSS ESTATE – DEDUCTIONS = ADJUSTED GROSS ESTATE – UNLIMITED MARITAL DEDUCTION AND CHARITABLE GIFTS = TAXABLE ESTATE.

To determine the value of the gross estate, add up the value of all assets shown in table 2 under the heading "Subject to Federal Estate Tax." (In establishing their value, you can use either the value at the time of the death or the value six months after the time of death, whichever is more advantageous.) To the sum of these values, add the total of all taxable gifts—gifts of more than $10,000 or more than $20,000 made with the consent of the deceased's spouse—that the deceased made during his lifetime. This grand total represents the gross estate.

Deductions that may be subtracted from the gross estate consist of hospital and medical expenses connected with the deceased's last illness, funeral and burial expenses, estate administration expenses (including the personal representative's expenses, compensation, and bond premium, probate court costs, and legal fees), and the deceased's debts, mortgages, and other liabilities. Subtracting the deductions from the gross estate produces the adjusted gross estate.

From the adjusted gross estate, you are entitled to deduct two items: (1) an unlimited marital deduction for all assets passing to the surviving spouse, and (2) all bequests to charitable organizations. When you have subtracted these deductions from the adjusted gross estate, the remainder comprises the taxable estate.

At this juncture, consult table 3. If the value of the taxable estate does not exceed those shown in the table, you need do nothing. If it does, you should seek professional help.

State Estate and Inheritance Taxes

Most states impose either of two kinds of death taxes: an estate tax, which is payable by the estate itself, or an inheritance or succession tax, which is payable by the beneficiary receiving an inheritance.

In some states, the estate tax is simply a percentage of the federal estate tax, and hence an estate that is not subject to federal estate tax will not be taxable. Other states are considerably less liberal but provide exemptions that range from $10,000 to $600,000. Table 5 indicates both the tax rates and the exemptions.

Many states levy a tax—variously called an inheritance, legacy, or succession tax—on the inheritance received by each beneficiary. This tax is payable to the state in which the deceased lived, regardless of the residence of the beneficiary. Various exemptions are allowed, depending on the size of the inheritance and the relationship of the beneficiary to the deceased. Table 6 illustrates both the rates and the exemptions.

Although inheritance taxes are payable by the beneficiary, the will may specify that the tax be paid by the estate on behalf of the beneficiary. In any event, however, it is the personal representative's responsibility to make sure that the tax is paid, because the probate court will normally require that he file a tax-clearance certificate, issued by the state treasurer's office, before the court will sign an order discharging the personal representative and closing the estate.

DISTRIBUTING THE ESTATE

Once all debts, taxes, and other liabilities of the estate have been discharged, the personal representative is ready to submit to the court a final accounting of his actions and to distribute the remaining assets to the beneficiaries or the heirs.

Certain changes in the distribution specified either by the will or by state law can be made provided that all beneficiaries or heirs give their written consent. For example, a parent who is a beneficiary can ask that his share be distributed equally to his two children, even though they were not mentioned in the will, or an heir who is affluent may ask that his share be added to that of his less affluent sister.

If one or more of the beneficiaries is a minor and the value of his share is not large, the distribution can be made to his parent or guardian. If, however, the amount is substantial—over $10,000 or $15,000—it must usually be paid to the conservator of the minor's estate, who is appointed by the probate court if one has not been designated in the will (see p. 181).

As soon as he has arranged all the details of the distribution, the personal representative prepares for signature by the probate judge an order allowing final account and assigning residue. Once it is signed, the order serves as a formal record indicating when, how, and to whom the assets were distributed.

Closing the Estate

After the distribution has been completed, the personal representative files with the probate court a closing statement certifying that he has discharged all his responsibilities—that he has notified all creditors, discharged all debts, distributed the residue in accordance with the terms of the will or with state law, and sent a copy of the closing statement to all interested parties.

Upon approval of the closing statement, the probate court issues to the personal representative an order discharging him from his position and relieving him of all further responsibilities. At this point the estate is closed.

INDEX